Annotated Legal Documents on Islam in Europe: United Kingdom

Annotated Legal Documents on Islam in Europe

VOLUME 25

The titles published in this series are listed at *brill.com/ldie*

Annotated Legal Documents on Islam in Europe

United Kingdom

Compiled, Annotated and Authored by

Prakash Shah

BRILL

LEIDEN | BOSTON

The Library of Congress Cataloging-in-Publication Data is available online at https://catalog.loc.gov

Typeface for the Latin, Greek, and Cyrillic scripts: "Brill". See and download: brill.com/brill-typeface.

ISSN 2214-1340
ISBN 978-90-04-73741-9 (paperback)

This book is printed on acid-free paper and produced in a sustainable manner.

Contents

Foreword by the Editors

This is the twenty-fifth volume in the series *Annotated Legal Documents on Islam in Europe*. The publication of this series responds to the widespread lack of sound information about the legal status of Islam in Europe. In principle, this information is easily available to those who are willing to make the effort and know enough about the subject to ask the right questions of the digital search engines. But that requires both expertise and effort, and it takes place in an environment where the public political debate on Islam in many European countries is characterised by increasing concern and fear. Islam has come to be broadly perceived as a security issue rather than a religion like others in Europe. But the concern has also moved into the legal field, most markedly, of course, with discussions about limitations on Muslim female dress enacted in a growing number of countries, or the ban on building minarets on mosques in Switzerland, or restrictions on building mosques in certain Austrian provinces. At the same time, in a number of European states like Austria and Germany, legislation is enacted and state treaties are negotiated which aim to establish a stable and reliable basis for Muslim life and organisation. Even so, such measures are under scrutiny by an increasingly sceptical European public, sometimes ignoring the legal principles of secularity, not least the demands of state neutrality towards and equal treatment of all religions and beliefs regardless of numbers of adherents or public reputation.

In addition, the religious status and rights of Muslims in the various European countries differ significantly, due to different historical developments regarding the organisation of the relations between the state and religions. Furthermore, while in some states laws regulating such matters introduced decades ago are still in force and have to be re-interpreted in the face of a 'newcomer' religion, others have introduced new laws that consider the increasing religious plurality within Europe. Despite the common legal and political foundations constructed since 1945 in instruments such as the European Convention on Human Rights and the more recently accumulated legislation of the European Union, this closer look reveals remarkable differences due to the extent of separating state and religion or establishing co-operative structures. In some countries Islam has an officially recognised status which in some cases originated in the first half of the 20th century. In other countries no such recognition of any religion is available even if informal ways of favouring one religion over another may exist. Since 1990 especially, European courts have moved to equalise the status of Islam with that of other religions in the practical exercise of religious freedom in various countries. Particular practices regarded as core religious obligations—in the case of Muslims dress codes and practices such as male circumcision, access to correctly slaughtered meat and otherwise *halal* food, free time for the main periods of worship and religious festivals, and the right to build mosques—can be controversial in some countries while less so in others. In the course of the ongoing process of self-organisation and the participation of Muslims in civil societies and their co-operation with the state, children's access to Islamic religious instruction or the education of Muslim theologians can be achieved in co-operation with the state education systems in some countries, while in others the community must rely on its own arrangements. The practically pressing issue of financing the religious infrastructure is still far from being settled in many countries.

The aim of this series is to make this legislation available to both the interested researcher and the practising lawyer. Altogether the series is expected to comprise 32 volumes, one for each of the 27 countries of the European Union plus Norway, Switzerland and the United Kingdom, and a volume each dealing with the European Union (treaties, directives and decisions of the Court of Justice of the European Communities) and the European Court of Human Rights. Excerpts of relevant legislation are introduced and summarised by the volume compiler/author, and where court cases have provided significant interpretation of the law they will also be referred to. The legislation itself is reproduced in the original language, as the editors and the publisher agreed early on in the preparation of the series that any attempt to translate legislation into English would be unsatisfactory and risked being misleading. The comments and analysis by the author should give sufficient guidance to users to allow a decision as to whether to arrange a translation for their specific purposes.

This volume, on the legislation of the United Kingdom, is markedly different—and longer—than other volumes in the series. The reason for this is the markedly different nature of law in the UK, where much of the law is made by judges reaching decisions which interpret parliamentary legislation with reference to the Common Law tradition and the binding precedent set by judges in the higher courts after a detailed account of the facts of the case. For this reason, this volume includes extensive citation of judicial decisions, presented in smaller type and indented.

An attempt has been made to ensure that the volumes are structured in as similar a manner as possible. The starting point for this has been the thematic organisation used variously in the *Yearbook of Muslims in Europe* which Brill has published annually since 2009. Normally one member of the editorial group takes responsibility for discussing the structure and compilation of each volume with the compiler: in this instance, this task was undertaken by Professor Marie-Claire Foblets. We are also grateful to Kate Elliott for the care shown in copy editing the volume. The initiative for this project came from the publisher, where Nicolette van der Hoek and Nienke Brienen-Moolenaar have played an invaluable role in ensuring that the project has maintained its momentum. As editors, we appreciate how much their expertise contributes to ensuring that a project like this can run smoothly.

The Editors, February 2025

General Introduction

This introduction provides a short background to the material covered in the remainder of this book. The first section provides a brief and general socio-demographic picture of Muslims in Britain who are a significant component of the population. The second section gives a short account of the character of British legal systems which Muslims encounter and before which they make their claims. The third section discusses the character of the *Shari'a* or Islamic law that still informs the Muslim conceptions of legality and the rule of law, and conditions Muslim expectations of the British legal systems. There is, however, a great deal of confusion about what *Shari'a* is or would entail today, and the discussion tries to clarify the extent to which British legal systems have come close to adopting parts of it. The final section provides a brief note on the criteria for selecting and arranging the material for this volume.

1 Muslims in Britain—A Demographic Picture

It was in the post-Second World War period that the UK saw an unprecedentedly large presence of Muslims. The Census and other figures demonstrate this, while statisticians have also altered their practices, for instance by adding a "religion" question in the 2001 Census specifically. Such a question would be unlawful in some European legal systems because of privacy concerns. Since the last Census, which was done online during the Covid crisis in 2021 (2022 in Scotland), how long it will function as a comprehensive population survey has been an open question.

In 2011, Muslims made up the largest non-Christian religious population in the UK as it totalled 2.8 million, and it still was during the 2021 Census, when the number had grown to around 4 million, 5.9 % for the United Kingdom as a whole. Muslims are unevenly distributed across the United Kingdom. In the 2021 Census of England and Wales, the total Muslim population was counted at 3,868,133, constituting 6.5 % of the population. In the Scottish census of 2022, the Muslim population count was 119,872, 2.2 % of the total Scottish population. In the Northern Ireland Census 2021, 10,870 Muslims were counted and constituted 0.57 % of the population.[1] The Pew Research Centre has predicted that

1 Unless otherwise stated, the statistics on England and Wales discussed in this section are drawn from the Office for National Statistics data, those for Scotland from Scotland's Census, and those for Northern Ireland from the Northern Ireland Statistics and Research Agency.

by 2050, in a zero-migration scenario, the UK's Muslim population would reach 9.7 %, 16.7 % with a medium level of migration, and 17.2 % with high migration.[2]

The last Census also showed that some 60 per cent of Muslims are from the Indian subcontinent, by either birth or ancestry. In England and Wales, 1,470,775 Muslims were in the Pakistani "ethnic group," 593,136 were Bangladeshis, and 246,968 Indians; while 378,219 were Black African and 277,737 were Arab. Some 176,645 were identified as Somali and made up more than 45 per cent of the Black African group.[3] The generalised picture of Muslims is often based on figures available only for Pakistanis and Bangladeshis. An overwhelming number of studies, reports and surveys refer to these two groups, whose countries of origin are overwhelmingly Muslim, while their representation in Britain is almost exclusively Muslim. However, there are reasons to think that similar social demographics and patterns can be found among other ethnic groups of Muslims, albeit with some variations. There are some variations between Pakistanis and Bangladeshis, too. The generalisability of conclusions about Muslims become more salient when one considers the comparisons with non-Muslims or those ethnic groups in which Muslims are not highly represented.

In comparison with that of the general population, the age profile of Muslims in general is far more skewed to the younger age groups, and this distribution holds true for both the Black African and Asian ethnic groups in which Muslims are prevalent. While, nearly half of Muslims in England and Wales were born overseas, the Black African groups are more likely (60 per cent) to have been born overseas than are the Asian groups (45 per cent). These figures are one indicator that the cultural reference points of Muslims in Britain, as elsewhere in Europe, tend to remain outside Europe in their countries and regions of origin.[4]

There are high rates of in-group marriage, which has a marked transnational dimension.[5] Concerns have been expressed that the high number of transna-

---

2 Pew Research Center, Europe's Growing Muslim Population, 29 November 2017, https://www.pewresearch.org/religion/2017/11/29/europes-growing-muslim-population/, accessed on 12 February 2025. The medium migration scenario is one where the then normal levels of regular migration were to continue, while the high migration scenario adds asylum-seeker migrants to these regular migrants.

3 It is likely that most Somalis are included within the African ethnic group, but smaller numbers also opted for Somali as their national identity or both their national identity and ethnic group.

4 For this point see Nielsen, J.S. and Otterbeck, J. (2016), *Muslims in Western Europe*. Edinburgh: Edinburgh University Press, p. 171.

5 Casey, L. (2016), *The Casey Review: A review into opportunity and integration*. London: Her Majesty's Stationery Office, p. 9.

tional marriages results in a "first generation in every generation", and children in each new generation growing up with a foreign-born parent.[6] Meanwhile, cousin marriages may be even more prevalent among Pakistanis in Britain than in Pakistan, and carries higher risks of medical congenital or genetic problems as well as psychosis and depression.[7]

England has the highest population and concentration of Muslims. The London Boroughs of Tower Hamlets, Newham and Redbridge and the cities of Blackburn, Luton and Bradford have a higher than 30 per cent Muslim population. Muslims constitute more than 20 per cent of the cities of Birmingham, Slough, Pendle, Oldham, Leicester, Manchester, as well the London Boroughs of Barking and Dagenham, Waltham Forest, Brent and Westminster. Compared to other minority faith groups, Muslims tend to live in higher residential concentrations at ward level, wards being the electoral units at local authority level. In 2011, the year of the previous census, Blackburn, Birmingham, Burnley and Bradford included wards containing between 70 and 85 per cent Muslims.[8]

This concentration of population is largely a matter of choice rather than discrimination or external compulsion.[9] The Muslim immigrants who arrived from Commonwealth countries enjoy the franchise at both local and national elections (as well as the European elections prior to Brexit). This allowed them considerable influence over decision-making, especially at local authority level, because of the ability to vote and elect representatives. Voter behaviour at local level can also influence the composition of and political attitudes in the Westminster Parliament. This influence has been used to exert political pressure on national issues such as the anti-discrimination law and foreign policy issues such as the Iraq War in 2003 and the Israel-Gaza conflict in 2023–

6 Ibid., p. 32: the "first generation in every generation" phenomenon is noted as a barrier to integration also by the Casey Report at p. 43.

7 Shaw, A. (2014), "Drivers of cousin marriage among British Pakistanis," *Human Heredity*, 77(1–4), pp. 26–36, Shaw, A. (2018), "Consanguineous marriage and the psychopathology of the progeny of first-cousin couples," *JAMA Psychiatry*, 75(5), pp. 426–427, Nash, P. (2022), *British Islam and English law: A classical pluralist perspective*. Cambridge: Cambridge University Press, pp. 266–268, Nash, P.S. (2024), "The case for banning cousin marriage," *Oxford Journal of Law and Religion*, 13(1), pp. 98–118.

8 Casey, L. (2016), *The Casey Review: A review into opportunity and integration*. London: Her Majesty's Stationery Office, p. 11.

9 For a similar earlier analysis see Nielsen, J.S. and Otterbeck, J. (2016), *Muslims in Western Europe*. Edinburgh: Edinburgh University Press, pp. 171–173. See also Pearl, D. and Menski, W. (1998), *Muslim family law*. London: Sweet & Maxwell, p. 61 on the multiple reasons Muslims have for this choice.

2025. Muslims of Pakistani origin in particular enjoy a high profile in terms of past or present elected or appointed political leadership.[10]

Muslim attitudes towards female participation in the labour market can be discerned through various available surveys, and their generally lower participation rate compared to that of men has been put down to "cultural-religious reasons."[11] Economic inactivity rates for Muslim men are also below those of the population as a whole. Pakistanis and Bangladeshis earn 16 per cent and 15 per cent less on average than do White British people, while Arabs earn 2.3 per cent less.[12] Those ethnic groups in which Muslims are highly represented such as Arabs, Bangladeshis and Pakistanis show greater receipt of state support.[13]

2 Distinctive Features of British Legal Systems

Despite some earlier and small-scale precedents, it is a commonplace that mass immigration to Europe by non-Europeans, including Muslims, took place only in the period after the Second World War. This applies to Britain also. This section sketches the legal context the recent arrivals could expect to encounter, and how that context has itself been changing as the settlement patterns were being established.

Given its long tradition of tolerance exemplified by the series of measures to remove legal disabilities against Catholics, Jews and Christian dissenters, in religious matters Britain has tended to proceed with an approach towards neutrality by adjusting policy, judicial or legislative frameworks for the enjoyment of civil rights.[14] The tradition of tolerance had already taken hold in Britain

10 For a critical analysis of the allegations of corruption and bloc voting in elections see Nash, P. (2022), *British Islam and English law: A classical pluralist perspective*. Cambridge: Cambridge University Press, pp. 219–248.

11 Casey, L. (2016), *The Casey Review: A review into opportunity and integration*. London: Her Majesty's Stationery Office, p. 108, and on Muslim women's (in)activity in the labour market p. 14. Equalities Review Panel (2007), *Fairness and freedom: The final report of the Equalities Review*, pp. 68–71. Available at: https://webarchive.nationalarchives.gov.uk/ukgwa/201008
06225818/http://archive.cabinetoffice.gov.uk/equalitiesreview/, pp. 68–71.

12 Casey, L. (2016), *The Casey Review: A review into opportunity and integration*. London: Her Majesty's Stationery Office, p. 110.

13 Figures are available from the annual Family Resources Surveys. For the year 2022–2023 see https://www.gov.uk/government/statistics/family-resources-survey-financial-year-2022-to-2023, accessed 12 February 2025. Cabinet Office (2018), *Race disparity audit: Summary findings from the Ethnicity Facts and Figures website*, p. 30.

14 For a list of such legislation see Robilliard, S.J.A. (1984), *Religion and the law: Religious liberty in modern English law*. Manchester: Manchester University Press, pp. 199–203,

by the time of significant imperial expansion, and aspects of that tradition conditioned the British approach to ruling and legal recognition in the British Empire also. Discounting the Mutiny of the mid-nineteenth century, Britain did not see significant revolts by Muslims in India, who overwhelmingly supported the idea initiated by the British of the creation of Pakistan, the eastern part of which later split during a bloody conflict, resulting in the creation of Bangladesh. The history of the colonial legal recognition of Muslim personal law was recalled in the arguments made in the 1970s, i.e., within three decades of decolonisation, for the implementation in Britain of a similar framework.

The earlier questions about how British legal systems could accommodate Muslim difference within the limits established by liberal toleration have shifted by the layering on of multicultural identity politics and the recognition of group level protected status which extends to religion and, therefore, to Muslims also.[15] What has been achieved in some other European legal systems, such as in Belgium, Italy or Spain,[16] through the formal legal framework of recognition of different religious communities to secure religious freedom has been done most often through less formal measures in Britain.[17] Leaving aside the situation of the established Christian churches, and subject to the adoption of more formalised structures available in company and charity law, religious groups are theoretically treated as voluntary associations, and there-

Rivers, J. (2010), *The law of organized religions: Between establishment and secularism*. Oxford: Oxford University Press, pp. 1–32, Sandberg, R. (2011), *Law and religion*. Cambridge; New York: Cambridge University Press, pp. 26–28.

15 While the often-cited liberal conception of multiculturalism is derived from the Canadian writer, Will Kymlicka, the non-liberal "Bristol School of multiculturalism," which includes Bhikhu Parekh, Tariq Modood, Naser Meer and Varun Oberoi, is arguably more influential and relevant to the British and Muslim context on which much of its writing is also focused. See Levey, G.B. (2019), "The Bristol school of multiculturalism," *Ethnicities*, 19(1), pp. 200–226. Its writing on the legal front remains somewhat low-resolution and the legal picture presented here may not match the Bristol school's theoretical framework, which requires reassessing. For other ways of categorising the frameworks, in terms of assimilation, accommodation and autonomy, see Ahdar, R.J. and Aroney, N. (2010), "The topography in the Western political landscape," in Ahdar, R.J. and Aroney, N. (eds.), *Shari'a in the West*. Oxford: Oxford University Press, pp. 1–31 at pp. 21–26.

16 Coglievina, S. (2016), *Annotated legal documents on Islam in Europe: Italy*. Leiden; Boston: Brill, Ferreiro, J. and Moreras, J. (2021), *Annotated legal documents on Islam in Europe: Spain*. Leiden, Boston: Brill, Janssens, Y. (2016), *Annotated legal documents on Islam in Europe: Belgium*. Leiden; Boston: Brill.

17 Cranmer, F. (2015), "Paying the piper? Public funding and supervision of religion in a secularized society (United Kingdom)," in Messner, F. (ed.), *Public funding of religions in Europe*. Farnham: Ashgate, pp. 171–198 at pp. 172 and 179.

fore presumed to be regulated by private and not public law; and this attitude of minimal regulation of religious groups is reinforced by the judicial principle of non-interference in their internal affairs.[18]

Apart from those areas in which legislation dictates otherwise, central government actions have traditionally not been restricted by more than a series of constitutional conventions. The powers of the central authorities depend on the exercise of the Royal Prerogative, nominally vested in the crown, but which effectively grants the executive a large area of discretion to make policies and pursue relationships, including those with religious groups, figures or organisations. Voluntary bodies and charities are among the "stakeholder" groups usually asked to respond to consultations on the planning of policy and legislation.

Scotland's separate legal system survived the Treaty and Acts of Union of 1706–1707 that united it with England under the Crown and the Westminster Parliament. Despite this settlement in the eighteenth century, separate decisions are required for legislation to apply in Scotland. Autonomy was widened in 1998 to the asymmetrically devolved assemblies and governments in Scotland, Wales and Northern Ireland and has since been deepening.[19] Devolution excludes defence, trade, immigration, foreign and constitutional policy, which still leaves many other areas of law and policy, such as health, education, and justice and policing, with the devolved governments. Essentially, the "British legal systems," referred to in the plural here, are those pertaining to these legal arrangements for the "nations" as well as that centred on Westminster.

Local government authorities are established in different and often confusing levels of tiers, and are responsible for areas such as managing common spaces, granting planning permission for buildings and change of property use, making decisions on social care, and maintaining schools. Other important decision-makers are large institutions such as health or police authorities and smaller ones such as individual schools or the contractors who provide goods and services to and for all of these authorities, and who have a muted but important role in a context in which the privatisation or contracting out of nominally public services has become standard. The provision for Muslims of burial sites, flexibility towards school dress, respect for dietary requirements,

18 Sandberg, R. (2011), *Law and religion*. Cambridge: Cambridge University Press, pp. 72–77.

19 The Royal Prerogative can be applied by the ministers in Scotland and Northern Ireland but not in Wales where other arrangements apply. See Torrance, D. (2024), *The royal prerogative and ministerial advice*. House of Commons Library.

and permission to build mosques and run madrasas have all become standard policies in these local contexts.[20]

The historical link between the common law and Christianity has become diluted over the past half-century in preference to a secular neutrality.[21] The religiously neutral stance of the common law is reflected in the following statement made in 2013 by Sir James Munby, when he was the President of the Family Division of the High Court:

> Religion—whatever the particular believer's faith—is not the business of government or of the secular courts, though the courts will, of course, pay every respect to the individual's or family's religious principles. Article 9 of the European Convention for the Protection of Human Rights and Fundamental Freedoms 1950 demands no less. The starting point of the common law is thus respect for an individual's religious principles, coupled with an essentially neutral view of religious beliefs and a benevolent tolerance of cultural and religious diversity. A secular judge must be wary of straying across the well recognised divide between church and State. It is not for a judge to weigh one religion against another. The court recognises no religious distinctions and, generally speaking, passes no judgment on religious beliefs or on the tenets, doctrines or rules of any particular section of society. All are entitled to equal respect, so long as they are "legally and socially acceptable" and not "immoral or socially obnoxious" or "pernicious".[22]

The reference to the common law points to the importance of case law and the precedents set by the higher courts, which in turn bind the lower courts and

20 Nielsen, J.S. and Otterbeck, J. (2016), *Muslims in Western Europe*. Edinburgh: Edinburgh University Press. pp. 57–59, Gale, R. (2005), "Representing the City: Mosques and the Planning Process in Birmingham," *Journal of Ethnic and Migration Studies*, 31(6), pp. 1161–1179, Gale, R. (2007), "Planning law and mosque development: The politics of religion and residence in Birmingham", in Shah, P. (ed.), *Law and ethnic plurality: Socio-legal perspectives*. Leiden: Brill Nijhoff, pp. 127–144.

21 Knights, S. (2021), *Law, rights, and religion*. Oxford: Oxford University Press, pp. 37–40.

22 Munby, S.J., "Law, morality and religion in the family courts," Lecture at the conference on *The sacred and the secular: religion, culture and the family courts*, London, 29 October 2013. A very similar view was expressed by the same judge when he was Munby J. in *Sulaiman v Juffali* [2001] EWHC 556 (Fam) [47]; and also *R. v Secretary of State for the Home Department Ex p. Moon* (1995) Admin LR 477, 480 cited in Knights, S. (2021), *Law, rights, and religion*. Oxford: Oxford University Press, p. 57. Similarly, see Cranmer, F. (2015), "Paying the piper? Public funding and supervision of religion in a secularized society (United Kingdom)," in Messner, F. (ed.), *Public funding of religions in Europe*. Farnham: Ashgate, pp. 171–198 at pp. 172–174, citing other judgments.

future courts, unless there are good legal or factual grounds for departing from earlier judgments. As in other common law countries, judgments given in British jurisdictions will typically contain detail in ways unfamiliar to other sorts of legal systems, and this carries some benefits. We get a greater sense of the factual background as well as the legal reasoning employed by the lawyers and judges. This accounts for the decision to include somewhat lengthier extracts from the relevant case law in this volume. Longer judgments also provide a window into the contemporary lifeworld of Muslims and some sense of how they are using the official law, notwithstanding its filtering through the language of British cultural and legal idioms.

If the older conception of tolerance meant the lifting of restrictions imposed on individuals because of their religion or their religious practices, its newer "multiculturalist" form has meant the imposition of several types of obligation. These rights and positive duties cut into the older traditional negative conception of liberty. They also provide a more definite legal expression for British multiculturalism. The enactment of civil anti-discrimination laws from the second half of the twentieth century as well as some criminal laws, which have been extended to cover religious groups at the behest of Muslim campaigners, has restricted contractual, expressive and other freedoms in the name of preventing and penalising certain acts that British legal systems now deem unacceptable.[23] These laws exist alongside a network of other legislation passed as the administrative and welfare state considerably widened its scope in British life in the post-Second World War period.

The last half century has seen the infusion of human rights norms, particularly from the European Convention on Human Rights (ECHR) and its Protocols as interpreted by the European and British judiciaries. While originally predicated on complaints being made directly to Strasbourg, judicial pronouncements made at the domestic level rendered the Convention more significant within British legal systems. The most obvious provision in the Convention concerning the status of Muslims and Islam is Article 9 of the ECHR on the freedom of thought, conscience, and religion. An early pronouncement on the significance of the Convention was given by Lord Denning in a case in which Article 9 was claimed in support of interpreting a statute to allow an employee time off for prayer during working hours:

23 For the claim that Muslim campaigning achieved some recognition for religious groups in this legislation see especially Meer, N. (2010), *Citizenship, identity and the politics of multiculturalism: The rise of Muslim consciousness*. Basingstoke: Palgrave Macmillan,Nash, P. (2022), *British Islam and English law: A classical pluralist perspective*. Cambridge: Cambridge University Press, pp. 45–80.

> The convention is not part of our English law, but, as I have often said, we will always have regard to it. We will do our best to see that our decisions are in conformity with it. But it is drawn in such vague terms that it can be used for all sorts of unreasonable claims and provoke all sorts of litigation. As so often happens with high-sounding principles, they have to be brought down to earth. They have to be applied in a work-a-day world.[24]

Some 20 years later the Human Rights Act 1998 was enacted, and it compelled courts and public authorities to act compatibly with the ECHR.[25] Lord Denning's foresight in warning about the ECHR's potential to "be used for all sorts of unreasonable claims and provoke all sorts of litigation" was salutary, albeit since ignored by legislators and lawyers.[26] The evidence compiled in this volume demonstrates how the ECHR is now routinely inserted into litigation claims concerning Muslims, demanding that judges take a view on its possible breach.

European Community and European Union membership over the last half century has meant the direct effect of norms of those legal orders and their mandatory implementation in British legal systems. From laws regarding the slaughter of animals for consumption to legal safeguards against religious discrimination in employment, the EU legal order has had its significant, if not widely noticed, effects. The influence of the Court of Justice of the EU has also been significant in some areas such as the impact on Britain in terms of immigration.[27] Brexit-related legislation allows for both the retention of and change to EU laws.[28]

---

24 *Ahmad v Inner London Education Authority* [1978] Q.B. 36 at 41.

25 See further ch. 1, section 1.

26 Lester, A. and Lyle, T. (2009), "History and context," in Lester, A., Pannick, D., and Herberg, J. (eds.), *Human rights law and practice*. 3rd ed. London: LexisNexis, pp. 1–26, at pp. 8–15.

27 See Guild, E. (2016), *BREXIT and its consequences for UK and EU citizenship or monstrous citizenship*. Leiden: Brill Nijhoff.; Shah, P. (2009), "Activism in the European Court of Justice and changing options for Turkish citizen migrants in the United Kingdom," in Hailbronner, K., Tiryakioğlu, B., Schneider, K., and Küçük, E. (eds.), *Vatandaşlık, göç, mülteci ve yabancılar hukukundaki güncel gelişmeler* (*Current developments in citizenship, immigration, refugee law and law of foreigners*). Ankara: Union of Turkish Bar Associations, pp. 299–326 for the migratory impact on the UK of the Turkey-EEC agreement (Ankara agreement) and its protocol which also arises out of the EU legal order.

28 The key legislation is the European Union (Withdrawal) Act 2018.

3 The Islamic Law or *Shari'a*

The question of Islamic law, the *Shari'a,* has seemed especially pertinent to a discussion of Britain and its legal systems, and perhaps more so than many other European legal systems.[29] The Archbishop of Canterbury's speech in 2008 has created the impression abroad that *Shari'a* is a part of British law, an impression that some in Britain also hold to. The fact that reportedly many *Shari'a* councils operate in Britain adds to the impression that *Shari'a* is officially recognised. The language frequently used by the press, of parallel legal systems and *Shari'a* courts, fuels the impression.[30] Further, several surveys point to the popularity of *Shari'a* among British Muslims who favour it in significant numbers. This may be not just talk in terms of ideals to be pursued but a part of the actual reconstruction process in Britain. Werner Menski remarks that:

> [I]t may appear today, from the outside, that Muslims in Britain are following English law, but in effect they are following a path which *they* consider appropriate. The classic Muslim term for this is nothing but *Shari'a,* but in the new environment of Britain, a new hybrid form of *Shari'a* was needed to avoid breaking the official law of the new home.

Menski goes on to name this hybrid form as "*angrezi Shari'at.*"[31] At the same time, what exactly is meant by those referring to, or making demands for, the *Shari'a* is quite unclear, and goes beyond the often observed point that the term "*Shari'a*" itself is "ambiguous" or, like the word "law," is just too general.[32]

---

29 The one obvious exception is Greece, where the *Shari'a* has official status for the Muslims of Western Thrace. See Tsitselikis, K. (2016), *Annotated legal documents on Islam in Europe: Greece.* Leiden: Brill.

30 Marotta, A. (2021), *A geo-legal approach to the English Sharia courts: Cases and conflicts.* Leiden, The Netherlands: Brill investigates in detail the representation of *Shari'a* bodies in Britain as "courts".

31 In Pearl, D. and Menski, W. (1998), *Muslim family law.* London: Sweet & Maxwell, pp. 57–59, the quotation being at p. 58. In the same text, at p. 84, the authors comment: "… Muslims, wherever they may be in the world, tend to claim that they remain governed by *Shari'a* principles."

32 See for the point about ambiguity, impression and generality, Rohe, M. (2014b), *Islamic Law in Past and Present.* Leiden: Brill, p. 10, Ahdar, R.J. and Aroney, N. (2010), "The topography of Shari'a in the Western political landscape," in Ahdar, R.J. and Aroney, N. (eds.), *Shari'a in the West.* Oxford: Oxford University Press, pp. 1–31, at pp. 3–6; Marotta, A. (2021), *A geo-legal approach to the English Sharia courts: Cases and conflicts.* Leiden, The Netherlands: Brill, pp. 19–22. See also the interesting case of *Shamil Bank of Bahrain EC v Beximco*

In his speech of February 2008, the then Archbishop of Canterbury, Rowan Williams, spoke at the Royal Courts of Justice before an invited audience of nearly 1,000 people regarding "the question of whether there should be a higher level of attention to religious identity and communal rights in the practice of the law, and to the larger issue ... of something like a delegation of certain legal functions to the religious courts of a community."[33] The tricky question was how to reconcile the British legal approach with the fact that the resolving of certain problems was happening in several unofficial Muslim fora, the *Shari'a* councils, which explains the reference by the archbishop to "religious courts."[34] Arguably, Dr. Williams was overplaying his hand by suggesting that it was necessary to address the "recognition of 'supplementary jurisdiction' in some areas, especially family law" even if he had merely raised the issue without providing any definite framework for or specific commitment to it.[35] If anything, his speech contains a series of warnings about the courts of a particular community acting in ways that could jeopardise the common rights of their members as citizens and, so, did not unequivocally favour either such courts or their official recognition. The Archbishop's intervention nevertheless gave impetus to the debate on legal pluralism in Britain for at least a few years afterwards, and some more detailed discussions have taken place since then, looking into how far English law ought to accommodate Islamic law and religion.[36]

Pharmaceuticals Ltd and others [2004] EWCA Civ 19, [2004] 1 W.L.R. 1784, extracted at ch. 12, section 2.

33 The text of the speech has been published in several sources: see Williams, R. (2008), "Civil and religious law in England: A religious perspective," *Ecclesiastical Law Journal*, 10(3), pp. 262–282 (the quotation is at p. 267); also Williams, R. (2013), "Civil and religious law in England: A religious perspective" in Griffith-Jones, R. (ed.), *Islam and English law: Rights, responsibilities and the place of Shari'a*. Cambridge: Cambridge University Press, pp. 20–34, Ahdar, R.J. and Aroney, N. (eds.) (2010), *Shari'a in the West*. Oxford; New York: Oxford University Press, pp. 293–308. For an account of the opposition see Griffith-Jones, R. (2013), "The 'unavoidable' adoption of shari'a law—the generation of a media storm," in Griffith-Jones, R. (ed.), *Islam and English law: Rights, responsibilities and the place of Shari'a*. Cambridge: Cambridge University Press, pp. 9–19 and Marotta, A. (2021), *A geo-legal approach to the English Sharia courts: Cases and conflicts*. Leiden, The Netherlands: Brill, pp. 135–146.

34 Grillo, R.D. (2015), *Muslim families, politics and the law: A legal industry in multicultural Britain*. Farnham: Ashgate, esp. pp. 13–36.

35 Williams, R. (2008), "Civil and religious law in England: A religious perspective," *Ecclesiastical Law Journal*, 10(3), pp. 262–282 at p. 268.

36 The controversy in the aftermath of Dr. Williams' lecture was initially tackled by Lord Phillips, then Chief Justice of England and Wales, in a speech at the East London Muslim Centre on 3 July 2008; extracted at Ahdar, R.J. and Aroney, N. (eds.) (2010), *Shari'a in the*

It is remarkable that, although British colonial policy tolerated a wide scope being given to Muslims in matters of personal law, within British legal systems a much narrower scope for recognition exists under private international law. This contrasts with the civil law countries of continental Europe, which only reluctantly granted recognition to Islamic personal law in colonial contexts, and, in the case of France, only on the condition that citizenship would be granted only to those who chose not to have their affairs regulated by personal law.[37] The same continental civil law countries today accord broader recognition to Islamic personal law via private international law, whereas British legal systems apply the law of the forum, and not the law that derives from one's nationality status.[38]

In Britain, multiculturalism has thus certainly not meant full-scale legal pluralism of the kind implemented in much of the British Empire, recognising distinct official spheres of personal laws and, among them, Islamic personal law, extending to a range of faith-related and familial matters.[39] While that framework derived from an ethic of Protestant tolerance proper to the eighteenth century, it would not have been thought suitable or acceptable in the twentieth century. Indeed, it was not. When the Union of Muslim Organisations of the UK and Eire demanded the application of just such a personal law system in 1975, it was repeatedly rejected by British ministers, although

West. Oxford: Oxford University Press, pp. 309–318. The more formal discussions, especially the lectures at Temple Church immediately following Dr. Williams' speech, have been published in Griffith-Jones, R. (ed.) (2013), *Islam and English law: Rights, responsibilities and the place of Shari'a*. Cambridge: Cambridge University Press. For some of the subsequent international commentary see the contributions in Ahdar, R.J. and Aroney, N. (2010), *Shari'a in the West*. Oxford: Oxford University Press.

37 Brett, M. (1988), "Legislating for inequality in Algeria: The Senatus-Consulte of 14 July 1865," *Bulletin of the School of Oriental and African Studies, University of London*, 51(3), pp. 440–461.

38 Shah, P. (2017), "South Asian legal systems and families in foreign courts: The British case," in Garimella, S.R. and Jolly, S. (eds.), *Private international law: South Asian states' practice*. Singapore: Springer Singapore, pp. 3–18. For Germany see Rohe, M. (2014), *Islamic law in past and present*. Leiden: Brill. pp, 468–490.

39 This sort of legal pluralism is the official one that legal anthropologists and others have contested and sought to confine through the use of terms such as "weak" or "classic legal pluralism". For theoretical overviews see Menski, W.F. (2006), *Comparative law in a global context: The legal systems of Asia and Africa*. Cambridge: Cambridge University Press, pp. 82–128, Shah, P. (2020), "Are there Asian diasporic laws in Britain? Reconsidering the presuppositions of legal pluralism," *Quaderni di diritto e politica ecclesiastica, Rivista trimestrale* (2020), 1, pp. 201–220, Tamanaha, B.Z. (2021), *Legal pluralism explained: History, theory, consequences*. New York: Oxford University Press, pp. 1–18.

of legal standards that conflict with some interpretation of *Shari'a* or Islam are reflected in the case law extracted in this book.

Since the early 1980s, *ulema* have organised to recreate an informal semblance of the old order by creating *Shari'a* fora to deal with legal problems. In Britain, they take the form of *Shari'a* councils although they are often labelled *Shari'a* courts in the press, while a link has been made between the South Asian and British versions.[56] They are known to exist in Canada, the United States and Australia, and therefore appear to be a particularly Anglo-Western development, where official multiculturalism holds sway.[57] Unlike in Ontario, where legislation was needed to remove the official imprimatur over the disputes they settled,[58] these fora do not have such an official status in British legal systems except that the commercial and inheritance disputes they resolve are covered, by election, under the Arbitration Act 1996. Their role is not formally recognised in other sorts of family disputes, even if their *de facto* presence is acknowledged in a variety of legal and other official contexts.[59] *Shari'a* councils in

(2007), "Revealed: Preachers' messages of hate," *The Guardian*, 7 January 2007. Available at: https://www.theguardian.com/media/2007/jan/07/broadcasting.channel4, Mirza, M., Senthilkumaran, A., and Ja'far, Z. (2007), *Living apart together: British Muslims and the paradox of multiculturalism*, London: Policy Exchange. Available at: https://policyexchange.org.uk/wp-content/uploads/2016/09/living-apart-together-jan-07.pdf, Taher, A. (2008), "A third of Muslim students back killings," *The Sunday Times*, 27 July 2008, Heath, A.F. Fisher, S.D., Rosenblatt, G., Sanders, D., and Sobolewska, M. (2013). *The political integration of ethnic minorities in Britain*. Oxford: Oxford University Press, pp. 70–71. For some claims of *Shari'a* which Islamists foresee as establishing, which would certainly conflict with British laws, see Perry, D.L. (2019), *Mainstream Islamism in Britain: Educating for the "Islamic Revival"*. Commission for Countering Extremism, pp. 9–15, Casey, L. (2016), *The Casey Review: A review into opportunity and integration*. London: Her Majesty's Stationery Office, pp. 69–71, citing a poll for Channel 4 published in 2016.

56 Jones, J. (2020), "Muslim alternative dispute resolution: Tracing the pathways of Islamic legal practice between South Asia and contemporary Britain," *Journal of Muslim Minority Affairs*, 40, pp. 48–66.

57 For Australia see Saeed, A. (2010), "Reflections on the establishment of Shari'a courts in Australia," in Ahdar, R.J. and Aroney, N. (eds.), *Shari'a in the West*. Oxford: Oxford University Press, pp. 223–238 at pp. 234–235 and Black, A. (2010), "In the shadow of our legal system: Shari'a in Australia," in Ahdar, R.T. and Aroney, N. (eds.), *Shari'a in the West*, pp. 239–254 at p. 244. For the United States see Broyde, M.J. (2017), *Sharia tribunals, rabbinical courts, and Christian panels: Religious arbitration in America and the West*. Oxford University Press.

58 Korteweg, A.C. and Selby, J.A. (eds.) (2012), *Debating Sharia: Islam, gender politics, and family law arbitration*. Toronto: University of Toronto Press.

59 There are some passing references to *Shari'a* councils in case law. See, e.g., *Luton Borough Council v Mr G, Mrs G, HG, AG (by her litigation friend, the Official Solicitor)* [2024]

Britain have nevertheless received disproportionate attention in the academic literature.[60]

An independent report commissioned by the British government advocated for measures to reduce the use of *Shari'a* councils.[61] It also found it unlikely that they had developed their operations beyond a certain measure i.e., beyond providing Islamic divorces to women who cannot otherwise obtain them from their husbands. While divorce seems to be the mainstay of *Shari'a* council use, it has been incorrectly related to the fact that a large proportion of Muslim marriages remain unregistered. The clientele of the *Shari'a* councils is mixed i.e., composed of women in religious-only marriages, those with both Islamic and officially registered marriages, and those whose marriages, although not registered, are nonetheless recognised in British legal systems if they are from jurisdictions such as India, Pakistan, or Bangladesh, where such marriages are valid or legally tolerated. Thus, although such "unregistered marriages" probably comprise the largest set of marriages among Muslims, the curbing of such marriages, which is the focus of some campaigners, need not be directly related to the use of *Shari'a* councils.[62] In addition, some unsuccessful attempts have been made to introduce statutory controls on the *Shari'a* councils, in part because they are deemed to misrepresent the

EWCOP 18, [2024] 3 WLUK 564, a case concerning an application by a local authority to continue a forced marriage protection order; *M v N* 2022 Fam. L.R. 102, concerning divorce proceedings brought by a husband where there was evidence that the marriage had been dissolved by a "Muslim council."

60 Bano, S. (2012), *Muslim women and Shari'ah councils: Transcending the boundaries of community and law*. Basingstoke: Palgrave Macmillan, Grillo, R.D. (2015), *Muslim families, politics and the law: A legal industry in multicultural Britain.* Farnham: Ashgate, Bowen, J.R. (2016), *On British Islam: Religion, law, and everyday practice in shari'a councils*. Princeton, NJ: Princeton University Press, Walker, T. (2016), *Shari'a councils and Muslim women in Britain: Rethinking the role of power and authority*. Leiden, The Netherlands: Brill, Marotta, A. (2021), *A geo-legal approach to the English Sharia courts: Cases and conflicts*. Leiden: Brill. In distinguishing his study from the conventional, Nash, P. (2022), *British Islam and English law: A classical pluralist perspective*. Cambridge: Cambridge University Press, p. 1 points out that areas such as Muslim marriages and *Shari'a* councils have been "done to death" and studies on them are "legion."

61 Siddiqui, M. (2018), *The independent review into the application of sharia law in England and Wales*. London: Her Majesty's Stationery Office. See Marotta, A. (2021), *A geo-legal approach to the English Sharia courts: Cases and conflicts*. Leiden, The Netherlands: Brill, pp. 183–187 for a contextualised discussion of the review.

62 The review by Siddiqui, M. (2018), *The independent review into the application of sharia law in England and Wales*. London: Her Majesty's Stationery Office also argues that unregistered marriages are not a necessary reason for *Shari'a* councils to be approached and cites several other possible reasons.

legal effects of their rulings and because they treat women in a discriminatory manner.[63] Although sex and religious discrimination are part and parcel of Islamic rules on marriage and divorce, *Shari'a* council proceedings that presuppose that such treatments are probably not unlawful under the Equality Act 2010.[64]

This volume gathers further evidence with respect to the ambivalent British legal approach to the *Shari'a* in its substantive sense. In some instances, such as Islamic finance, the rules of Islam have been incorporated especially because of the financial benefits perceived to accrue.[65] In many other instances, as varied as whether adults who lack capacity should fast during Ramadan or how far extremism is reprimanded by Islam, courts do go on to consider evidence as to compliance with Islamic rules and their bearing on disputes in the courts. Although the neutrality principle mentioned above may be being adhered to, it has certainly not meant a blindness to religious factors with respect to Islam, but rather an engagement with its rules in so far as they are discernible. Meanwhile, there have also been many attempts in the judgments and by legislation to keep within bounds some of the more unsavoury practices, from terrorism to forced marriage, associated with Muslims. In the early days of the UK's membership of the EEC, Lord Denning used the phrase the "incoming tide" to describe how the influence of the rules of European law upon British legal systems could not be held back.[66] As the evidence in this volume testifies, after suitable conceptual adaptation, the phrase may be aptly used of the influence of Islam too.[67]

63 Grillo, R.D. (2015), *Muslim families, politics and the law: A legal industry in multicultural Britain*. Farnham: Ashgate, pp. 137–246, Marotta, A. (2021), *A geo-legal approach to the English Sharia courts: Cases and conflicts*. Leiden, The Netherlands: Brill, pp. 146–159.

64 The Equality Act 2010, Schedule 23, para. 2 makes an exception for religious organisations providing a service on a discriminatory basis.

65 Nash, P. (2022), *British Islam and English law: A classical pluralist perspective*. Cambridge: Cambridge University Press, pp. 131–152.

66 *H P Bulmer Ltd and another v J Bollinger SA and others* [1974] 2 All ER 1226 at pp. 1232–1233.

67 Only a few years later, Lord Denning seemed more perplexed, warning that: "… the flowing tide of Community law is coming in fast. It has not stopped at high-water mark. It has broken the dykes and the banks. It has submerged the surrounding land. So much so that we have to learn to become amphibious if we wish to keep our heads above water." *Shields v E Coomes (Holdings) Ltd* [1979] 1 All ER 456 at 462.

4 Material Covered in This Volume

This volume reproduces primary documents that provide the reader with the raw material for understanding the impact of the Muslim presence in British legal systems in some of its forensic detail. In this text Britain means the whole of the United Kingdom.[68] This material is admittedly biased towards providing the contemporary picture, rather than being a step-by-step historical record of the development of the legal approaches towards Islam and Muslims which would have generated a different sort of book. This bias also satisfies the necessity of providing the reader with the current, prevailing legal picture, a sort of status quo. It will be obvious to the legally informed that old material ceases to be legally relevant as the new replaces it either by repeal or by the creation of new precedents.

It is hoped that the commentary or "annotation" and the further references that accompany each chapter will to some extent compensate for the bias. Their purpose is to provide the required context, to draw the reader's attention to the important and relevant elements of the legal sources provided, to make connections between the various topics covered in the book, and to refer the reader to further material on the topics. In addition to the references in the text and footnotes, the reader may check the bibliography for further material. Of the primary sources, mainly the legislation and case law, only those extracts thought to be the most relevant and interesting are reproduced. Often, however, the length of extracts chosen breaches the "less is more" heuristic, errs on the side of comprehensiveness, and avoids the inconvenience of the reader having to access the full documents by other means, even if their online availability makes for full access to most material. The arrangement of chapters and sections follows, as much as was sensibly possible, the general tenor of this series, when a one-off volume on British legal systems might have demanded a different sort of structure. This consistency within the series should make for easier cross-checking by readers interested in comparisons with the other countries covered by the series. At times, however, this consistency is sacrificed because of the uniqueness of British legal systems, and when maintaining a rigid structure did not make sense.

A significant number of texts has already discussed some of the material displayed here in some depth. However, no one text covers or could cover the breadth of the material now available, which is staggering. Despite the

68 This book does not discuss the legal or other situations in the Isle of Man, the Channel Islands or any British Overseas Territory.

advances made in recent years, generating this sort of compilation makes one realise just how much more could have been included, the limits of the existing work on Islam and Muslims, the sheer number of relevant legal areas, new and emerging research questions, and the range of further work that has yet to be prepared.

CHAPTER 1

Status of Religious Communities

Unlike some other European legal systems, where a specific, formal legal framework of recognition of different religious communities obtains in order to secure religious freedom, British legal systems have tended to adopt a stance of informality and voluntarism.[1] This observation should, however, be read subject to the fact that there are established Christian churches in Britain to which special legal regimes are applicable and, to that extent, the legal regime for the status of religious communities is asymmetrical. This can be seen in many ways, such as the fact that parliamentary legislation governs the functioning of the established churches, the appointment of Bishops to the House of Lords, and the fact that certain laws such as that on marriage place the Anglican church in a special position. Otherwise, religious groups are theoretically treated as voluntary associations, and therefore presumed to be regulated by private law and not public law; and this attitude of minimal regulation of religious groups is reinforced by the judicial principle of non-interference in the internal affairs of religious groups.[2] More formal structures are available however, through innumerable means which include the legal frameworks applicable to companies and charities and the ability of those celebrating marriages to become registrars of marriage. Although none of these is compulsory, they are accompanied by certain benefits as well as obligations to those groups or individuals who seek to comply with them. In this chapter specific mention is made of human rights law, the law on the registration of religious buildings and charity law.

In the introduction above, a quotation was reproduced from Lord Justice Munby when he was President of the Family Division. In an earlier judgment, given in the case of *Sulaiman v Juffali*, which concerned the recognition of a *talaq* divorce pronounced in England and communicated to the authorities in Saudi Arabia, he anticipated his later remarks thus:

> Before leaving this topic I should make it clear, and I trust he will accept, that my decision is not in any way founded upon any lack of respect either for the

1 Cranmer, F. (2015), "Paying the piper? Public funding and supervision of religion in a secularized society (United Kingdom)," in Messner, F. (ed.), *Public funding of religions in Europe*. Farnham: Ashgate, pp. 171–198 at pp. 172 and 179.

2 Sandberg, R. (2011), *Law and religion*. Cambridge: Cambridge University Press, pp. 72–77.

> husband's religion or for his culture. Although historically this country is part of the Christian west, and although it has an established church which is Christian, I sit as a secular judge serving a multi-cultural community of many faiths in which all of us can now take pride, sworn to do justice "to all manner of people". Religion—whatever the particular believer's faith—is no doubt something to be encouraged but it is not the business of government or of the secular courts. So the starting point of the law is an essentially agnostic view of religious beliefs and a tolerant indulgence to religious and cultural diversity. A secular judge must be wary of straying across the well-recognised divide between church and state. It is not for a judge to weigh one religion against another. All are entitled to equal respect, whether in times of peace or, as at present, amidst the clash of arms.[3]

While this quotation from Lord Justice Munby does not incorporate a reference to the ECHR, it will be recalled that his statement made in 2013 did refer to Article 9 ECHR.[4] It is to the Human Rights Act 1998 which incorporates the ECHR into domestic UK law to which we now turn.

1 The Human Rights Act 1998 and European Convention on Human Rights

The Human Rights Act 1998 (HRA) incorporates the European Convention on Human Rights (ECHR) into domestic UK law. Although it was one of the original drafters of the ECHR, the UK did not see fit to enable the domestic courts to apply its provisions until the HRA came into force. The ECHR is the only major human rights treaty that receives such recognition, while other prominent international human rights instruments have not received domestic recognition in the same manner, even if there may be references to them or their provisions in separate legislation.[5]

3 *Sulaiman v Juffali* [2001] EWHC 556, para. 47.

4 Munby, S.J., "Law, morality and religion in the family courts," Lecture at the conference on *The sacred and the secular: religion, culture and the family courts*, London, 29 October 2013. See the Introduction for the quotation.

5 For example, the Children Act 1989, section 1 which somewhat reflects the wording of the UN Convention on the Rights of the Child 1989, Article 3 with respect to a child's welfare. The Asylum and Immigration Appeals Act 1993, section 2 provides that nothing in the Immigration Rules should lay down any practice that would be contrary to the Refugee Convention of 1951 and its 1967 Protocol.

The kind of incorporation that the HRA enacts is important if one takes into account that the UK follows a dualist conception of international law and therefore keeps international and domestic law separate. British courts and tribunals will recognise the norms of international law in only a limited way (for instance as an aid to the interpretation of statutes which are presumed not to conflict with international obligations) unless they are instructed to do more by parliamentary legislation. An act of incorporation such as the HRA is therefore necessary for them to have full effect in the courts and tribunals.

The HRA obliges courts and tribunals to decide cases, whether brought under statute or common law, compatibly with the ECHR and requires all public authorities to act compatibly with it. Courts and tribunals must interpret existing and future legislation in conformity with the ECHR where possible and, where that is not possible, to make a "declaration of incompatibility." They must take Strasbourg case law into account in all cases in which it is relevant to do so.[6] Bodies whose "functions are of a public nature" (section 6(3)(b)) will also attract human rights claims when those bodies are privatised.[7]

The ECHR's incorporation into domestic law in this manner is important primarily because of its Article 9 on the right to freedom of thought, conscience and religion. The ECHR's non-discrimination provision in Article 14 includes religion but a claim invoking religion must also be linked to one of the other substantive rights. It thereby considerably expands the scope of religion-based claims by linking them to the enjoyment of the other rights. The potential width of the non-discrimination provision in Article 14 might also be quite considerable, given that it extends to direct and indirect forms of discrimination.[8] While the notions of direct and indirect discrimination are also contained in the Equality Act 2010, currently the main anti-discrimination statute in UK law, the HRA, endows the ECHR provisions with greater importance because they may be wider in scope and the higher courts can use the HRA to make "declarations of incompatibility" in respect of provisions of primary legislation, which the Equality Act cannot be used for.[9] The UK has not, however, acceded

6 Human Rights Act 1998, sections 6, 3, 4 and 2 respectively.

7 Knights, S. (2021), *Law, rights, and religion*. Oxford: Oxford University Press. p. 64.

8 Ibid., p. 89.

9 Human Rights Act 1998, section 4; Wadham, J. et al. (2011), *Blackstone's guide to the Human Rights Act 1998*. 6th edn. Oxford: Oxford University Press, pp. 85–91. This mechanism strikes a balance between parliamentary sovereignty, a traditional constitutional doctrine since the English revolution of the 17th century, and the importance given to the ECHR. Also see Knights, S. (2021), *Law, rights, and religion*. Oxford: Oxford University Press, p. 87.

to Protocol 12, which provides for a free-standing right to non-discrimination including on grounds of religion. In addition, Protocol 1, Article 2, provides for respect to be given to the right of parents to ensure that education and teaching are provided in conformity with their religious and philosophical convictions.

During the passage of the HRA concerns were raised that it might lead to questions about whether the Church of England, for example, could refuse to marry gay couples or to dismiss schoolteachers who had lost their faith. An obligation was therefore added in section 13 of that Act that a court or tribunal must have "particular regard" to the importance of the right in Article 9 ECHR with respect to a religious organisation and its members.

Human Rights Act 1998

13 Freedom of thought, conscience and religion.
(1) If a court's determination of any question arising under this Act might affect the exercise by a religious organisation (itself or its members collectively) of the Convention right to freedom of thought, conscience and religion, it must have particular regard to the importance of that right.[10]

It has been said that this provision does not add anything substantial to the obligation already contained in Article 9 and that it functions more as a political signal to religious interests.[11] Parliamentary assurances were also given by the government minister during the passage of the HRA that churches need not fear being subject to its provisions because they do not act as public authorities for the purposes of the Act. However, that claim is difficult to square with the argument that, when they act on behalf of the state, they perform some functions of a public nature, such as performing marriages, providing burials, or providing education in church schools.[12]

---

10 Section 13(2) provides that "court" includes a tribunal.

11 Pannick, D., and Steele, I. (2009), "Human Rights Act 1998," in Lester, A., Pannick, D., and Herberg, J. (eds.), *Human rights law and practice*. 3rd ed. London: LexisNexis, at pp. 89–91, Wadham, J. et al. (2011), *Blackstone's guide to the Human Rights Act 1998*. 6th edition, pp. 62–63, Knights, S. (2021), *Law, rights, and religion*. Oxford: Oxford University Press, p. 66.

12 Pannick, D., and Steele, I. (2009), "Human Rights Act 1998," in Lester, A., Pannick, D., and Herberg, J. (eds.), *Human rights law and practice*. 3rd ed. London: LexisNexis, pp. 89–90. *Parochial Church Council of the Parish of Aston Cantlow and Wilmcote with Billesley, Warwickshire v Wallbank and another* [2003] UKHL 37 at [13]–[15], per Lord Nicholls. See also Knights, S. (2021), *Law, rights, and religion*. Oxford: Oxford University Press, p. 65.

This means that human rights claims could emerge at some point in the future against Muslim bodies also in those sorts of areas i.e., performing marriages and providing education in schools. It is already the case that segregation on grounds of sex in co-educational schools of a religious character has attracted a school's liability under the Equality Act 2010, and it would not be beyond the realm of possibility that such schools could also be made liable under the HRA.[13] It is an open question whether a Muslim religious body such as a *Shari'a* council can be construed as performing functions of a public nature. Would the granting of Islamic religious divorces, which are one of the main activities that *Shari'a* councils carry out, be construed as performing a function of a public nature?

1.1 *Standard of Review by the Domestic Courts under Article 9*

R (Begum) v Headteacher and Governors of Denbigh High School [2006] UKHL 15 (per Lord Hoffmann)

In the *Begum* case, that of a Muslim pupil whose school refused her claim to be allowed to wear a *jilbab*, a full-length gown that covered her neck, the House of Lords held that Article 9 involves a substantive test and not a procedural one of the kind that might be typical of judicial review claims:

> [68] In domestic judicial review, the court is usually concerned with whether the decision-maker reached his decision in the right way rather than whether he got what the court might think to be the right answer. But article 9 is concerned with substance, not procedure. It confers no right to have a decision made in any particular way. What matters is the result: was the right to manifest a religious belief restricted in a way which is not justified under article 9.2? The fact that the decision-maker is allowed an area of judgment in imposing requirements which may have the effect of restricting the right does not entitle a court to say that a justifiable and proportionate restriction should be struck down because the decision-maker did not approach the question in the structured way in which a judge might have done. Head teachers and governors cannot be expected to make such decisions with textbooks on human rights law at their elbows. The most that can be said is that the way in which the school approached the problem may help to persuade a judge that its answer fell within the area of judgment accorded to it by the law.

13 See the extracts at ch. 7, section 2 from *Regina (Interim Executive Board of Al-Hijrah School) v HM Chief Inspector of Education, Children's Services and Skills (Secretary of State for Education and others intervening)* [2017] EWCA Civ 1426.

1.2 *Use of Human Rights Grounds to Limit Recognition*

It has been argued that any claims for recognition of ethnic minority religious and cultural practices should also be measured against the international human rights obligations, such as the ECHR, which the UK has undertaken. Therefore, not only might the adherence to human rights require "positive" recognition of the norms and practices of Muslims; it could also provide the justification for their non-recognition.[14] As was held by the European Court of Human Rights in the *Refah Partisi* case, a threat posed to the stability of the democratic institutions of the state can amount to a pressing social need to curb human rights otherwise recognised in the ECHR.[15]

2 Registration of Places of Worship

It has been noted that the idea of a public religion is an unfamiliar one to English lawyers. However, there are two principal candidates for a regime of public religion: the registration of places of worship and charitable status.[16] There are two ways in which registration by religious bodies of their places of worship can be made under the Places of Worship Registration Act 1855. This Act provides for registration and certification by the Registrar-General, an application for which is made through the Superintendent Registrar of Births, Deaths and Marriages at local level. Furthermore, registration is a precondition for a number of privileges including protection by the criminal law from disturbance, exemption from local taxation, registration for the solemnisation of marriages, and exemption from registration with the Charity Commission.

14 Poulter, S. (1998), *Ethnicity, law, and human rights: The English experience*. Oxford: Clarendon.

15 *Refah Partisi (The Welfare Party) v Turkey* (2003) 37 E.H.R.R; McGoldrick, D. (2013), "The compatibility of an Islamic shari'a law system or shari'a rules with the European Convention on Human Rights," in Griffith-Jones, R. (ed.), *Islam and English law: Rights, responsibilities and the place of Shari'a*. New York: Cambridge University Press, pp. 42–71, Pannick, D. and Steele, I. (2009), "Human Rights Act 1998," in Lester, A. and Pannick, D., and Herberg, J. (eds.), *Human rights law and practice*. 3rd ed. London: LexisNexis, pp. 117–118, 121 noting that, although not directly referred to, the ECtHR used an idea already contained in Article 17 (destruction or limitation of Convention rights and freedoms). See ch. 2, section 1 for further discussion.

16 Rivers, J. (2010), *The law of organized religions: Between establishment and secularism*. Oxford: Oxford University Press, p. 147.

Places of Worship Registration Act 1855

…

II Places of Worship to be certified to Registrar General.

Every Place of Meeting for Religious Worship of Protestant Dissenters or other Protestants, and of Persons professing, the Roman Catholic Religion … not heretofore certified and registered or recorded in a manner required by Law, and every Place of Meeting for Religious Worship of Persons professing the Jewish Religion, not heretofore certified and registered or recorded as aforesaid, and every Place of Meeting for Religious Worship of any other Body or Denomination of Persons, may be certified in Writing to the Registrar General of Births, Deaths, and Marriages in *England*, through the Superintendent Registrar of Births, Deaths, and Marriages of the District in which such Place may be situate; and such Certificate shall be in Duplicate, and upon Forms in accordance with Schedule A. to this Act, or to the like Effect, such Forms to be provided by the said Registrar General, and to be obtained (without Payment) upon Application to such Superintendent Registrar as aforesaid; and the said Superintendent Registrar shall, upon the Receipt of such Certificate in Duplicate, forthwith transmit the same to the said Registrar General, who, after having caused the Place of Meeting therein mentioned to be recorded as herein-after directed, shall return One of the said Certificates to the said Superintendent Registrar, to be re-delivered by him to the certifying Party, and shall keep the other Certificate with the Records of the General Register Office.

III Places of Meeting to be recorded.

The said Registrar General shall cause all Places of Meeting for Religious Worship certified to him under this Act to be recorded in a Book to be kept by him for that Purpose at the General Register Office, and no such Place of Meeting as aforesaid shall be certified to or registered in any Court of any Bishop or Archdeacon, or be certified to or recorded at any General or Quarter Sessions; and the certifying to the said Registrar General of any such Place of Meeting for Religious Worship of Protestant Dissenters or other Protestants or Roman Catholics, or Persons professing the Jewish Religion, and of any Place of Meeting for Religious Worship of any other Body or Denomination of Persons, shall, subject to the Provisions herein contained, have the same Force and Effect as if such Place had been duly certified and recorded or registered and recorded as before the passing of the said Act of the Fifteenth and Sixteenth Years of Her Majesty, Chapter Thirty-six, was required by Law, and such Act and this Act had not been passed.

3 Charity Law

The second of the two possible candidates for a regime of public religion in British legal systems is charity law. It has been suggested that the charitable trust was a substitute for the lack of availability of forms of corporate personality for public institutions.[17] Charities will tend to be trusts, but they do not have to be incorporated under company law, although many are because company law may be seen as advantageous. In addition to charity law, therefore, charities could simultaneously be subject to a combination of different legal frameworks, particularly those on trusts and companies.

3.1 *Charity Status*

With respect to charitable status in England and Wales, a comprehensive reform was undertaken in the Charities Act 2006, but the current regime for England and Wales is contained in the Charities Act 2011, from which the provisions below are reproduced. The statutory basis for charity law in Scotland and Northern Ireland is distinct and contained in the Charities and Trustee Investment (Scotland) Act 2005 and the Charities Act (Northern Ireland) 2008 respectively. The regulatory bodies are, respectively, the Charity Commission of England and Wales, the Office of the Scottish Charity Regulator and the Charity Commission for Northern Ireland.

Prior to the 2006 Act, it was presumed that the advancement of religion constitutes a "charitable purpose" per se, but this is no longer the case. Candidates for charitable status have to establish that theirs is a purpose that not only pursues the advancement of religion (Charities Act 2011, section 3(1)(c)) but is also for the "public benefit" (sections 2(1)(b) and 4). A charity, even if it has some sort of religious character, need not only pursue the advancement of religion; the Charities Act 2011, section 3(1), allows for other purposes such as the relief of poverty, education, health and the saving of lives, etc. A charity must, however, have exclusively charitable objects, meaning that all its activities must be directed towards charitable purposes.[18]

The Charities Act 2011, section 3(2)(a) attempts to provide an inclusive definition of religion for the purposes of the Act beyond the monotheistic presuppositions of the Semitic religions, to include belief in more than one god or in no god. This expansive concept is not directly relevant to Muslims or Islam, except that it may provoke objections by Muslims because entities recognised

17 Ibid., p. 160.

18 These changes are reflected in Scotland and Northern Ireland too.

as a result would go beyond the religions of the book and would be considered not as religions proper, but as either heretical or false religions. The primary benefit of charity status means that gifts made to charities are exempt from taxation, a topic which is taken up later (ch. 3, section 1).

Charities Act 2011

2 Meaning of "charitable purpose"

(1) For the purposes of the law of England and Wales, a charitable purpose is a purpose which—
  (a) falls within section 3(1), and
  (b) is for the public benefit (see section 4).

(2) Any reference in any enactment or document (in whatever terms)—
  (a) to charitable purposes, or
  (b) to institutions having purposes that are charitable under the law relating to charities in England and Wales, is to be read in accordance with subsection (1).

3 Descriptions of purposes

(1) A purpose falls within this subsection if it falls within any of the following descriptions of purposes—
  (a) the prevention or relief of poverty;
  (b) the advancement of education;
  (c) the advancement of religion;
  (d) the advancement of health or the saving of lives;
  (e) the advancement of citizenship or community development;
  (f) the advancement of the arts, culture, heritage or science;
  (g) the advancement of amateur sport;
  (h) the advancement of human rights, conflict resolution or reconciliation or the promotion of religious or racial harmony or equality and diversity;
  (i) the advancement of environmental protection or improvement;
  (j) the relief of those in need because of youth, age, ill-health, disability, financial hardship or other disadvantage;
  (k) the advancement of animal welfare;
  (l) the promotion of the efficiency of the armed forces of the Crown or of the efficiency of the police, fire and rescue services or ambulance services;
  (m) any other purposes—

(i) that are not within paragraphs (a) to (l) but are recognised as charitable purposes by virtue of section 5 (recreational and similar trusts, etc.) or under the old law,

(ii) that may reasonably be regarded as analogous to, or within the spirit of, any purposes falling within any of paragraphs (a) to (l) or sub-paragraph (i), or

(iii) that may reasonably be regarded as analogous to, or within the spirit of, any purposes which have been recognised, under the law relating to charities in England and Wales, as falling within sub-paragraph (ii) or this sub-paragraph.

(2) In subsection (1)—

(a) in paragraph (c), "religion" includes—

(i) a religion which involves belief in more than one god, and

(ii) a religion which does not involve belief in a god,

...

4 The public benefit requirement

(1) In this Act "the public benefit requirement" means the requirement in section 2(1)(b) that a purpose falling within section 3(1) must be for the public benefit if it is to be a charitable purpose.

(2) In determining whether the public benefit requirement is satisfied in relation to any purpose falling within section 3(1), it is not to be presumed that a purpose of a particular description is for the public benefit.

...

15 The Commission's general functions

(1) The Commission has the following general functions—

1 Determining whether institutions are or are not charities.

2 Encouraging and facilitating the better administration of charities.

3 Identifying and investigating apparent misconduct or mismanagement in the administration of charities and taking remedial or protective action in connection with misconduct or mismanagement in the administration of charities.

4 Determining whether public collections certificates should be issued, and remain in force, in respect of public charitable collections.

5 Obtaining, evaluating and disseminating information in connection with the performance of any of the Commission's functions or meeting any of its objectives.
6 Giving information or advice, or making proposals, to any Minister of the Crown on matters relating to any of the Commission's functions or meeting any of its objectives.

3.2 *Management of Charities*

The Charity Commission, whose powers now appear in part 2 of the Charities Act 2011 (as amended by the Charities (Protection and Social Investment) Act 2016 and the Charities Act 2022), has a variety of supervisory and disciplinary functions over charities on behalf of the Crown, including deciding whether or not a body is a charity and keeping a register of such charities.

Trustees of a charity are ultimately responsible for managing a charity in accordance with its governing document and the general law. Prior to the introduction of the Charities (Protection and Social Investment) Act 2016, the Commission's ability to remove an individual from trusteeship was limited and could be done only as a result of their misconduct and/or mismanagement in a given charity and being satisfied that it was necessary or desirable to act to protect that charity's property. Since the 2016 Act, as a result of which trustees' decision-making can amount to failure to observe obligations, the Charity Commission can take a whole variety of measures to investigate a charity, direct it to take measures, suspend trustees, disqualify trustees from holding trustee or senior management functions in them, appoint interim managers, and make an order to wind up and dissolve them. These failures can involve misconduct or mismanagement in the administration of a charity, including not adequately managing inherent conflicts of interest and/or loyalty, misapplying funds and not using them for exclusively charitable purposes, and trustees receiving unauthorised personal benefits.[19]

19 See, e.g., *Bhaiyat v Charity Commission for England and Wales*, Case Reference: CA/2021/0021, First-tier Tribunal (General Regulatory Chamber) Charity, [2023] UKFTT 307 (GRC), 2023 WL 02588213; the Charity Commission Decision in *Charity Inquiry on the Islamic Research Foundation International*, 19 May 2022, https://www.gov.uk/government/publications/charity-inquiry-islamic-research-foundation-international/charity-inquiry-islamic-research-foundation-international, accessed on 12 February 2025. For broader criticism of the ability of the Charity Commission to be able to monitor and enforce the law on charities see Nash, P. (2022), *British Islam and English law: A classical pluralist perspective*. Cambridge: Cambridge University Press, pp. 153–184.

The guidance on extremism is discussed later (ch. 2, section 1), and it may have some bearing on the way in which charitable purposes and public benefit are construed by the Charity Commission in order to scrutinise whether certain organisations can continue to benefit from charity status. By the Charities (Protection and Social Investment) Act 2016, section 10, a new section 181A was introduced into the Charities Act 2011 and carried discretionary power to disqualify trustees, enabling the Commission to consider a broader range of conduct by an individual beyond the management and administration of a charity. The case below illustrates how such a power of disqualification under section 181A is applied.

Dr Zakir Abdul-Karim Naik v The Charity Commission for England and Wales, 4 December 2020, Appeal Reference: CA/2019/0014 V, First-tier Tribunal (General Regulatory Chamber) Charity, 2020 WL 11421621

The following case tests one of the powers given to the Charity Commission, introduced by the Charities (Protection and Social Investment) Act 2016 (inserting a new section 181A to the Charities Act 2011). That power allows the Commission to issue an order to disqualify a person from being a charity trustee if their past or continuing conduct is deemed to be damaging or likely to be damaging to public trust and confidence in charities generally. In this case, a trustee was deemed to have so conducted himself. The specific facts are provided in the extracts from the judgment of the Tribunal.

> 1. Dr Zakir Abdul-Karim Naik appeals against an order of the Charity Commission by which he was disqualified from being a charity trustee for 15 years. That order ("the Disqualification Order") is dated 26 April 2019 and was made under section 181A of the Charities Act 2011 ("the 2011 Act"). It disqualified Dr Naik from being a charity trustee and/or trustee for a charity in relation to any or all charities generally, whether registered with the Charity Commission or not. It also disqualified Dr Naik from holding any office or employment with senior management functions in any such charity.
>
> …
>
> 8. Dr Naik is an Indian national living in Malaysia. He is a renowned international speaker and author of books on Islam and comparative religion. He has at all material times been a director and charity trustee of the charitable company known as Islamic Research Foundation International ("the Charity"). He is the founding chairman of the Charity and is currently one of its four directors. The Charity was established in 2007, primarily for religious and educational purposes

and purposes concerned with the relief of poverty and distress, but also for such other charitable objects as its board of trustees may think fit. Dr Naik has never been a charity trustee of another English charity.

9. In 2010, the then Home Secretary directed that Dr Naik be excluded from the UK on the grounds that his presence would not be conducive to the public good. The Home Secretary took the view that Dr Naik had engaged in unacceptable behaviour, namely (in her view) making statements that attempt to justify terrorist activity and foster hatred. Dr Naik sought to challenge his exclusion in judicial review proceedings but this challenge was rejected by the High Court in 2010 and by the Court of Appeal in 2011. On 11 February 2019, the Home Office confirmed that, as far it is concerned, Dr Naik remains excluded from the UK.

...

11. The Charity's activities have included the raising and provision of funds for the Peace TV network, which was founded by Dr Naik in 2006 and which broadcasts religious television programmes from an Islamic perspective via an online streaming service from Dubai. The Peace TV network has a very extensive audience worldwide and was formerly regulated by Ofcom,[20] until its UK broadcast licences were surrendered in 2018 and 2019. The Charity no longer provides it with funds.

...

24. The Charity Commission concluded that these past statements of Dr Naik can be seen as justifying or glorifying terrorist violence and/or fostering hatred. The Commission was concerned that the statements were therefore at odds with at least some of the Charity's objectives and that Dr Naik's conduct fell short of what would be expected of a trustee or a senior manager in the wider charitable sector. The Commission was also unconvinced that Dr Naik had done enough to repudiate the statements he had previously made or to address their republication (see paragraph 23 above). Consequently, it concluded that his continued association with the Charity, or charities in general, would be damaging or likely to be damaging to public trust and confidence in charities generally. In the Commission's view, Dr Naik's status, prominence and influence only served to increase the risk of such damage occurring.

...

20 Ofcom is the Office of Communications, the approved regulatory and competition authority for the broadcasting, telecommunications and postal industries.

37. For these reasons, we find that all of the conduct relied upon by the Charity Commission in deciding to make the Disqualification Order is conduct falling within the scope of Condition F provided that it has the quality of being damaging, or of being likely to be damaging, to public trust and confidence in charities generally or in specific charities or classes of charity.

…

43. Ofcom's review in 2012 focused on comments made by Dr Naik, whilst answering questions on Islamic theology in front of an audience on programmes broadcast by the Peace TV network, about whether or not apostates should be put to death and about individuals who criticise Islam. In its decision on whether the Broadcasting Code had been breached by virtue of these comments, Ofcom stated:

> In Item 1, a scholar on Islam, Dr Naik, expressed his views on two interpretations of Qur'anic texts on how apostates from Islam should be treated. He set out both views and said he tended to "agree more" with the interpretation of Qur'anic texts which states that a Muslim who converts to another religion and who then propagates that religion "should be put to death", as opposed to being put to death simply for becoming a non-Muslim. In Ofcom's view, it is potentially offensive for any service to broadcast comments suggesting that it is acceptable to apply a "penalty" and kill any individual for renouncing their faith.
>
> In Item 2, Dr Naik answered a question about individuals who criticise Islam. As part of his reply Dr Naik stated that, according to the Qur'an, the appropriate response against those who "wage war against Islam" is to execute them, chop off their limbs, or exile them. Dr Naik did not specify how he defined waging war against Islam. Ofcom noted that his reply was given in response to a question about individuals who criticise Islam. Ofcom considered that for an individual to state on air that it was acceptable to execute, chop off limbs or exile anyone who waged "war against Islam", where it was not specified what this phrase actually meant in practice, was potentially offensive.

44. Ofcom found that the potential offence caused by these statements was not justified by the context and that the broadcaster did not apply generally accepted standards. Rule 2.3 of the Broadcasting Code had therefore been breached.

45. Ofcom's subsequent review, in 2019, found that there had been further breaches of the Broadcasting Code in later broadcasts. Again, the breaches arose from comments made by Dr Naik. One of the programmes concerned, broad-

cast in 2017, was described by Ofcom as consisting of Dr Naik answering questions from an Islamic perspective on the interpretation of a variety of Christian and Islamic scriptures in front of an audience of hundreds of Muslim and non-Muslim people in Nigeria. In response to one question, Dr Naik said:

> The brother asked the question that in an Islamic state if somebody comes out of Islam can he be killed? Like I said in a normal country if a person sells the secrets of his country, can he be killed? Yes, he can be killed. But by whom, by the court of law of that country. Similarly, if the country has a trial, in the trial it is proven that the person has sold the secrets of the country, he can be put to death, he can do life imprisonment. Same thing in Islamic State, in an Islamic State where Islamic Shariah is followed, in an Islamic State if the Qazi takes the trial of the person, if he's caught and he is changing the religion and if it's proven, in an Islamic State only a Qazi can see to it, that if he has done treason, if he has done apostasy he can be put to death.

46. Ofcom found that the comments made in this programme breached its Broadcasting Code in several ways, as did comments made by Dr Naik in another programme in which he discussed the Islamic perspective on marriage (in particular, child marriage for girls).

…

59. … we are satisfied that the wider public interest considerations outweigh any benefit the Charity might gain by retaining Dr Naik's services as a trustee. Nor do we accept the contention that disqualifying Dr Naik from being a trustee would be likely to undermine the trust and confidence which members of the Muslim community have in the charity sector generally. The fact that Dr Naik is well-known and has a high profile adds weight to the case for disqualifying him from being a trustee on public interest grounds.

4 Muslim Litigants in Courts and Islamophobia

In a different context, it can be noted that the latest July 2024 edition of the Equal Treatment Bench Book, which is meant to increase the awareness and understanding of the different circumstances of people appearing in courts and tribunals, contains the following exhortations with respect to Muslims.[21]

21 Equal Treatment Bench Book, July 2024, https://www.judiciary.uk/about-the-judiciary/diversity/equal-treatment-bench-book/, accessed on 12 February 2025.

Equal Treatment Bench Book

Treatment of Muslims in court

49. Given the above experiences, Muslim people might arrive at court uncertain and anxious about how they are perceived by the court and whether they will get a fair hearing.

50. It is important to avoid applying any stereotyped assumptions, eg about the attitudes, allegiances, level of education etc to Muslim individuals.

51. As in all cases, it is important to demonstrate respect for cultural difference. This includes:
- Taking care to get a person's name right. For details, see "Names and naming systems".
- Showing understanding regarding correct practice on taking the oath. For details, see "Islam" in the Glossary of religions.
- Showing awareness of fasting practice if the hearing takes place during Ramadan and making any necessary adjustments, eg offering additional breaks. For more detail, see "Islam" in the Glossary of religions.
- Showing understanding of any issues regarding times when a Muslim person cannot attend court, eg because of an important holy day, or because they need time off or facilities to pray. For more detail, see "Islam" in the Glossary of religions.
- Not making any unnecessary objections regarding dress code. Regarding wearing a full face veil, see further comments in chapter 9.

More details can be found the hyperlinks provided by the Bench Book. Besides this specific guidance, the immediately preceding section (paragraphs. 43–48) is entitled "Anti-Muslim racism: Islamophobia" and the Bench Book observes that the term "Islamophobia" is in common use and generally taken to mean "anti-Muslim racism in its broadest sense." The Bench Book also refers to the definition of Islamophobia adopted by the All-Party Parliamentary Group on British Muslims: "Islamophobia is rooted in racism and is a type of racism that targets expressions of Muslimness or perceived Muslimness."[22] Although this definition is contested and has been criticised, it has also been observed, crit-

22 APPG on British Muslims (2018), *Islamophobia defined*. All Party Parliamentary Group on British Muslims.

ically, that it has been adopted by more than 50 local authorities in the UK.[23] While it can therefore be taken to have some quasi-normative status, the question of its adoption by the central government or in any specifically binding legal form is still being debated. The prosecution guidance on hate crimes in England and Wales does not yet incorporate a specific reference to "Islamophobia."[24] Evidence from the case law extracted in this book reveals that claims of Islamophobia have been made against defendants or appear in the background.[25]

---

23 Singh, H. (2023), *"Islamophobia" revisited*, London: Civitas.

24 Racist and Religious Hate Crime—Prosecution Guidance, https://www.cps.gov.uk/legal-guidance/racist-and-religious-hate-crime-prosecution-guidance, updated 3 March 2022, accessed on 12 February 2025.

25 See *R. (on the application of TTT) v Michaela Community Schools Trust* [2024] EWHC 843 (Admin), extracted at ch. 5, section 2 and *Erlam v Rahman* [2015] EWHC 1215 (QB), extracted at ch. 2, section 2.

CHAPTER 2

Relations between the State and Islam

There is no one set method for the recognition of a religion as having status in British legal systems. Any number of different devices may be used, including the legal forms of a trust, a company or a charity. By default, religious groups are regarded as voluntary and private associations, and the aforementioned legal forms may confer some benefits as well as some obligations on those taking them up. Apart from the questions of legal form, the British state follows an informal paradigm when establishing relations between the state and a religious association or those representing religious groups. This can be viewed in the context of British multiculturalism and what has been noted as its dynamic relationship with different parts of diverse society involving assertion of differences, claims making, recognition and accommodation.[1] The difficulties experienced by successive British governments of all political persuasions in dealing with religions in recent decades have been driven by a fear of Islamic extremism. One of the consequences is a more rigorous regime imposed more generally in religious matters, which the terminology of "faith" is often used to capture.[2]

1 Islamic Extremism Colours the Direction of State Policy

During Tony Blair's prime ministership, the Muslim Council of Britain (MCB) was among the favoured bodies that the government would use as a pipeline to establish its relations with Muslim communities. It became a successful campaigning voice in convincing the British government to enact legislative and other reforms in a variety of areas including the law on religious discrimination, incitement to religious hatred and *halal* slaughter; state funding for Islamic schools; and the introduction of faith identification in the decennial census.[3]

1 Modood, T. (2013), *Multiculturalism: A civic idea*. Cambridge: Polity, p. 36.

2 One consequence not often recognised is in relation to visa requirements for ministers of religion as noted by Cranmer, F. (2015), "Paying the piper? Public funding and supervision of religion in a secularized society (United Kingdom)," in Messner, F. (ed.), *Public funding of religions in Europe*. Farnham: Ashgate, pp. 171–198 at p. 181.

3 O'Toole, T., DeHanas, D.N., Modood, T., Meer, N., and Jones, S.H. (2013), *Taking part: Muslim participation in contemporary governance*. University of Bristol, pp. 18–20. For a discussion

The same government then diversified the Muslim bodies and spokespersons with which it sought to create a dialogue, and eventually suspended dialogue with the MCB after one of its office-holders signed a declaration that appeared to condone violence against British armed forces if it was deemed necessary to support Gaza.[4]

Although evidence of British Muslims taking part in terrorism abroad was increasing through the 1990s and into the 2000s, relations between the British government and Muslim communities took a different turn after the terrorist attacks of 7 July 2005. In the 2007–2010 period, as part of the Prevent strategy, £60 million was channelled through three government departments and local authorities to Muslim third-sector organisations to counter violent extremism.[5] A new Prevent Strategy was launched in 2013, and under the Counter-Terrorism and Security Act 2015 it acquired a statutory footing and an obligatory character that includes duties imposed on schools and universities.[6]

After the release of an anonymous letter entitled "Operation Trojan Horse", which alleged that there was a strategy to take over a number of schools in Birmingham and run them on strict Islamic principles, an investigation was conducted by a Government appointed Education Commissioner into 14 Birmingham schools. The Commissioner concluded in his 2014 report that there was clear evidence that there were a number of people, associated with each other and in positions of influence in schools and governing bodies who espoused, endorsed or failed to challenge extremist views.[7] The report also found "a sustained and coordinated agenda to impose upon children in a number of Birmingham schools the segregationist attitudes and practices of a hardline and politicised strand of Sunni Islam."[8]

---

of the changes achieved see Meer, N. (2010), *Citizenship, identity and the politics of multiculturalism: The rise of Muslim consciousness*. Basingstoke: Palgrave Macmillan, Nash, P. (2022), *British Islam and English law: A classical pluralist perspective*. Cambridge: Cambridge University Press, pp. 45–80.

4 O'Toole, T., DeHanas, D.N., Modood, T., Meer, N., and Jones, S.H. (2013), *Taking part: Muslim participation in contemporary governance*. University of Bristol. pp. 19–22, on pluralisation. Khan, S. and McMahon, T. (2016), *The battle for British Islam: Reclaiming Muslim identity from extremism*. London: Saqi, pp. 53–54, on the suspension of dialogue with the MCB.

5 O'Toole, T., DeHanas, D.N., Modood, T., Meer, N., and Jones, S.H. (2013), *Taking part: Muslim participation in contemporary governance*. University of Bristol. p. 20.

6 These duties are discussed in ch. 8.

7 Clarke, P. (2014), *Report into allegations concerning Birmingham schools arising from the 'Trojan Horse' letter*. London: Her Majesty's Stationery Office, p. 12.

8 Ibid., p. 48. Perry, D.L. and Stott, P. (2022), *The Trojan Horse Affair: A documentary record. A report from Policy Exchange's Understanding Islamism project*. London: Policy Exchange reject claims that the "Operation Trojan Horse" was being used by the government to expand the

The core aim of Prevent is to provide a pre-criminal route of intervention through its Channel programme, which directs those at risk of radicalising to preventative measures through the intervention of health, social services and other professionals.[9] One of the consequences of the Prevent programme was to diversify how the state interacted with Muslim communities by bringing in a large number of organisations to counter violent extremism. The money that followed the programme was also the largest injection of funds in British Muslim civil society. Organisations received unprecedented levels of funding to launch new initiatives allowing substantial creativity and flexibility in how funds were used. Prevent had a decentralised management structure across three central government departments and local authorities. It also represented an attempt to distance state bodies from Islamist ideology, cultivate the idea of mainstream moderate Islam and support those spokespersons and bodies who became its proponents.[10] Meanwhile, with the support of some trade unions, universities and student unions, Islamist organisations have criticised Prevent by misrepresenting its role as an assault on Muslims by unfairly criminalising them, while supressing evidence of the involvement of British Muslims in terrorism.[11]

In addition to direct relations with the central government and local authorities, one can point to more informal relations cultivated within the Inter Faith Network for the United Kingdom. As its Articles of Association state, it is "established to advance public knowledge and mutual understanding of the teachings, traditions and practices of the different faith communities in Britain including an awareness both of their distinctive features and their common ground and to promote good relations between persons of different faiths".[12]

Prevent duty and make it statutory. It emphasises that concerns about extremism in schooling, including in Birmingham, were already present prior to the letter and investigation.

9 Khan, S. and McMahon, T. (2016), *The battle for British Islam: Reclaiming Muslim identity from extremism*. London: Saqi, pp. 89–96. For a court's description of an intervention by a Channel "Intervention Provider" in a case concerning a special guardianship order for a child of a radicalised mother who supported the Islamic State (ISIL) see *A Local Authority v A Mother, A Father, BB, CC, J (by her Children's Guardian)* [2020] EWHC 3496 (Fam).

10 O'Toole, T., DeHanas, D.N., Modood, T., Meer, N., and Jones, S.H. (2013), *Taking part: Muslim participation in contemporary governance*. University of Bristol, pp. 20–22; Maher, S. and Frampton, M. (2009), *Choosing our friends wisely*. London: Policy Exchange, pp. 26, 37–47.

11 Khan, S. and McMahon, T. (2016), *The battle for British Islam: Reclaiming Muslim identity from extremism*. London: Saqi, pp. 96–117.

12 Schedule, para. 3, of the Articles of Association of The Inter Faith Network for the United Kingdom, last updated July 2022. The Interfaith Network takes the legal form of a company limited by guarantee as well as a charity under the Charities Act 2011.

Based at the national level, however, this is only one of a number of means by which faith bodies interact between each other and sections of national and local government. It was noted in the first decade of this millennium that there "has been an exponential rise in new consultation processes between public and religious bodies over the last decade",[13] that ten regional multi-faith forums in England and Wales existed which provided information, training, consultation and input into regional governmental structures, and over 200 inter-faith or multi-faith bodies were established in England and Wales.[14] These fora are supported and provided with funding by a variety of means including from the central government, the Church of England and local authorities. The account below refers to a potential change in direction which may or may not be permanent considering that it is subject to changes in the political colour of government.

The Inter-Faith Network has not escaped becoming embroiled in concerns about Islamic extremism and the MCB in particular. The prospect of withholding funding from the Department for Levelling Up, Housing and Communities (DLUHC) to the national-level Inter-Faith Network resulted from the potential reputational risk to the government posed by the membership of the MCB. In turn, the Inter-Faith Network Board of Trustees replied that it could not expel the MCB and would dissolve itself as a charity.[15]

In recent years, British government policy has been moving towards countering extremism beyond its violent form. Given the earlier discussion (ch. 1, section 1.2) regarding threats posed to the stability of the democratic institutions of the state, questions may arise whether action may be taken to curb the activities of Islamist groups or political parties in ways that are compatible with the ECHR. The British government's Department of Levelling Up, Housing and Communities appears to have followed the kind of reasoning that the

13 Rivers, J. (2010), *The law of organized religions: Between establishment and secularism*. Oxford: Oxford University Press, p. 304. For an account of inter-faith networks being one among among a number of means of extending Muslim influence over decision making see O'Toole, T., DeHanas, D.N., Modood, T., Meer, N., and Jones, S.H. (2013), *Taking part: Muslim participation in contemporary governance*. University of Bristol.

14 Rivers, J. (2010), *The law of organized religions: Between establishment and secularism*. Oxford: Oxford University Press, p. 304.

15 Statement by the Interfaith Network, "IFN Funding," https://www.interfaith.org.uk/about/ifn-funding, and "Key Points Drawn on in a letter of 22 January 2024 from IFN's Co-Chairs to Secretary of State," https://www.interfaith.org.uk/about/key-points-drawn-on-in-letter-of-22-january-2024-from-ifn-co-chairs-to-secretary-of-state, accessed on 12 February 2025.

ECtHR offered in the *Refah Partisi* case when, on 14 March 2024, it set out a new definition of extremism and guidance on how to implement it.[16]

This guidance is additional to what already exists in various statutes on terrorism and that issued as part of the government's Prevent strategy, which is more closely related to radicalisation and terrorism. The guidance fills the gap left in regulation by extremist materials and activities that are not necessarily illegal and do not meet the threshold required for terrorism or national security. It targets groups, some of which have not been proscribed and operate lawfully, but which are seeking to replace democracy with an Islamist and Nazi society respectively, including by actively radicalising others and openly advocating for the erosion of fundamental democratic rights. The definition of extremism is intended to be used by government departments and officials to ensure that they do not inadvertently provide a platform, funding or legitimacy to groups or individuals who attempt to advance extremist ideologies that negate fundamental rights and freedoms and overturn the UK's system of liberal parliamentary democracy. However, not being statutory, the definition is not meant to affect the existing criminal law, but applies to the operations of the government itself.[17] It should nevertheless influence the way in which British government departments support, fund and consult with some Muslim groups. The relinquishing of funding to the Inter-Faith Network because of the presence of an MCB member on its board of trustees (discussed at 2 above) provides an indicator of the kind of consequences that might follow from this more general guidance on extremism. It remains to be seen, in light of the change of government in July 2024, whether there could be a change in policy. However, if it remains in place, it could be seen as a further consolidation of a notion of "militant democracy" in the UK.

New definition of extremism (2024)

…

2. The definition

Extremism is the promotion or advancement of an ideology based on violence, hatred or intolerance, that aims to:

---

16 See https://www.gov.uk/government/publications/new-definition-of-extremism-2024/new-definition-of-extremism-2024#introduction, 14 March 2024, accessed on 12 February 2025.

17 See Press release, Government strengthens approach to counter extremism, https://www.gov.uk/government/news/government-strengthens-approach-to-counter-extremism, 14 March 2024, accessed on 12 February 2025.

1. negate or destroy the fundamental rights and freedoms of others; or
2. undermine, overturn or replace the UK's system of liberal parliamentary democracy and democratic rights; or
3. intentionally create a permissive environment for others to achieve the results in (1) or (2).

The types of behaviour below are indicative of the kind of promotion or advancement which may be relevant to the definition, and are an important guide to its application. The further context below is also an essential part of the definition.

3. Behaviour that could constitute extremism

Aim 1 (negate or destroy fundamental rights and freedoms): Behaviour against a group, or members of it, that seeks to negate or destroy their rights to live equally under the law and free of fear, threat, violence, and discrimination. Including:

- Using, threatening, inciting, justifying, glorifying or excusing violence towards a group in order to dissuade them from using their legally defined rights and freedoms.

Aim 2 (undermine, overturn or replace liberal democracy): Attempts to undermine, overturn, or replace the UK's system of liberal parliamentary democracy and democratic rights. Including:

- Advocating that the UK's parliamentary democracy and democratic values and rights are not compatible with their ideology, and seeking to challenge, overthrow, or change our political system outside of lawful means.
- Using, threatening, inciting, justifying, glorifying or excusing violence towards citizens, in order to dissuade them from participating freely in the democratic process.
- Subverting the way public or state institutions exercise their powers, in order to further ideological goals, for example through entryism, or by misusing powers or encouraging others to do so.
- Using, threatening, inciting, justifying, glorifying or excusing violence towards public officials including our armed forces, police forces and members of local, devolved or national legislatures, in order to dissuade them from conducting their obligations freely and fearlessly, without external interference.
- Establishing parallel governance structures which, whether or not they have formal legal underpinning, seek to supersede the lawful powers of existing institutions of state.

Aim 3 (enabling the spread of extremism): Intentionally creating a permissive environment for behaviour in aim 1 or aim 2. Including:

- Providing an uncritical platform for individuals or representatives of groups or organisations that have demonstrated behaviour in either aim 1 or aim 2.
- Facilitating activity of individuals or representatives of groups or organisations that have demonstrated behaviour in either aim 1 or aim 2, including through provision of endorsement, funding, or other forms of support.
- The dissemination of extremist propaganda and narratives that call for behaviour in either aim 1 or aim 2.
- Attempts to radicalise, indoctrinate and recruit others to an ideology based on violence, hatred or intolerance, including young people.
- Consistent association with individuals or representatives of groups or organisations that have demonstrated behaviour in either aim 1 or aim 2 without providing critical challenge to their ideology or behaviour.
- If any behaviour listed in aim 1 or aim 2 has occurred previously, a refusal by the individual, group or organisation that conducted the behaviour to rescind, repudiate or distance themselves from the behaviour.

2 Electoral Law

There have been intermittent concerns that the conduct of politics and participation or campaigning in elections is corrupt or otherwise inappropriate. The basic provisions are contained in the Representation of the People Act 1983, as amended by the Elections Act 2022. According to an Electoral Commission review, areas with high concentrations of Pakistani- and Bangladeshi-origin residents were thought to be particularly prone to allegations of fraud, and the Pakistani and Bangladeshi communities were perceived to be more vulnerable to fraud.[18] It has been found that "*biraderi*" (clan and kinship) networks which reinforce candidate selection lead to undue influence where access to individual ballots of women and adult children can be refused by the elders and votes are cast by men on behalf of their wives or daughters.[19] Electoral malpractices legally termed "personation," i.e. the use of forged postal votes in their

18 Electoral Commission (2014), *Electoral fraud in the UK: Final report and recommendations*. London: The Electoral Commission. For a discussion of the cases and investigations into corruption and fraud in voting see Nash, P. (2022), *British Islam and English law: A classical pluralist perspective*. Cambridge: Cambridge University Press. esp. at pp. 225–242.

19 Sobolewska, M., Heeg, S.W., Hill, F., and Borkowska, M. (2015), *Understanding electoral fraud vulnerability in Pakistani and Bangladeshi origin communities in England*. Electoral Commission.

thousands, was discovered to be used in Birmingham to elect some candidates in local government elections, leading to prosecutions and convictions.[20]

The provisions to do with spiritual injury and undue spiritual pressure were originally introduced to avoid the Catholic clergy being able to influence electoral outcomes. This provision of the 1983 Act was initially section 115 but that was replaced by two separate provisions, retaining the wording of the original section 115 in a new section 114A and creating a newly worded provision in section 115 for local government elections in Scotland and Wales. The original section 115 remained unused until the mayoral election in the London Borough Tower Hamlets. In that case there were found to have occurred personation and other electoral offences in elections for the local council and mayor. Extracts from one of the ensuing cases, *Erlam v Rahman*, where the issue of spiritual injury was specifically considered are given below.

Representation of the People Act 1983

114A Undue influence

(1) A person is guilty of a corrupt practice if the person is guilty of undue influence.

(2) A person ("P") is guilty of undue influence if P carries out an activity falling within subsection (4) for the purpose of—

(a) inducing or compelling a person to vote in a particular way or to refrain from voting, or

(b) otherwise impeding or preventing the free exercise of the franchise of an elector or of a proxy for an elector.

(3) A person ("P") is also guilty of undue influence if P carries out an activity falling within any of paragraphs (a) to (f) of subsection (4) on account of—

(a) a person having voted in a particular way or refrained from voting, or

(b) P assuming a person to have voted in a particular way or to have refrained from voting.

20 *R. (on the application of Khan) v Election Commissioner* [2005] EWHC 2365 (Admin). Use of postal votes and personation was found by Hill, E., Sobolewska, M., Wilks-Heeg, S., and Borkowska, M. (2017), "Explaining electoral fraud in an advanced democracy: Fraud vulnerabilities, opportunities and facilitating mechanisms in British elections," *The British Journal of Politics and International Relations*, 19(4), pp. 772–789, Sobolewska, M., Heeg, S.W., Hill, E., and Borkowska, M. (2015), *Understanding electoral fraud vulnerability in Pakistani and Bangladeshi origin communities in England*. Electoral Commission.

(4) The following activities fall within this subsection—
(a) using or threatening to use violence against a person;
(b) damaging or destroying, or threatening to damage or destroy, a person's property;
(c) damaging or threatening to damage a person's reputation;
(d) causing or threatening to cause financial loss to a person;
(e) causing spiritual injury to, or placing undue spiritual pressure on, a person;
(f) doing any other act designed to intimidate a person;
(g) doing any act designed to deceive a person in relation to the administration of an election.
(5) For the purposes of subsections (2) and (3) an activity is carried out by a person ("P") if it is carried out—
(a) by P,
(b) by P jointly with one or more other persons, or
(c) by one or more other persons on behalf of P and with P's authority or consent.
(6) In subsection (4)(f) and (g) "act" includes an omission (and references to the doing of an act are to be read accordingly).
(7) This section does not have effect in relation to an election in Scotland or Wales under the local government Act.

115 Undue influence: local government elections in Scotland and Wales.
(1) A person shall be guilty of a corrupt practice if he is guilty of undue influence in relation to an election in Scotland or Wales under the local government Act.
(2) A person shall be guilty of undue influence in relation to an election in Scotland or Wales under the local government Act—
(a) if he, directly or indirectly, by himself or by any other person on his behalf, makes use of or threatens to make use of any force, violence or restraint, or inflicts or threatens to inflict, by himself or by any other person, any temporal or spiritual injury, damage, harm or loss upon or against any person in order to induce or compel that person to vote or refrain from voting, or on account of that person having voted or refrained from voting; or
(b) if, by abduction, duress or any fraudulent device or contrivance, he impedes or prevents, or intends to impede or prevent, the free exercise of the franchise of an elector or proxy for an elector, or so compels, induces or prevails upon, or intends

> so to compel, induce or prevail upon, an elector or proxy for an elector either to vote or to refrain from voting.

Erlam v Rahman
[2015] EWHC 1215 (QB)

A number of electoral offences were considered to have taken place in the election for the London Borough of Tower Hamlets in 2014. The extracts below constitute the parts of the judgment in which the issue of "spiritual injury," as originally contained in the Representation of the People Act 1983, section 115, is considered by the court. (The provision has now been replaced by section 114(4)(e).) The detail in the judgment that is not otherwise extracted here also covers the historical context of the provision. The court also recounted an event at which a formal invitation from the Council had been given to the Imam of Mecca to pay a visit to the Borough, as well as other incidents in 2014 when the mayor shared a platform with the Chairman of the Council of Mosques and another in which prominent Islamic scholars and community leaders in Tower Hamlets urged the general public to vote for Mayor Lutfur Rahman to retain equal rights and the development of the borough. The extracts below focus on the effect of a letter which was signed by some 101 imams supporting the election of the mayor.

> 546. On 16 May 2014 (6 days before the election) the Weekly Desh, a newspaper published in Bengali and in English with a circulation of about 20,000 (mainly in the Borough), carried a letter. The letter was solely in Bengali and no English version appeared in the paper. There is an accepted translation of the letter which the court will adopt.
>
> 547. The letter was signed by 101 Imams and other religious leaders and scholars. Leading the list was Mr Hoque [Chairman of the Council of Mosques]. There was no suggestion that any of the signatures on the letter was other than genuine—the letter had indeed been signed by 101 Muslim leaders. It was said, at one stage, that the number 101 has a special significance in Islam but this was not expanded upon. Patently, however, for 101 prominent clerics and scholars to sign a letter in a single London Borough, albeit one with a large Muslim population, is a serious matter and the letter was intended to be taken seriously.
>
> 548. Before dealing with the letter itself, it is necessary to recall that this election campaign was widely conducted in the media (by all parties). The letter in the Weekly Desh was not just a matter between the newspaper and its readers. It

was given enormous prominence in the other media, especially the Bangladeshi media, and, inevitably, on social media. The effect of the letter, therefore, went a great deal wider than the 20,000 readership of the Desh.

549. Bearing in mind that any grammatical infelicities are the responsibility of the translator and not the authors of the Bengali original, the text of the letter is as follows:

BE UNITED AGAINST INJUSTICE

MAKE LUTFUR RAHMAN VICTORIOUS

Creating opportunities, making provisions and providing services to the citizens on behalf of Her Excellency the Queen. In this case everyone has a freedom of right to choose a candidate who is suitable and able to provide the services. However we are observing that the media propagandas, narrow political interests etc involving the Mayoral election of Tower Hamlets Council have created a kind of a negative impression which in turn have created confusions amongst the public, divided the community and put the community in question. We are further observing that today's Tower Hamlets have made significant and enviable improvements in the areas of housing, education, community cohesion, interfaith harmony, road safety and youth developments. In order to retain this success and make further progress it is essential that someone is elected as Mayor of the Tower Hamlets Borough on 22nd May who is able to lead these improvements and who will not discriminate on the basis of language, colour and religious identities.

We observe that some people are targeting the languages, colours and religions and attempting to divide the community by ignoring the cohesion and harmony of the citizens. This is, in fact, hitting the national, cultural and religious 'multi' ideas of the country and spreading jealousy and hatred in the community. We consider these acts as abominable and at the same time condemnable.

With utmost concern we observe that by shunning the needs and opportunities of the Tower Hamlets Council and its citizens, Islamophobia, which is the result of the current political stance and which has derived from false imagination, has been made an agenda for voting and voters. The mosques and religious organisations have been targeted. It is being publicised that any relationship [involvement] with the religious scholars and clerics are condemnable and is an offence. Religious beliefs and religious practice are being criticised. One of the local former councillors of the Labour Party has stated in the BBC's Panorama programme that 'Religions divide people'. Even in the same programme the honourable Imam of the Holy Kaba Sharif was presented in negative and defaming ways and thus all the religious people, particularly the Muslims, have been insulted and thrown in to a state of anxiety. We cannot support these ill attempts under any circumstances. We believe that it is not an offence to be a Muslim voter, an imam or Khatib of a mosque and have involvement with all these. Under no circumstances it is acceptable to give a voter less value or to criticise them on the basis of their identity. As voters, like in any other elections we also have a right to vote in the forthcoming Tower Hamlets Mayoral Election and we should have the opportunity to cast our votes without fear. As a cognisant group of the community and responsible voters and for the sake of truth, justice, dignity and development we express our unlimited support for Mayor Lutfur Rahman and strongly call upon you, the residents of Tower Hamlets, to shun all the propagandas and slanders and unite against the falsehood and injustice.

550. Although this document speaks of "the community" throughout in a neutral fashion, it must be recalled that the letter was published solely in the Bengali language in a newspaper whose readership (at least in its Bengali editions) was restricted to Bengali speakers. It had not appeared in the English section of the newspaper. In the context "the community" means, and is intended to be taken as "the Bangladeshi community."

…

555. What was the effect of the letter? First, as has been pointed out, it was widely reported in the other press and broadcast media and on social media. Its influence stretched well beyond the readers of the Weekly Desh.

556. Secondly there is a substantial body of credible evidence that the Imams' message that it was the duty of faithful Muslims to vote for Mr Rahman entered the general campaign, with religious duty being mentioned in canvassing before the poll and to voters attending polling stations on election day (see below under "intimidation").

557. How the letter came to be written is shrouded in mystery. In addition to Mr Hoque, evidence was called from one of the other 100 Imams but he shed little light on the logistics of the letter's production. Mr Hoque maintained that someone else must have drafted it and that it was presented for his signature (he signed first) when it was in its final form. Who actually drafted it was never made clear. Experience would indicate that to compile a letter and to get 101 different people to agree with it and to sign it is a major undertaking.

558. Then there is the timing—carefully arranged to appear on the last Friday before the election, doubtless in order to be much discussed at Friday prayers.

559. Although the official line was that this document was compiled entirely by the clerics involved, it is noticeable that much of the language does bear a striking resemblance to that of the political messages put out by Mr Rahman's campaign. Although Mr Rahman claims to have been taken by surprise by the appearance of the letter, it beggars belief that neither he nor his close associates knew that it was coming out. Given the close relationship between Mr Rahman and Mr Hoque it would be astonishing if, during the arduous process of obtaining the agreement and signature of all the Imams, no word of it slipped out to Mr Rahman.

560. The only inference one can draw from the evidence is that, at a relatively early stage, Mr Rahman decided to run his campaign on the basis that it was the religious duty of faithful Muslims to vote for him and to enlist the support of Mr Hoque to deliver what might be termed the imprimatur of the senior Muslim clergy.

561. This brings one back to the target audience. As has been set out above, everybody in the case agreed that a high proportion of the Bangladeshi population of Tower Hamlets were traditionalist, conservative and strongly religious. The letter was deliberately pitched at Bengali speakers (to the exclusion of English speaking Bangladeshis) and lined up a very large number of very senior clerics to sign it. There can be no doubt that the target audience would take advice about their religious duties from so many senior clerics and scholars very seriously indeed. A sophisticated metropolitan readership might smile patronisingly on the earnest strictures of the Bishops of the Church of England but many traditionalist and pious Muslim voters of Tower Hamlets are going to accept the word of their religious leaders as authoritative.

562. Though it is true to say that the world has moved on considerably since 1892, there is little real difference between the attitudes of the faithful Roman Catholics of County Meath at that time and the attitudes of the faithful Muslims of Tower Hamlets. To some extent the proof of the pudding is in the eating. If Dr Nulty had not known his target audience well, he would not have couched his pastoral letter in the terms he did. If those responsible for the Imams' letter had not thought that it would have a significant influence on the votes of the Bengali-speaking devout Muslim voters of Tower Hamlets, they would not have gone to the considerable trouble of organising the letter and obtaining 101 signatures to it. One cannot put a document of that kind into the public domain and then say 'I didn't think it would have any effect.' If that were the case, why do it?

563. If this part of s 115 of the 1983 [Act] is still good law—and in the judgment of the court, it is—and if the interpretation placed on the statute by the courts (albeit in the 19th century) is still valid—and in the judgment of the court, it is—then it must be said that no meaningful distinction can be drawn between the conduct of Mr Hoque and the others responsible for organising the Imams' letter and that of the Bishop of Meath.

564. Controversial though it may be, and likely to cause offence, it is none the less the clear duty of this court to hold that the participation of the Muslim clerics in Mr Rahman's campaign to persuade Muslim voters that it was their religious duty to vote for him and, in particular, the Imams' letter, did, however unwittingly for most of the signatories, cross the line identified by Andrews J [the judge in the 1892 case] between what is permissible and what is impermissible.

565. Sadly, therefore, the court feels it has no option but to find that there was undue spiritual influence contrary to s 115(2) of the 1983 Act.

566. But that is not the end of the story. If, as is clearly the case, the influence was likely to affect the result of the election, such a finding would avoid the election but, by itself does so only under the general corruption provisions of [the Representation of People Act 1983] s 164 [to do with avoidance of an election]. The next question is thus whether the candidate or his agents have been guilty of undue influence.

567. In view of the findings of the court as to the close relationship between Mr Rahman and Mr Hoque and what may, I hope not too facetiously, be described as their 'double act' at various functions, it is right to class Mr Hoque as being within the category of 'agents' in the wider sense required by electoral law.

568. Is Mr Rahman, however, assisted by s 158? If the candidate himself commits a corrupt practice, then he is personally guilty. If he does not commit it himself but it is committed with his knowledge and consent he is personally guilty unless the corrupt practice is treating or (as here) undue influence. Thus knowledge and consent of undue influence do not, by themselves, make the candidate personally guilty. Where undue influence is committed by an agent of the candidate, the candidate is guilty by his agents of the corrupt practice unless he can prove the four elements of s 158(3).

569. In the light of the findings above, it seems inescapable that Mr Rahman was himself a party to the undue spiritual influence of the clerics, in which case s

158(3) does not arise. If, however, the court is wrong about that, subs (3) must be considered. Mr Rahman does not fare well with this subsection.

570. Can Mr Rahman prove that "(a) … the offences mentioned in the report were committed contrary to the orders and without the sanction or connivance of the candidate or his election"? Clearly not: they were carried on with his sanction and connivance and he gave no contrary orders. Indeed he seems both to have invited and to have approved of the exhortations delivered by Mr Hoque in his presence.

571. Can he assert "(b) that the candidate and his election agent took all reasonable means for preventing the commission of corrupt and illegal practices at the election"? The evidence is all to the contrary.

572. Under (c), can one say "that the offences mentioned in the report were of a trivial, unimportant and limited character"? Again, no.

573. Finally can it be shown "(d) that in all other respects the election was free from any corrupt or illegal practice on the part of the candidate and of his agents"? Given the findings of personation, other voting offences, making false statements, paying canvassers and bribery, this cannot be shown.

574. Though it may thus be academic whether Mr Rahman is regarded as personally guilty of undue influence or guilty through his agents, as set out above the court finds Mr Rahman personally guilty.

CHAPTER 3

State Support for Islamic Religious Communities

State support comes in many different forms, from direct funding from central government or local authorities or in-kind support from state institutions. Some of these, especially the ones related to funding often do not require legislative assent in order to be dispensed because they may be part of the discretionary funding which is available to be distributed from within the powers those state bodies already enjoy. This chapter is focused on those legal mechanisms in which there is specific legislative sanction or an obligation to grant state support or exemption from taxation which serves as an indirect means of support or subsidy.

1 Charities

As already noted (ch. 1, section 3), one of the chief attractions of being registered as a charity with the Charity Commission is to benefit from tax advantages which donations attract and because charities themselves have some tax exemptions.[1]

1.1 *Giving to Charities*

When individuals give to charity, both the individual donor and the recipient charity receive tax advantages. Employees can specify that part of their salary or pension is paid directly to a charity. Relief is given at the marginal rate of income tax, because the deduction is made before deducting tax under the Pay As You Earn (PAYE) scheme. Persons donating money to a charity will qualify for Gift Aid, which provides relief from higher and additional rates of income tax. The donation to the charity is treated as being made net of income tax at the basic rate, which the charity can recover from His Majesty's Revenue and Customs (HMRC), provided the donor's tax bill covers the tax reclaimed. Gift aided donations made between the end of the tax year and the date the tax

1 Rivers, J. (2010), *The law of organized religions: Between establishment and secularism*. Oxford: Oxford University Press, pp. 171–175. Cranmer, F. (2015), "Paying the piper? Public funding and supervision of religion in a secularized society (United Kingdom)," in Messner, F. (ed.), *Public funding of religions in Europe*. Farnham: Ashgate, pp. 171–198 at 181–185.

return is submitted can be backdated for tax purposes, to be treated as paid in the year covered by the tax return. This can reduce the tax liability of donors whose income may otherwise fall into a higher tax bracket. Gifts of assets to a charity are exempt from capital gains tax. Transfers of value, which would otherwise be chargeable to inheritance tax, are exempt if passed on to a charity. In certain circumstances, a gift to a charity on death can reduce the rate of tax payable on the remainder of the estate which is not being passed on to the charity.

The extract below is a sample of the kind of provision that allows for tax relief to be claimed. It is from the Income Tax Act 2007 and, especially in chapters 2 and 3 of that Act, other provisions cover other eventualities which also benefit donors and charities.

Income Tax Act 2007

414 Relief for gifts to charity

(1) An individual who makes a gift to a charity which is a qualifying donation is entitled to the relief set out in subsection (2).

(2) The Income Tax Acts have effect in their application to the individual for the tax year in which the gift is made as if—

 (a) the gift had been made after deduction of income tax at the basic rate, and

 (b) the basic rate limit ... were increased by an amount equal to the grossed up amount of the gift

...

1.2 *Tax Reliefs Available to Charities*

Trustees are liable to pay income tax, and companies to pay corporation tax, on all their income. But when funds are held by a charity, for use for charitable purposes, various exemptions apply to taxes which would otherwise be payable. Subject to certain requirements, charitable trusts and companies are exempt from those taxes. Charities are exempt from capital gains tax on the sale of assets, provided the gains are applied for charitable purposes. Premises occupied by charities or charity trustees and used wholly or mainly for charitable purposes are eligible for a mandatory 80 per cent reduction in business rates, with a further reduction of up to 20 per cent available at the discretion of the local authority. When they are unoccupied, the premises are subject to zero local taxation (see extracts from the Local Government Finance Act 1988). In addition to this, charities may also be exempt from Stamp Duty Land Tax on the purchase of land or property.

A "hereditament" is a "property which is or may become liable to a rate ..." (General Rate Act 1967, section 115). The values in the calculation are as follows: A is the rateable value shown for the day as regards the hereditament, B is the non-domestic rating multiplier for the financial year, and C is the number of days in the financial year (Local Government Act 1988, section 44).

Local Government Finance Act 1988

...

Section 43 Occupied hereditaments liability.

(5) Where subsection (6) applies the chargeable amount for a chargeable day shall be calculated in accordance with the formula—

$$\frac{A \times B}{C \times 5}$$

(6) This subsection applies where on the day concerned
   (a) the ratepayer is a charity or trustees for a charity and the hereditament is wholly or mainly used for charitable purposes (whether of that charity or of that and other charities).

...

45A Unoccupied hereditaments: zero-rating

(1) Where section 45 applies in relation to a hereditament, the chargeable amount for a chargeable day is zero in the following cases.

(2) The first case is where—
   (a) the ratepayer is a charity or trustees for a charity, and
   (b) it appears that when next in use the hereditament will be wholly or mainly used for charitable purposes (whether of that charity or of that and other charities).

2 Taxation Benefits for Registered Religious Buildings

We saw in ch. 1, section 2 that the Places of Worship Registration Act 1855 allows for the registration of places of worship and that one of the benefits of registration is an exemeption from local taxation. Currently, this exemption is set out in the Local Government Finance Act 1988, Meanwhile, the case of *Ludkin v Trustees of Anjuman E Isthahul Muslimeen of UK* illustrates the kind of interpretive problems regarding whether there is exemption from local taxation when use of an building adjacent to a registered mosque is made for activities such as running a school.[2]

Local Government Finance Act 1988

…

SCHEDULE 5

…

NON-DOMESTIC RATING: EXEMPTION

…

Registration as a religious building attracts exemption from local taxation.

11(1) A hereditament is exempt to the extent that it consists of any of the following—
- (a) a place of public religious worship which belongs to the Church of England or the Church in Wales (within the meaning of the Welsh Church Act 1914) or is for the time being certified as required by law as a place of religious worship;
- (b) a church hall, chapel hall or similar building used in connection with a place falling within paragraph (a) above for the purposes of the organisation responsible for the conduct of public religious worship in that place.

(2) A hereditament is exempt to the extent that it is occupied by an organisation responsible for the conduct of public religious worship in a place falling within sub-paragraph (1)(a) above and—
- (a) is used for carrying out administrative or other activities relating to the organisation of the conduct of public religious worship in such a place; or
- (b) is used as an office or for office purposes, or for purposes ancillary to its use as an office or for office purposes.

(3) In this paragraph "office purposes" include administration, clerical work and handling money; and "clerical work" includes writing, book-keeping, sorting papers or information, filing, typing, duplicating, calculating (by whatever means), drawing and the editorial preparation of matter for publication.

---

2 *Ludkin v Trustees of Anjuman E Isthahul Muslimeen of UK* [1988] RA 209.

CHAPTER 4

Anti-discrimination Law

Until the 2000s, anti-discrimination law did not clearly provide for religious groups unless they could claim to have suffered discrimination on grounds of ethnic or national origin under the Race Relations Act 1976. The clear recognition of Muslims as claimants under anti-discrimination law began once the Human Rights Act 1998 came into effect, on 1 October 2000, with respect to acts by public authorities or those bodies exercising functions of a public nature (see ch. 1, section 1). Then, when the EU Employment Equality Framework Directive (2000/78/EC) was implemented in UK law (by SI 2003/1660) with effect from 2 December 2003, recognition was extended to discrimination *inter alia* on religious grounds though only in employment contexts. More general recognition was extended to religion as a ground of discrimination under the Equality Act 2006.

The current regime is contained in the Equality Act 2010, where religion is one of its "protected characteristics." Like the earlier instruments it allows claims for direct and indirect discrimination, harassment and victimisation. The Equality Act 2010 covers discrimination in the areas of the provision of services, public functions,[1] the disposal and management of premises, employment and education.[2] It ought to be noted that while the Human Rights Act 1998 and the Equality Act 2010 can provide a basis for Muslims to make religion-based claims, discrimination claims under the Equality Act 2010 can also be made against Muslims as alleged perpetrators of discrimination on any of the mentioned protected characteristics.

Whereas in some jurisdictions the typical approach to discrimination has been to adopt hate crimes legislation, the British model has only more recently given greater emphasis to the use of the criminal law. The adoption in the Crime and Disorder Act 1998 of the notion of racially aggravated offences was extended, by the Anti-terrorism, Crime and Security Act 2001, to include religiously

1 Although, unlike the Human Rights Act 1998, the Equality Act 2010 does not apply to acts done in compliance with primary or secondary legislation or for the purpose of safeguarding national security, the definition of public function in the Equality Act 2010 directly refers to the notion of "a function of a public nature" as contained in the Human Rights Act 1998 (see Equality Act 2010, section 31(4)).

2 The parts of the Equality Act 2010 relevant to the provision of goods, facilities and services are extracted in ch. 12. Section 85, which is important for schools, is reproduced at ch. 7, section 1.2.

aggravated offences. Further, the Racial and Religious Hatred Act 2006 added to existing criminal offences related to public order.[3]

The provisions of the Equality Act 2010 reproduced below are particularly important, not least because they can be seen to recur regularly in claims of discrimination made in the distinct areas covered in the other chapters in this volume.

1 Frequently Used Provisions of the Equality Act 2010

Equality Act 2010

…

4 The protected characteristics

The following characteristics are protected characteristics—

age;
disability;
gender reassignment;
marriage and civil partnership;
pregnancy and maternity;
race;
religion or belief;
sex;
sexual orientation.

…

10 Religion or belief

(1) Religion means any religion and a reference to religion includes a reference to a lack of religion.

(2) Belief means any religious or philosophical belief and a reference to belief includes a reference to a lack of belief.

(3) In relation to the protected characteristic of religion or belief—

(a) a reference to a person who has a particular protected characteristic is a reference to a person of a particular religion or belief;

(b) a reference to persons who share a protected characteristic is a reference to persons who are of the same religion or belief.

3 These are addressed in ch. 14 on criminal law.

13 Direct discrimination

(1) A person (A) discriminates against another (B) if, because of a protected characteristic, A treats B less favourably than A treats or would treat others.

19 Indirect discrimination

(1) A person (A) discriminates against another (B) if A applies to B a provision, criterion or practice which is discriminatory in relation to a relevant protected characteristic of B's.

(2) For the purposes of subsection (1), a provision, criterion or practice is discriminatory in relation to a relevant protected characteristic of B's if—
  (a) A applies, or would apply, it to persons with whom B does not share the characteristic,
  (b) it puts, or would put, persons with whom B shares the characteristic at a particular disadvantage when compared with persons with whom B does not share it,
  (c) it puts, or would put, B at that disadvantage, and
  (d) A cannot show it to be a proportionate means of achieving a legitimate aim.

26 Harassment

(1) A person (A) harasses another (B) if—
  (a) A engages in unwanted conduct related to a relevant protected characteristic, and
  (b) the conduct has the purpose or effect of—
    (i) violating B's dignity, or
    (ii) creating an intimidating, hostile, degrading, humiliating or offensive environment for B.

(2) A also harasses B if—
  (a) A engages in unwanted conduct of a sexual nature, and
  (b) the conduct has the purpose or effect referred to in subsection (1)(b).

(3) A also harasses B if—
  (a) A or another person engages in unwanted conduct of a sexual nature or that is related to gender reassignment or sex,
  (b) the conduct has the purpose or effect referred to in subsection (1)(b), and
  (c) because of B's rejection of or submission to the conduct, A treats B less favourably than A would treat B if B had not rejected or submitted to the conduct.

(4) In deciding whether conduct has the effect referred to in subsection (1)(b), each of the following must be taken into account—
  (a) the perception of B;
  (b) the other circumstances of the case;
  (c) whether it is reasonable for the conduct to have that effect.

(5) The relevant protected characteristics are—
  age;
  disability;
  gender reassignment;
  race;
  religion or belief;
  sex;
  sexual orientation.

Bakkali v Greater Manchester Buses (South) Ltd (trading as Stagecoach Manchester)
[2018] I.C.R. 1481, Mrs Justice Slade, Employment Appeal Tribunal

This case was an appeal from a decision of the first instance Employment Tribunal (ET). It is important for establishing what relationship there is between discrimination under the Equality Act 2010, section 13, and harassment under section 26. The claimant challenged the ET's decision to refer to its finding that there was no direct discrimination when deciding whether there had been harassment. In effect, the challenge before the Employment Appeal Tribunal (EAT) raised the question whether the lower tribunal had confused the tests for direct discrimination and harassment. The dispute arose when another employee mentioned a previous conversation with the claimant, a Moroccan Muslim, regarding a news report about the actions of ISIS in Syria which the claimant had positively commented on. The fellow employee had remarked, "Are you still promoting IS/Daesh." The issue then involved other employees who alleged that the claimant had been aggressive, and he was eventually dismissed after in-employment disciplinary hearings. In the event, the ET concluded that there had been no direct discrimination or harassment against the claimant under the Equality At 2010, sections 13 and 26 respectively. The EAT held that although the wording of the tests for direct discrimination and harassment differs, the ET did not err in referring back to the facts that had been relevant to the finding with respect to direct discrimination.

> 31. In my judgment the change in the wording of the statutory prohibition of harassment from "unwanted conduct on grounds of race …" in the Race Relations

Act 1976 section 3A to "unwanted conduct related to a relevant protected characteristic" affects the test to be applied. Paragraph 7.9 of the Code of Practice on the Equality Act 2010 encapsulates the change. Conduct can be "related to" a relevant characteristic even if it is not "because of" that characteristic. It is difficult to think of circumstances in which unwanted conduct on grounds of or because of a relevant protected characteristic would not be related to that protected characteristic of a claimant. However, "related to" such a characteristic includes a wider category of conduct. A decision on whether conduct is related to such a characteristic requires a broader enquiry. In my judgment the change in the statutory ingredients of harassment requires a more intense focus on the context of the offending words or behaviour. … "the mental processes" of the alleged harasser will be relevant to the question of whether the conduct complained of was related to a protected characteristic of the Claimant. It was said that without such evidence the ET should have found the complaint of harassment established. However such evidence from the alleged perpetrator is not essential to the determination of the issue. A tribunal will determine the complaint on the material before it including evidence of the context in which the conduct complained of took place.

32. The issue in this appeal is whether the ET failed to apply the statutory test for harassment in the Equality Act 2010, section 26: whether the conduct complained of was "related to" the religious belief or race of the Claimant, instead wrongly applying the test for direct discrimination in section 13, whether the conduct was because of those protected characteristics.

…

34. The facts giving rise to the allegation of harassment were not disputed. Those facts included the offending words used by Mr Cotter on 19 October 2015. They also included the context in which they were spoken. It was not disputed that the Claimant had initiated a conversation with Mr Cotter earlier in October in which he had recounted the report of a German journalist which could be understood as being of a positive nature about ISIS. The Claimant relayed that the reporter had said that ISIS were very good fighters and had managed to run the country.

35. Based on the unchallenged facts the ET found at paragraph 20:

> 20. … We find that Mr Cotter made the remark because of the previous conversation. There is no evidence that Mr Cotter made the remark because of the claimant's race or religion.

The ET made a similar observation in relation to those unchallenged facts in paragraph 69:

> 69. … If the comment had been made without the context, and the speaker knew the claimant was Muslim, it would have appeared that the speaker was linking the claimant's religion to the possibility of him promoting ISIS. However, the context in which Mr Cotter made this remark was that it followed a conversation where the claimant had informed Mr Cotter about positive sounding comments from a German journalist about ISIS. Mr Cotter had understood that, by making these comments, the claimant was promoting ISIS. Given the context, we conclude that the claimant has not proved facts from which we could conclude that the respondent treated him less favourably because of his religious belief. …

36. In dealing with the claim of direct discrimination the ET rightly considered whether the conduct of Mr Cotter on 19 October 2015 was *because* of his race and/or religious belief.

37. In addition to the Equality Act 2010, section 13, direct discrimination, the ET set out the Equality Act 2010, section 26, the definition of harassment, which contains the words "relevant to a protected characteristic".

38. The same facts were relied upon by the Claimant in support of his claim of harassment as that of direct discrimination. Findings of fact on the evidence before them were made in paragraphs 20, 68 and 69. Those included findings about the context in which the conduct complained of, the language used by Mr Cotter on 19 October 2015, took place.

39. As the complaint of harassment was based on the same facts as those relied upon for the complaint of direct discrimination the ET did not err in referring back in paragraph 82 to those findings. In deciding the complaint of harassment, in paragraph 82 the ET addressed the test applicable to harassment: whether the conduct complained of was or was not *related* to religious belief. They concluded in respect of the offending words that there was "no evidence it was *related* to race". The ET held:

> 82. … given our conclusion that, in the context, the remark was not related to religious belief, this complaint fails. There is no evidence it was related to race so the complaint of harassment related to race also fails.

The ET were entitled to take into account the context in which the offending words were spoken. Whilst another ET may have reached a different conclusion, this ET applied the correct test for whether the conduct complained of constituted harassment within the meaning of the Equality Act 2010, section 26.

Heathrow Express Operating Co Ltd, Redline Assured Security Ltd
[2022] EAT 54, [2022] 4 WLUK 93, [2022] I.R.L.R. 558, Employment Appeal Tribunal

The first respondent was an airport rail link operator. The second respondent had a contract with Heathrow airport for security-related services, which extended to stations operated by the first respondent. Security testing for Heathrow airport included the deploying of suspect packages by the second respondent, who was contracted to do so by the first respondent, to test whether they were treated appropriately by employees. To that end a carrier bag was concealed at one of the stations. It contained a piece of paper with the words "Allahu Akbar," which words the tribunal found had been used in terrorist attacks. Although the employee, a Muslim, had not been on duty on the day of the test, he had received an email with details of the test results and images of the bag and note. His claim for harassment under the Equality Act 2010, section 26, was rejected by the first instance Employment Tribunal (ET) which found that the employee should have understood that the security team were not seeking to associate Islam with terrorism and that it had not been reasonable for him to have taken offence. The employee contended that the ET's decision was perverse and that it had failed to provide adequate reasons. He argued that the ET had failed to address the fact that the vast majority of Muslims did not support terrorist extremists and would be deeply offended by the association of their religion with terrorism; that it was wrong to tarnish Muslims generally by using their sacred terms in association with possible terrorist acts; and that it had been unnecessary for the purposes of the test to have placed such a note inside the bag.

> 53. The propositions that the vast majority of Muslims do not behave as the terrorists do, or support their actions, that it is wrong to tarnish the vast majority in that way, and that they are deeply offended by the association of their religion with terrorism (grounds 1(a) and (b)) are all, surely, wholly unexceptionable. But they do not point to the conclusion that this tribunal should, and only could, have found that what the second respondent did itself amounted to that form of egregious and fundamentally misconceived stereotyping.
>
> 54. Similarly, the proposition that the idea that a religious phrase, itself, makes a bag more suspicious is going to be offensive to adherents of the religion (ground 1(d)), does not point to the conclusion that this tribunal should have concluded that the second respondent's use of the phrase was, in effect, not materially different from the use of the phrase by terrorists themselves, or from the actions of those who stereotype Muslims as terrorists or terrorist sympathisers.

55. The fifth strand of the perversity challenge (ground 1(e)) makes the point that it was not necessary to use the note as part of the scenario. Other ways could have been found, which would not offend the followers of Islam. There are a number of points to make about this.

56. First, a strand of Mr Toms' argument was, more specifically, that the note was pointless, because a member of staff or the security team finding the bag would be advised not to open it up or delve inside it. However, the tribunal specifically found as a fact at [27] that the bag was left open and the note was placed at the top so as to be visible on close inspection. The tribunal was entitled to find that this was done in order to ensure that a security guard finding, or being shown, the bag would not fail immediately to treat it as suspicious.

57. A different point, however, is that there was nothing in the service agreement or protocols that obliged the second respondent to use this particular writing, or any writing at all, to make the object or prop used in a security test appear obviously suspicious. However, that does not appear to have been disputed, as such; and certainly there is nothing in the decision to suggest that the tribunal thought otherwise. Nor can it be said that the tribunal did not appreciate, or agree, with the proposition that the use of the holy phrase was liable to cause offence to Muslims. The tribunal specifically referred at [27] to the fact that it was not in dispute that this was an important and significant phrase for Muslims, which may be used many times a day in the course of religious devotion.

58. But, once again, this feature does not point to the tribunal's conclusion at [55] being in the legal sense perverse. It is not said, on appeal, that the tribunal should have concluded that these words had been chosen gratuitously with the deliberate purpose of causing upset, still less with one of the purposes proscribed by section 26.

59. We understand that a strand of the claimant's case was that the use of this phrase was particularly insensitive, and offensive to him, not merely because it referenced Islam, but because of the sacred nature and significance of this particular phrase in religious observance. While we do not accept that it was perverse not to regard the conduct of the second respondent as amounting in itself to the stereotyping of Muslims generally as terrorists or terrorist sympathisers, we do understand that he also says that, because such stereotyping is a significant and serious blight on the lives of Muslims, the use of these words in this context was particularly charged for him, more than, say, the use of an animal-rights slogan co-opted by some terrorists would be for a vegan. However, we cannot say that

these features point to the conclusion that the tribunal could only properly have found that the claimant's perception that the conduct had the effects on him of the kind referred to in section 26(1)(b) was a reasonable one.

60. We remind ourselves again that the application of the reasonableness test was "quintessentially" a matter for the tribunal, not the EAT. Further, although the tribunal said, at [55] that it was not reasonable for the claimant to "take offence" at this incident, that was plainly itself a shorthand for his perception that it had effects referred to in section 26(1)(b): violating his dignity or creating an intimidating, hostile, degrading, humiliating or offensive environment for him. Reading the decision as a whole, the tribunal plainly was alive to this test, and had it in mind. They cited it when first summarising the law, specifically reminded themselves again of it, when considering this particular complaint, at [52], used its language when referring to the claimant's evidence, at [53], and referred back to it again at the start of [55] by referring to "that effect".

61. The tribunal made proper findings that the conduct was not directed at the claimant because of his religion, that the phrase had been used in connection with recent high-profile terrorist attacks, that it was, for that particular reason, chosen to reinforce the suspicious nature of the package, and that the claimant should have reasonably appreciated that. These were all features of the circumstances to which it was entitled to have regard when deciding whether it was reasonable for him to perceive the conduct as having the proscribed effect. We do not think any of these other points or arguments show that it was bound nevertheless to decide otherwise.

62. In argument Mr Toms advanced the further point that the claimant could not have known what was inside the minds of Mr Rutherford, or his team, when they devised this test. But the tribunal's point precisely was that, within the context of this being a security test, and against the background of a recent spike of terrorist attacks, in which these words had been invoked, of which the claimant was aware, the purpose reasonably should have been appreciated by him.

63. It may be said, nevertheless, that the claimant did not appreciate at the time that other phrases were used in other tests, but we do not consider that the tribunal's reference to Mr Rutherford's evidence in this regard makes good the perversity challenge. The two particular circumstances that the tribunal highlighted and relied upon in the main part of [54] were the recent past use of the phrase by terrorists, and the associated use by the second respondent of it as a means of provoking suspicion by referencing those topical incidents. The evid-

ence that other phrases were used on other occasions was added as something that the tribunal said they "also bear in mind"; and it was the former two, linked, features that are the ones to which it specifically returned at [55]. The tribunal was, in any event, fully entitled to reach the view that they did on the reasonableness question, having regard to those features alone.

64. We stress again, in conclusion on this ground, that it would not be sufficient to a perversity challenge that another employment tribunal might, properly, have come to a different conclusion as to whether the claimant reasonably viewed this conduct as having the proscribed effect. The perversity hurdle is only surmounted if no reasonable tribunal, applying the correct legal test, could have reached the conclusion that this tribunal did. Whether or not the second respondent's actions, notwithstanding their found purpose, might be thought to have been ill-judged, or insensitive, we do not find that hurdle to have been surmounted in this case. inadequate because of a failure to address the same five matters that were referred to in ground 1 at sub-paragraphs (a) to (e).

...

66. As to the points made at (a) and (b), true it is that, in his closing skeleton argument to the tribunal, Mr Toms referred to them in support of his contention that it was reasonable for the claimant "to be offended", which, we assume, was intended by him to be a shorthand for the statutory test. True it is that the tribunal did not expressly mention them in its decision. However, it was, in our view, not necessary for it do so. That is for the following reasons.

67. First, there is no reason at all to suppose that the tribunal's failure to mention these propositions—that the vast majority of Muslims do not behave in the manner of the terrorist extremists, or support them, that it is wrong to tarnish Muslims generally by using their sacred terms in association with possible terrorist acts, and that law-abiding Muslims would be deeply offended by the association of their religion with terrorism—was because it had failed to consider them, or took issue with them as such. Their nature is such that the tribunal did not need to confirm if it regarded them as uncontroversial as such. Rather, it would have been necessary for the tribunal to spell out if for some reason it took issue with any of them.

68. Secondly, as we have discussed, the significance, or not, of these propositions, for the issue that the tribunal had to decide, was largely parasitic on the submission that the claimant reasonably regarded the second respondent's conduct as itself inherently amounting to an act of stereotyping or tarnishing of Muslims in

general as terrorists or terrorist sympathisers. The tribunal gave, in substance, in its decision, its reasons for rejecting that core proposition. That being so, we do not think it was incumbent on it to go on to address these propositions in terms.

69. As to point (c) this expressly refers to something that was stated in the tribunal's reasons, at [55], so it cannot be said that the tribunal erred by failing to address it; and we note that this strand of ground 2 was not pursued in Mr Toms' submissions.

70. As to point (d) this too featured in Mr Toms' skeleton to the tribunal. It is, however, in its first part, effectively a restatement of points (a) and (b). Its second part makes points about stereotyping and its effects, which, once again were relied upon in support of the underlying proposition that the claimant reasonably considered that the second respondent was itself engaging in such stereotyping. Once again, the nature of the proposition about the stereotyping of Muslims and its perniciousness, is such that we do not think it can be inferred, because it did not mention it, that the tribunal had overlooked or took issue with it. Once again, the particular significance said to attach to this point was that it was relied upon in harness with the proposition that the second respondent had itself engaged in such stereotyping, which the tribunal did, as such, address.

71. As to (e), again the point was raised in Mr Toms' skeleton. But there is nothing in its decision to suggest that the tribunal had overlooked this, or otherwise thought that the second respondent was obliged to use material of this sort as part of a test prop, or relied upon any such assumption. The tribunal accepted that the claimant had been deeply offended by it, and noted at [57] that the second respondent had not used any religious phrases in its tests since receiving his complaint, which it commended as sensible. As we have stated, we do not think that the tribunal was obliged to regard this feature as pointing to the conclusion that the claimant's perception, by reference to section 26(1)(b)(i) and (ii), was, in all the circumstances, a reasonable one. All of that being so, we do not think it was necessary for it, in its decision, specifically to refer to this submission.

72. We note that the tribunal was, in this decision, concerned with a number of complaints of which this was only one. Perhaps it would have been better if its conclusion in relation to this particular complaint had been expressed a little bit more fully. But in rule 62 terms, all the essential facts are set out. As to the law, some reference to the key authorities or principles emerging from them might usefully have been included. But, as we have said, the tribunal plainly had the

section 26 definition firmly in mind, understood how to apply section 26(4) and did apply it. Standing back, and applying the fundamental test in Meek and English, the tribunal set out the facts at [34] to [30]. It opened paragraphs [54] and [55] by referring to what the other circumstances “include”. It went on, there, to identify the features among all the circumstances of the case, those that were critical to its decision on this particular complaint. It thereby told the claimant why this complaint was unsuccessful.

73. Ground 2 accordingly fails.

2 The Public Sector Equality Duty

The Equality Act 2010, section 149, is somewhat modelled on section 71 of the Race Relations Act 1976, section 76A of the Sex Discrimination Act 1975, and section 49A of the Disability Discrimination Act 1995. These provisions imposed similar public-sector equality duties in relation to race, sex and disability respectively. There were no equivalent public-sector equality duties for age, religion or belief or sexual orientation in previous legislation. Therefore, section 149 extended the new public-sector equality duty to include gender reassignment in full, age, religion or belief and sexual orientation. One of the examples which the explanatory notes to this section provides is as follows: “[t]he duty could lead a local authority to introduce measures to facilitate understanding and conciliation between Sunni and Shi’a Muslims living in a particular area, with the aim of fostering good relations between people of different religious beliefs.” The explanatory notes mention other activities including a review of recruitment procedures, targeting training and mentoring schemes, providing staff with education and guidance, and reviewing an anti-bullying strategy. All these measures aim at one or other of the objectives in section 149(1)(a)–(c). Although section 149 does not refer to “intersectional” needs it does provide another illustration which may be relevant. It says: “[t]he duty could lead a local authority to provide funding for a black women’s refuge for victims of domestic violence, with the aim of advancing equality of opportunity for women, and in particular meeting the different needs of women from different racial groups.” The example shows that a combination of protected characteristics may be used to design a particular policy. Thus, given predominantly low levels of Muslim women being economically active (see Introduction), a consideration of a policy by a public authority or a body that exercises public functions that improve their involvement in the workplace may be obligatory under section 149(1)(b) and (3). Although such an initiative might be considered to breach section 149(6) by treating some people more favourably than others, in fact, it would appear to be envisaged (though permitted, not obliged) by the Equality Act 2010, sections 158 and 159, which relate to positive action.

Equality Act 2010

149 Public sector equality duty

(1) A public authority must, in the exercise of its functions, have due regard to the need to—
  (a) eliminate discrimination, harassment, victimisation and any other conduct that is prohibited by or under this Act;
  (b) advance equality of opportunity between persons who share a relevant protected characteristic and persons who do not share it;
  (c) foster good relations between persons who share a relevant protected characteristic and persons who do not share it.

(2) A person who is not a public authority but who exercises public functions must, in the exercise of those functions, have due regard to the matters mentioned in subsection (1).

(3) Having due regard to the need to advance equality of opportunity between persons who share a relevant protected characteristic and persons who do not share it involves having due regard, in particular, to the need to—
  (a) remove or minimise disadvantages suffered by persons who share a relevant protected characteristic that are connected to that characteristic;
  (b) take steps to meet the needs of persons who share a relevant protected characteristic that are different from the needs of persons who do not share it;
  (c) encourage persons who share a relevant protected characteristic to participate in public life or in any other activity in which participation by such persons is disproportionately low.

(4) The steps involved in meeting the needs of disabled persons that are different from the needs of persons who are not disabled include, in particular, steps to take account of disabled persons' disabilities.

(5) Having due regard to the need to foster good relations between persons who share a relevant protected characteristic and persons who do not share it involves having due regard, in particular, to the need to—

(a) tackle prejudice, and
(b) promote understanding.

(6) Compliance with the duties in this section may involve treating some persons more favourably than others; but that is not to be taken as permitting conduct that would otherwise be prohibited by or under this Act.

(7) The relevant protected characteristics are—

age;
disability;
gender reassignment;
pregnancy and maternity;
race;
religion or belief;
sex;
sexual orientation.

(8) A reference to conduct that is prohibited by or under this Act includes a reference to—

(a) a breach of an equality clause or rule;
(b) a breach of a non-discrimination rule

CHAPTER 5

Mosques and Prayer

This topic can be broadly divided up into the question of planning issues that arise with respect to mosques and individual requests for permission, space or time off for prayer, especially in conditions where the requirements of work, education, medical treatment or confinement restrict their availability. However, the issues are often not so conveniently circumscribed because, in practice, other questions intrude. For example, mosques are often planned together with a madrasa and the seeking of permission may therefore be more complicated.[1]

1 Mosques

The number of mosques or masjids in Britain is difficult to measure. One survey that tried to identify mosques and prayer rooms estimated that there were around 2,000 active ones in total in 2017.[2] While they have their origins in many parts of the Muslim world, the largest number are managed by Muslims from the Indian subcontinent, and the largest groups are affiliated to the Deobandi and Barelvi movements, both of which also emerged in the subcontinent. The increase in the Muslim population leads to a great demand for places of worship and mosques in particular.[3] In the UK, mosque attendance has been positively associated with voting, volunteering in political affairs, participating in demonstrations, donating money for a political cause and getting involved in local community organisations.[4]

1 *R. (on the application of Umar) v Secretary of State for Communities and Local Government* [2009] EWHC 1770 (Admin), where the application involved a mosque and a madrasa. In *Newham London Borough Council v Ali and others* [2014] EWCA Civ 676 an appeal against a mandatory injunction requiring the trust to carry out the removal of works to a mosque and faith centre, one of the concerns expressed by the appellants was about learning and schooling facilities.

2 Naqshbandi, M. (2017), *UK mosque statistics*. Available at: https://www.muslimsinbritain.org/resources/masjid_report.pdf. The survey adds figures collected through a variety of different methods and is a work in progress.

3 In *Newham London Borough Council v Ali* and others [2014] EWCA Civ 676 one of the claims against an injunction to remove an unauthorised building was that "all other mosques are already at full capacity."

4 Oskooii, K.A.R. and Dana, K. (2018), "Muslims in Great Britain: The impact of mosque attend-

Much of the challenge might lie in the varied types of planning permission which is sought and over which planning authorities have a large discretion under the applicable legislation.[5] This is not restricted just to the erection of new buildings as mosques but can also involve a variety of different types of issues including certificates of lawfulness, change of use (of a building either to or from a place of worship) or planning conditions, demolition, extension, listed building consent, redevelopment (demolition and reconstruction), renewal and variation of applications.[6] Planning authorities enjoy a wide discretion in granting, refusing or setting conditions on planning permission. They have to take account of the relevant local development plan and any other material considerations. A decision by the planning authority which acknowledges the existence of the religious dimension may proof it against judicial review including a human rights challenge.[7]

Research has indicted that the number of applications and approvals for mosques and madrasas has increased and there is some reason to believe that there is an increase in awareness among planning authorities of what kinds of needs Muslims have. That does not necessarily mean the easy approval of mosques or madrasas, considering that often their applications envisage a change of use from residential premises to religious ones. This seems a peculiar demand of Muslims who tend to prefer mosques to be within walking distance. It carries with it the penalty that the envisaged disruption to residential areas will result in the greater likelihood of refusal for such applications.[8] Another matter which can give rise to disputes is the call to prayer (*azan*) which local

---

ance on political behaviour and civic engagement," *Journal of Ethnic and Migration Studies*, 44(9), pp. 1479–1505.

5 The main piece of legislation is the Town and Country Planning Act 1990 although planning law has numerous other potentially applicable statutes and secondary legislation. See Bowes, A. (2019), *A practical approach to planning law*. Oxford: Oxford University Press.

6 CAG Consultants et al. (2008), *Responding to the needs of faith communities: Places of worship*, London, which surveyed applicants, planning applications and planning appeals in London Boroughs.

7 Rivers, J. (2010), *The law of organized religions: Between establishment and secularism*. Oxford: Oxford University Press, pp. 195–199.

8 See Gale, R. (2005), "Representing the city: Mosques and the planning process in Birmingham," *Journal of Ethnic and Migration Studies*, 31(6), pp. 1161–1179 on Birmingham. See *R. (on the application of Umar) v Secretary of State for Communities and Local Government* [2009] EWHC 1770 (Admin), where the application was to replace residential premises that were already being used as a mosque and madrasa with a new purpose-built building. Traffic problems and the adverse effect on the other occupants of neighbourhood premises were cited by the planning inspector who heard the appeal against refusal of permission, and the refusal was upheld by the court.

planning authorities might refuse or restrict.[9] Bearing in mind greater official and political representation of Muslims and greater residential concentration, it is to be expected that hurdles in the way of planning approval are becoming easier to overcome.

Newham London Borough Council v Ali and others
[2014] EWCA Civ 676, Court of Appeal

After a series of events that lasted more than a decade, which included the construction of buildings on a site of strategic importance on the city plan for London and temporary planning permission, the trustees of the site did not submit the required planning permission and a further application was refused because it was not in compliance with the city's plan. They were ordered by the planning authority to cease use of and take down the constructed buildings. After further proceedings, an injunction was granted with the same requirements. While the appeal against the injunction was refused, part of the claim concerned the human rights implications of the rejection of the planning application and injunction. The Court of Appeal noted as follows:

> 33. In other words, the judge was aware of and took into account the harmful effect that an injunction would have, but concluded that this was insufficient to justify withholding the remedy that would ordinarily be granted in such a situation. It is true that he did not make any reference to articles 9 and 11 of the Convention. But article 9.2 states that "freedom to manifest one's religion or beliefs shall be subject only to such limitations as a prescribed by law and are necessary in a democratic society … for the protection of the rights and freedoms of others." There is a similar provision in article 11.2. The enforcement of planning obligations by a local planning authority in the public interest falls squarely within the scope of articles 9.2 and 11.2. I do not consider that an argument based on the Convention takes the debate any further.

2 Prayer

Individual requests for permission, space or time off in order to pray can be raised most often in conditions where the requirements of work, education,

9 See Gale, ibid. for a discussion of this issue in Birmingham.

medical treatment or confinement restrict their availability. As in many other areas, such claims are most frequently based on ECHR, Article 9 (freedom of religion), and the Equality Act 2010 (religious discrimination).

The original version of the Education Act 1944, section 30, contained a provision to ensure the protection of schoolteachers from being disadvantaged because of their religious opinions or acts of worship. Section 30 of the Education Act 1944 has been superseded by later legislation and is now contained in the School Standards and Framework Act 1998, section 59. (These updated provisions are extracted at ch. 7, section 6.2.) Meanwhile, section 30 was tested in the case of *Ahmad* before the Court of Appeal, whose judgment may still be considered of some relevance to the requirements of ECHR, Article 9, and its application to requests by employees for time off for prayers.

Education Act 1944

30 Saving as to position of teachers.
Subject as hereinafter provided, no person shall be disqualified by reason of his religious opinions, or of his attending or omitting to attend religious worship, from being a teacher in a county school or in any voluntary school, or from being otherwise employed for the purposes of such a school; and no teacher in any such school shall be required to give religious instruction or receive any less emolument or be deprived of, or disqualified for, any promotion or other advantage by reason of the fact that he does or does not give religious instruction or by reason of his religious opinions or of his attending or omitting to attend religious worship:
Provided that, save in so far as they require that a teacher shall not receive any less emolument or be deprived of, or disqualified for, any promotion or other advantage by reason of the fact that he gives religious instruction or by reason of his religious opinions or of his attending religious worship, the provisions of this section shall not apply with respect to a teacher in an aided school or with respect to a reserved teacher in any controlled school or special agreement school.

Ahmad v Inner London Education Authority
[1978] Q.B. 36, Court of Appeal (Civil Division)

Ahmad, a schoolteacher, had refused an offer of employment on a 4½-day week basis, and then left his full-time employment because his employers would not allow him to be absent from school for ¾ of an hour every Friday to attend a mosque. The question was raised whether section 30, read in conformity with Article 9 ECHR, could allow a schoolteacher to take time off for prayers on Fridays in such a way that intruded on the school teaching day. Lord Denning MR and Orr LJ were in the majority and agreed that that was not the effect of the provisions. Scarman LJ dissented. Some of the factual background is set out in the judgment of Orr LJ:

> Mr. Ahmad did not before entering into the contract disclose to the I.L.E.A. that the practice of his religion would or might require that he should be absent from school for a period of time after the lunch-time break on Fridays in order to attend prayers in a mosque. From his appointment C until 1974 he was employed in Division 8 of the I.L.E.A. where his respective schools were some distance away from any mosque with the result that during that period he made no request to be allowed time off for this purpose, but after his transfer in 1974 to Division 5 he found himself nearer to mosques and at his first school in that division, in which he was a supernumerary teacher, the headmaster (Mr. Foley), of his own volition and without consulting the Divisional Office of the I.L.E.A., allowed him to be absent from school for a short period after the midday break in order to attend Friday prayers at a mosque. Mr. Foley's evidence as to this matter was that Mr. Ahmad had a teaching period after the Friday midday break but that the staff did not object to his having time off to attend the mosque and were prepared to accommodate him in this respect. If, however, there had been other Muslim teachers who wished to go to a mosque for Friday prayers the school could not have managed, and there was in fact in the school another Muslim teacher who had never made such a request.
>
> Mr. Ahmad was next employed, still as a supernumerary teacher, at the Chisern Hall School, Bethnal Green, and there he did not at first ask for permission to attend a mosque for Friday prayers but the headmistress, Miss Gadd, heard of his intention to do so and obtained advice from the Divisional Office that she could not stop him from going but should not give him permission to do so, and on his later asking for permission to go she gave him these answers and insisted that he should be back by 1.30, at the end of the midday break, but he never returned before 2.20 with the result that Friday afternoon teaching periods had to be adjusted until he returned and, although this adjustment was not difficult, the other staff, Miss Gadd said, had to accommodate him all the time.
>
> Mr. Ahmad was next employed at the Bonner Primary School at Bethnal Green where he asked for similar permission to attend a mosque for Friday prayers

and the headmaster, Mr. Wilford, refused this request and reported his refusal to the Divisional Office, but Mr. Ahmad disregarded the refusal and attended the mosque with the result that on one Friday the headmaster had a class without a teacher until Mr. Ahmad returned.

Mr. Ahmad was next employed, still as a supernumerary teacher, at the Bethnal GreenPrimary School for one term from September 1974, where the headmaster, having previously consulted the Divisional Office, refused his request to be allowed to attend a mosque on Fridays, but Mr. Ahmad attended the mosque in spite of this refusal, and the deputy headmaster reported that there were grumbles about this from the staff.

Finally, for the first term of 1975, the appellant was employed as a stand-in teacher at a Roman Catholic primary school in Mile End, the headmaster of which was informed by the Divisional Office that Mr. Ahmad had been refused permission to be absent during school hours on Fridays, but B Mr. Ahmad, although allowed at this school to use a room for prayers, said that he would take time off on Fridays in spite of the refusal and did so.

…

The industrial tribunal heard evidence from Mr. Ahmad himself, from Dr. Pasha, an Islamic religious leader, on his behalf, and also from the head teachers to whom I have referred and members of the I.L.E.A. staff. Dr. Pasha's evidence was that Friday is a day on which a Muslim is by the Koran required to attend prayers and thereafter return to work. If F there were three others in the school Mr. Ahmad could pray with them but if not he is required to attend a mosque unless it is too far from the school, in which case he may say his prayers in a quiet place of worship at the school. Dr. Pasha accepted that it would be advisable for a Muslim not to become involved in an employment which prevents his attending a mosque for Friday prayers but said that if he had such an employment he should convince his employer of this requirement, and he took the view that in this respect it was the duty of an employer to consider the needs of his employees. He added that outside an Islamic state there is no penalty for failure to attend the mosque but it is for the individual to reconcile his own conscience. Sickness would be accepted as a good reason for not attending, but not the nature of the employment.

Lord Denning set out the legal grounds for construing section 30 read together with Article 9 ECHR as not allowing the schoolteacher to take time off work for prayers:

If the words [of section 30] were read literally without qualification, they would entitle Mr. Ahmad to take time off every Friday afternoon for his prayers without loss of pay. I cannot think this was ever intended. The school time-table was well known to Mr. Ahmad when he applied for the teaching post. It was for the usual teaching hours from Monday to Friday, inclusive. If he wished to have every Friday afternoon off for his prayers, either he ought not to have applied for this post: or he ought to have made it clear at the outset and entered into a 41/2-day engagement only. This was the sensible thing for him to do. Instead he undertook full-time work without making any disclosure that he wanted Friday afternoon off for prayers.

I think that section 30 can be applied to the situation perfectly well by reading it as subject to the qualification "if the school time-table so permits." So read, it means that he is to be entitled to attend for religious worship during the working week if it can be arranged consistently with performing his teaching duties under his contract of employment. It has been so interpreted by the great majority of Muslim teachers in our schools. They do not take time off for their prayers. Nor should Mr. Ahmad if he wants to get his full pay for a five-day week. The industrial tribunal said:

> … none of the other education authorities has ever received such a A request from Muslim staff and the problem would seem to be unique to the applicant, Mr. Ahmad.

I have no doubt that all headmasters will try to arrange their time-table so as to accommodate devout Muslims like Mr. Ahmad: but I do not think they should be compelled to do so, if it means disrupting the work of the school and the well-being of the pupils.

During the argument Scarman L.J. drew attention to article 9 of the European Convention on Human Rights (Convention for the Protection of Human Rights and Fundamental Freedoms, Cmd. 8969), to which this country has subscribed. It says: "(1) Everyone has the right to freedom of thought, conscience and religion; this right includes freedom to change his religion or belief and freedom, either alone or in community with others and in public or private, to manifest his religion or belief in worship, teaching, practice and observance. (2) Freedom to manifest one's religion or beliefs shall be subject only to such limitations as are prescribed by law and are necessary in a democratic society in the interests of public safety, for the protection of public order, health or morals, or for the protection of the rights and freedoms of others." The convention is not part of our English law, but, as I have often said, we will always have regard to it. We will do our best to see that our decisions are in conformity with it. But it is drawn

> in such vague terms that it can be used for all sorts of unreasonable claims and provoke all sorts of litigation. As so often happens with high-sounding principles, they have to be brought down to earth. They have to be applied in a work-a-day world. I venture to suggest that it would do the Muslim community no good—or any other minority group no good—if they were to be given preferential treatment over the great majority of the people. If it should happen that, in the name of religious freedom, they were given special privileges or advantages, it would provoke discontent, and even resentment among those with whom they work. As, indeed, it has done in this very case. And so the cause of racial integration would suffer. So, whilst upholding religious freedom to the full, I would suggest that it should be applied with caution, especially having regard to the setting in which it is sought. Applied to our educational system, I think that Mr. Ahmad's right to "manifest his religion in practice and observance" must be subject to the rights of the education authorities under the contract and to the interests of the children whom he is paid to teach. I see nothing in the European Convention to give Mr. Ahmad any right to manifest his religion on Friday afternoons in derogation of his contract of employment: and certainly not on full pay.

R.* (*on the application of Hussein*) *v Secretary of State for the Home Department

[2018] EWHC 213 (Admin), [2018] 2 WLUK 27, [2018] A.C.D. 32

A challenge was mounted by two Muslim claimants, from Ethiopia and Bangladesh respectively, who had been held in immigration detention, and were subject to a mandatory lock-in regime between the hours of 21.00 and 08.00. This impacted on three obligatory prayer times during which they were not allowed to use the prayer room and therefore forced to pray in their rooms, which were shared, near an uncovered toilet. They brought proceedings for judicial review claiming that their rights under Article 9, ECHR were breached and they were subject to indirect discrimination under the Equality Act 2010, section 19. The Secretary of State had already conceded that she had not considered the "public sector equality duty" contained in section 149 of the Equality Act. Given that the decision in this case was made provisionally, it ought to be read together with the case that follows it.[10]

10 See below for extracts from the case of *The Queen, on the Application of Nemat Soltany, Abdul Nasir Ebadi, Abidullah Oriakhail v Secretary of State for the Home Department v G4S* [2020] EWHC 2291 (Admin).

28. In my view, this evidence, and in particular that of the Imam, clearly establishes that Article 9 is engaged in this case and that a combination of the required hours of prayer, the lock in, room sharing, and unclosed lavatories within the rooms, does result in an interference with, or a limitation upon, the rights of a Muslim protected by Article 9.

29. Relying upon the observations of Lord Wilson in *Mathieson v Secretary of State for Work and Pensions* [2015] UKSC 47, [2015] 1 WLR 3250 at paragraph 17 Mr Roe [counsel for the defendant] submitted that although the facts and circumstances of this claim are "within the scope of" or "ambit of" Article 9, and the Article is thus engaged, there is nevertheless no interference. I cannot accept that submission. Article 9 protects the freedom to manifest one's religion in worship, practice and observance. It must not be subject to any limitations save those which fall within Article 9(2).

30. The Imam states that "it is highly discouraged in Islam that the place of prayer is near to a toilet" and that this should only be done "in extreme circumstances … (when no other option or place is available) …"

31. The claimants were compulsorily detained, and then compulsorily locked in between hours during which they were required to say at least one or, depending on the season, two or three prayers. They were thus forced to worship and practise their religion in what are "extreme circumstances" which are "highly discouraged" in the tenets of that religion. Mr Hussein says that it distracted him from his prayer to have to pray in the smelly room and that he was unable to concentrate on his prayers in the presence of noisy room-mates. Mr Rahman says that he could not pray, or pray properly, in a room with a toilet and smell. He simply could not concentrate on prayer given the odour and uncleanliness.

32. During his oral submissions Mr Roe submitted that any interference with the freedom protected by Article 9 was "minimal" in the sense of the legal maxim *de minimis non curat lex*. At paragraph 4 of their written "Secretary of State's supplementary skeleton argument" dated 24th January 2018, Mr Roe and Ms Hafsah Masood [counsel for the defendant] repeatedly say that any impact was not "significant".

33. I make clear that I do not by this judgment, after a relatively short hearing during which I have not heard any oral evidence, attach any adjective to qualify or quantify the degree of interference, or to place it on a spectrum. I do not say

whether it was minor (but not de minimis), significant, or grave; but in my view it went beyond the de minimis, and constituted an actual interference with the protected freedom.

34. That being so, Article 14 of the European Convention on Human Rights is also engaged. So far as is material, that provides as follows:

> 14. The enjoyment of the rights and freedoms set forth in this Convention shall be secured without discrimination on any ground such as … religion, …

35. There is indirect discrimination in these circumstances on the ground of religion. Muslims are required to pray at the stated hours, and the lock-in has the differential and discriminatory consequence that they have to pray in conditions (viz in the shared rooms with the lavatories) in which adherents of other faiths, or of none, do not have to do. However great the impact of the lock-in, the lavatories and room sharing may be on other detainees, it has a greater and discriminatory impact upon practising Muslims because of the requirements of their religion. As the European Court of Human Rights said in *Thlimmenos v Greece* (2001) 31 EHRR 15 at paragraph 44:

> The right not to be discriminated against in the enjoyment of the rights guaranteed under the Convention is also violated when States without an objective and reasonable justification fail to treat differently persons whose situations are significantly different.

…

38. Patently the SSHD applies a provision, criterion or practice which puts persons who share the protected characteristic of being practising adherents of the Muslim faith at a particular disadvantage when compared with persons who do not share that characteristic. There is thus a burden on the SSHD under section 19(2)(d) to show that the relevant provision, criterion or practice is a proportionate means of achieving a legitimate aim. It thus follows that both under the Convention and under section 19 of the domestic Equality Act 2010 there is a burden upon the SSHD to justify, if she can, the discrimination in point.

…

65. The blunt truth and reality is that the SSHD has never previously thought about the differential discriminatory effect upon practising Muslims of the combination of their required times of prayer, the night state, the unclosed lavatories and the shared rooms. It may in the end be justifiable, but, as already indicated, there may be a range of steps which the SSHD may be able to take to mitigate or avoid it. Unless and until she, who is the policymaker, has fully and con-

> scientiously considered those steps (and others) and thought this whole problem through, I am quite unable to hold, meantime, that it is justified.
>
> 66. For these reasons, I will make a declaration in terms to be drafted and agreed by counsel ... to the effect that the night state or lock-in regime at Brook House in conjunction with the presence of internal unclosed lavatories and shared rooms (i) constitutes indirect discrimination contrary to Article 9 of the European Convention on Human Rights read with Article 14 which is unlawful unless justified; and (ii) unless justified, constitutes unlawful indirect discrimination contrary to section 19 of the Equality Act 2010. No such justification has yet been shown by the SSHD.

The above case of *R. (on the application of Hussein) v Secretary of State for the Home Department* was not decisive because the holding was provisional and conditional on the provision of a justification by the Secretary of State. The same issues as arose in the *Hussein* case above therefore arose again in a follow-up challenge, one which involved three other claimants, but without the two claimants in the *Hussein* case (spelt "Hussain" in the subsequent case).

The Queen, on the Application of Nemat Soltany, Abdul Nasir Ebadi, Abidullah Oriakhail v Secretary of State for the Home Department v G4S
[2020] EWHC 2291 (Admin)

> 31. ... Holman J made clear [in the *Hussein* case] that he was not ruing that the Defendant had discriminated unlawfully against the Claimants on religious grounds. Rather, the effect of his ruling was that the treatment would be unlawful religious discrimination, contrary to Articles 9 and 14 and EA 10, s19, unless it could be justified by the Defendant as being a proportionate means of achieving a legitimate aim. Noting that the Defendant had not, at that stage, carried out an equality impact assessment ("EIA") or complied with her obligations under the PSED [public sector equality duty], Holman J said that no such justification had as yet been shown by the Defendant (paragraph 66).
>
> 32. It is clear from the judgment of Holman J that, in so saying, he was not making a finding that the treatment complained of was not capable of being justified. Rather, he was, in effect, postponing consideration of the justification issue, until after the Defendant had carried out an EIA.
>
> 33. The current proceedings are, in in a sense, and to an extent, Stage Two of the litigation which began with the *Hussain and Rahman* proceedings. Whether or

not, as a matter of procedural formality, these proceedings are the second stage of the *Hussain and Rahman* proceedings, the practical reality is that I am being asked to address the issues, relating to religious discrimination, which Holman J did not deal with both because there was insufficient time and because the Defendant had not yet conducted an EIA. …

…

Article 9

…

366. … The evidence which has been placed before me, however, was much more extensive than the evidence that was placed before Holman J. As a result, I am not bound by the conclusion of Holman J in this regard [i.e., with respect to interference with freedom of religion].

…

369. In my judgment, notwithstanding the impact that the night state and conditions at Brook House had upon the prayers of observant Muslims, the Defendant took reasonable and appropriate measures to secure Muslim detainees' rights. The interferences resulting from having to pray during night state in a shared room, and in close proximity to the toilets, did not completely prevent Muslim detainees from manifesting their religion, or go against the very essence of their freedom to do so.

370. The starting-point is that the Defendant went to great lengths to respect Muslim detainees' religious beliefs and to provide a supportive and respectful environment for them at Brook House. The Imams and chaplaincy provided an excellent service. Space was made available for communal prayers, and Qurans and the other materials that Muslim detainees might require for religious purposes were made available. Muslim detainees were assisted in performing their prayers in their rooms by being provided with prayer mats and jugs to perform their ablutions in-room, if they required them. G4S looked to place Muslim detainees in rooms together to minimise the risk that roommates might be disruptive to detainees whilst they prayed, and were prepared to move detainees to a different room if a problem arose in that regard. As I have found, curtains were available to block the aperture at the entrance to the toilet, and cleaning materials were made available to detainees to clean the toilet areas. Imams, at Friday Prayers, encouraged detainees to clean their toilet areas. The risk of having to pray very close indeed to the toilet area arose only where there were three Muslim detainees in a room, but this problem could be averted by the residents of a room

agreeing to stagger the times when they prayed within a particular prayer time-window. Similarly, if a roommate chose to use the toilet whilst a Muslim detainee was praying, or if there were particularly strong odours emanating from the toilet, the Muslim detainee could pause in his prayers until the roommate had finished and/or the worst of the odours had dissipated.

371. None of this means that the situation was ideal. The expert evidence, and that of Mr Qayum, made clear that it is highly discouraged in Islam that the place of prayer is near a toilet, and that it is important that, whilst praying, believers should avoid being distracted by matters such as strong and unpleasant odours and loud noises. However, I did not understand the expert evidence, even that from Professor Haleem, to mean that the proximity of a toilet completely invalidated and rendered nugatory the prayers of a believer. If it is unavoidable, it is permissible to pray near to a toilet, and this was unavoidable for those who were detained at Brook House. It was not a matter for their personal choice, for which they could be criticised. As I understood Professor Haleem's evidence, whilst he said that particularly offensive toilet odours could invalidate a prayer, what he meant was that in such circumstances the believer should pause and wait for the worst of the smells to dissipate, before resuming his prayers. This is consistent with the evidence from Mr Ebadi and Mr Oriakhail themselves. Neither said that they were prevented from completing their prayers. Mr Oriakhail said that the conditions did not stop him from praying completely.

372. The circumstances in which Professor Haleem said that prayers should be performed were "clean, quiet conditions." However, in my view, this was a counsel of perfection. In practice, in many places, it is not possible to guarantee such conditions for practising Muslims, and believers manage to perform their prayers in less ideal conditions. I note that Professor Haleem said that a loud television could distract believers during their prayers, but there was no suggestion that the presence of TVs in the rooms was an interference with Muslim detainees' Article 9 rights. Even if there had been no night state, this would not have meant that the prayer hall would have been open during the night hours, or that all of the Muslim detainees at Brook House could have gathered to pray together.

373. I do not think that there was any real, significant, difference, apart from in emphasis, between the two expert witnesses.

374. In my judgment, two other points are highly relevant to the question whether the Defendant had failed to take reasonable and appropriate measures to secure

the Claimants' rights under Article 9(1). The first is that neither Mr Ebadi nor Mr Oriakhail complained whilst he was in Brook House. The second is that it was clear from Ms Harrison QC's submissions that the Claimants accepted that there would have been no breach of Article 9(1) if the night state had been only eight hours long, even though this would still have meant that, in the summer, one of the prescribed prayers, the Fajr, would have had to be performed in the detainee's room during the night state. In my view, if it is acceptable under Article 9(1) for one prayer to be performed in the detainee's room during the night state, notwithstanding the conditions, then it is hard to see why it would be a breach of Article 9(1) for it to be necessary for two or three prayers to be performed in the same conditions.

375. Even if I am wrong, and there was an interference with the Defendant's rights under Article 9(1), any such interference is justified under Article 9(2). For the reasons given earlier in this judgment, the limitations imposed by and consequent upon the night state were lawful. In my judgment, they were necessary in a democratic society in the interests of public safety, for the protection of public order, health or morals, or for the protection of the rights and freedoms of others.

376. There were good reasons for the existence of night state. It was important, for the safety, security, comfort and wellbeing of detainees, that there was a quiet night-time period. The Defendant was entitled to take the view that, where the infrastructure existed, in the form of in-room toilets, it was preferable to lock detainees in their rooms during night state. Otherwise, detainees might congregate on the corridors and disturb those nearby. Some of these detainees would have been difficult and possibly even dangerous. If detainees were able to move around, then there would be two equally unsatisfactory options for the Defendant. Either the same regime would have to be operated, in terms of staff, as during the day, which would have been noisy and expensive, or a small night staff would have been on duty, with attendant dangers for safety and security.

377. As for the length of the night state, this was within the scope of the Defendant's lawful discretion, in my view. Once it is accepted, as the Claimants accept, that a night state which required one of the daily prayers to be performed in the detainees' room was lawful for Article 9 purposes, then in my judgment it is difficult to see why a night state which required one prayer for part of the year and two to three prayers in other parts of the year was impermissible for the purposes of Article 9(1).

Article 14

378. There was no dispute between the parties as regards the applicable legal principles.

379. For Article 14 to apply, it is not necessary that there was a breach of one of the other Articles. It is enough if the facts of the case fall within the ambit of another substantive provision of the Convention or its Protocols: … The Defendant accepts that this case falls within the ambit of Article 9.

380. The Defendant does not dispute the finding of Holman J that, for the purposes of Article 14, the night state at Brook House had a greater and discriminatory impact upon practising Muslims because of the requirements of their religion. It is common ground that the only issue is whether this prima facie discriminatory treatment is objectively and reasonably justified, in the sense that it pursues a legitimate aim, and there is a reasonable relationship of proportionality between the means employed and the aim sought to be realised …

381. It is also common ground that a failure to treat differently persons whose situations are significantly different can be in breach of Article 14 ECHR, in the absence of objective and reasonable justification …

…

387. It is clear, therefore, that appropriate respect should be given to the decision-maker. In my judgment, it is relevant in matters such as this, that the decision is a specialist one, involving operational considerations.

388. In my judgment, there was no breach of Article 14, when read with Article 9.

389. The night state pursues a legitimate aim. That aim is to maintain a safe and quiet centre through the night for detainees of all religions.

390. There is a reasonable relationship of proportionality between the means employed and the aim sought to be realised. For the reasons given at paragraph 376, above, the night state is effective to achieve the aim for which it was designed. That aim would not be achievable if Muslim detainees were exempted from night state, and the Claimants' skeleton argument makes clear that this is not being contended for. Rather, the Claimants contend that, in so far as night state pursues a legitimate aim, that aim could have achieved by a shorter night

state for all detainees, which would have meant that, at most, only one daily prayer would have to be performed during the night state.

391. In my judgment, the duration of the night state at the relevant time at Brook House did not mean that there was no reasonable relationship of proportionality between the means employed and the aim sought to be realised. The duration of the night state at a particular IRC was an operational matter, decided upon by making use of specialist expertise, which had to take into account matters such as the configuration of the buildings and the profile of the detainees. In my view, the decision to accept a bid from GSL which provided for a night state from 9 PM to 8 AM was a reasonable one and was within the measure of discretion afforded to the decision-maker.

392. Whilst the situation was not ideal, this was not a case in which the treatment complained of meant that observant Muslim detainees were completely prevented from practising their religion. As I have explained, at paragraphs 368–373, above, Muslim detainees had a reasonable opportunity to observe their religious practices, including their daily prayer obligations, notwithstanding the existence of the night state. It is accepted by the Claimants that a night state can be lawful, for Article 14 purposes, even if it means that, sometimes, one of the daily prayers is performed in the detainee's room.

393. Muslim detainees were not singled out to be treated differently from other detainees.

394. An integral part of the conditions which led to the Claimant's concerns about night state was that there was an in-room toilet. This had disadvantages, relating to odour and the scope for embarrassment, but on the other hand, there are benefits in having an in-room toilet which detainees can use throughout the night, without needing to use toilets elsewhere in the building. The fact that the rooms had in-room toilets was not, therefore, of itself something that made the treatment in general, or the treatment of Muslim detainees in particular, unreasonable or unlawful.

395. It is worth noting, also, that none of those who reported on the conditions … said that the lock in at Brook House excessively interfered with the religious observance of Muslim detainees.

396. It is true that, since the period with which this case is concerned, the Defendant has taken the decision to limit the night state at Brook House to no more than

9 hours, but this does not mean that a longer night state was necessarily unreasonable or unlawful, for the purposes of Article 14. A less intrusive measure could have been used, in the sense that any shorter night state would, inevitably, be less intrusive than the one that was adopted, but this does not mean, in my judgment, that the night state as actually operated in 2017–2018 was disproportionate and in breach of Article 14. It was within the scope of the discretion that is afforded to the state. Even if the night state was eight hours long, Muslim detainees would still have had to perform their prayers in their rooms once a day in the summer months.

397. Ms Harrison QC points out that cost alone cannot justify discrimination, and submits that the reason longer night state hours at Brook House was cost, because the night state hours were an integral part of the GSL bid in 2007 which was lowest in price. However, there was no evidence that the reason why GSL proposed a night state of 11 hours was solely in order to save costs. As I have said, night states of similar duration were in place at other IRCs. The main reason why there was a night state was not connected with cost.

398. For these reasons, in my judgment, and taking account of the findings of fact that I have made, the treatment complained of struck a fair balance between the rights of the individual and the rights of the community.

Indirect religious discrimination contrary to [the Equality Act 2010] …

399. Both the Claimants and the Defendant, in their submissions, proceeded on the basis that the considerations that were relevant to the Article 14 challenge were equally applicable to the indirect discrimination challenge under the EA 10 [the Equality Act 2010]. In my view, they were correct to do so. In both cases, the central question was whether the prima facie discriminatory treatment complained of was a proportionate means of achieving a legitimate aim. The only relevant difference between Article 14 and the EA 10 is that the *Thlimmenos* principle [*Thlimmenos v Greece* (2001) 31 EHRR 15] only applies to claims under Article 14.

400. For the reasons already given in relation to the challenges under Article 9, ECHR, and Article 14 when read with Article 9, in my judgment, the night state and the conditions surrounding the night state at Brook House was not unlawful under the EA 10. The prima facie discriminatory treatment complained of was a proportionate means of achieving a legitimate aim, taking account of the extent of the discriminatory impact and the importance of the aim.

R. (on the application of TTT*) v Michaela Community Schools Trust* [2024] EWHC 843 (Admin)

The claimant was a year-10 student at a secular secondary school in London with approximately 700 students from various ethnic and religious backgrounds. Around half of the student body, including the claimant, are Muslims. The school has a reputation for academic excellence and enforces a strict disciplinary code, fostering a "team" environment that reduces social distinctions, encourages integration among students of different faiths and cultures, and emphasises the collective interests of the school community over individual needs. In March 2023, the school enacted a policy [the prayer ritual policy or PRP] prohibiting the performance of prayer rituals by students on school property. The ban clearly affected Muslim students who sought to pray during school hours. Up to the implementation of the PRP, the school had not banned prayer rituals and had no dedicated prayer space. The student claimed that, as a Muslim, she was required to pray five times a day. During the autumn and winter months, one of these prayers, Duhr, coincides with the school's lunch period, which the school had reserved for eating and socialising in small groups of students guided and supervised by teachers. The claimant wished to perform Duhr prayers during the guided socialising period which was prevented by the effecting of the PRP banning prayer.

Seeking judicial review of the school's PRP and related decisions, the claimant argued that: (1) the PRP infringed her right to manifest her religious beliefs under ECHR Article 9; (2) the PRP constituted indirect discrimination against Muslim students, against the Equality Act 2010, section 85(2),[11] when read with section 19; (3) the school failed to fulfil its public-sector equality duty under the Equality Act 2010, section 149, by not adequately considering the need to eliminate discrimination, advance equality of opportunity and foster good relations between Muslim and non-Muslim students;[12] and (4) two fixed-term exclusions (FTES) she received in early 2023 (one for alleged threats to other students, the other for alleged rudeness and defiance towards a teacher) were procedurally unfair, as she was not given the opportunity to respond to these allegations.

Linden J found in favour of the claimant only on the way one of the exclusion periods was dealt with. The case became somewhat of a *cause célèbre* about the

11 The Equality Act 2010, section 85, is extracted at ch. 7, section 1.2.

12 The Equality Act 2010, section 149 is extracted at ch. 4, section 2.

allowing of prayers in schools. The extracts below provide greater detail on the facts and the way grounds (1)–(3) were approached by the court.

> 7. The School's case is that the PRP [prayer ritual policy] does not "interfere" with the Claimant's freedom to manifest her religion or belief for the purposes of Article 9 ECHR. Nor does it subject her to a "detriment" for the purposes of section 85(2)(f) of the 2010 Act. Islam permits the Claimant to make up for missing Duhr by performing Qada prayers later in the day and, even if this were not so, she chose a secular school which she knew to have a strict behavioural regime and she is free to transfer to a school which would permit her to pray if she wishes to do so. The School argues that any interference with the Claimant's religious freedom is in any event justified, as is any indirectly discriminatory effect of the PRP itself, principally because the performance of ritual prayer would conflict with the School's ethos and its behavioural rules, and because the practicalities of pupils doing so mean that it cannot be accommodated by the School.
>
> …
>
> 30. The Claimant says that in Year 8 she started to take prayer seriously. The question of praying came up in conversation amongst her friends, and her mother and other parents also discussed it. She and her friends knew that they should be praying as they were getting older and reaching puberty, but they did not feel that they could ask fora prayer room because they believed that prayer was not permitted: "In general if we were not explicitly allowed to do something we could not do it". They had also heard rumours of a request for a prayer room being made in the past which had been ignored. The Claimant says that her mother had telephoned the School to raise a concern that, when she was fasting during Ramadan, the Claimant was uncomfortable about sitting with children at "family lunch" who were eating and drinking, but the question of prayer had not been raised with the School. Although her mother says that she thinks she is likely to have raised prayers in the same call, she does not appear actually to recall doing so. The School's evidence is that prayer was not raised as an issue before the events of March 2023 which I describe below.
>
> …
>
> 38. In relation to the School's reliance on Qada as a substitute for praying at the right time, at [90] of her first witness statement the Claimant says:
>
>> 90 … Doing Qadaa is less meaningful than performing the prayer at the proper time. Qadaa is when one makes up prayers when one has inadvertently missed them. This could be for very straightforward reasons (being asleep at the time

> that the prayers are supposed to have been undertaken) or for more substantive ones—*i.e. a surgeon performing a complex operation clearly could not break from that to perform prayers … Being in the middle of, say a biology lesson on a winter's afternoon would in my view be a reason for Qadaa, given the inconvenience that* seeking to pray at that time would cause to myself and to others. Qadaa seems to me to be a reasonable way of dealing with that, and accommodating my religion to the world within which I live. If I have time free to pray I think it is right to pray rather than not pray. At school, because of the lunchbreak, the opportunity is there at the relevant time and in my view I should use that opportunity. I really do not think it right to seek to apply Qadaa to a situation such as this. It upsets me that somebody suggests that I should. That is not what Qadaa is for. (emphasis added)

…

42. Professor Siddiqui's evidence about the importance of prayer was broadly consistent with the Claimant's, although perhaps with some differences of emphasis. She confirms that prayer is one of the five pillars of Islam, and that it is regarded as an obligation. She confirms that children are normally expected to begin to pray on reaching puberty. She says that prayers last no more than 5–10 minutes at a time, and she confirms that prayers should take place early within the allotted time and not left until it is coming to an end.

43. In relation to Qada, Professor Siddiqui says that *"If one fails for any reason to perform a prayer within the specified time period, one can (and should) make it up later (qada)."* It appears from her report that Qada is the performance of the prayer—the fulfilling of the obligation—at the first opportunity, in contrast to seeking divine forgiveness, which is an *"ever present possibility."*

44. As I understand her report, consistently with [21] of the Claimant's pleaded case, Professor Siddiqui draws a distinction between freely choosing not to pray at the allotted time—"intentionally or deliberately" choosing not to do so—and missing a prayer through forgetfulness or oversleeping or circumstances beyond the person's control. Professor Siddiqui says that:

> The dominant view is that qada prayers are prayers which compensate for prayers which have been missed owing to forgetfulness or oversleeping, not prayers which have been deliberately not observed. Therefore, qada should not be regarded as an alternative practice to missed prayers. For some scholars, if one missed a prayer deliberately, that prayer could never be made up by qada, rather, the person should seek God's forgiveness and repent.

45. She goes on to give the example of a surgeon (also given by the Claimant in her evidence) who may forgo prayer during an operation and says:

> … a pupil at a school should not miss a lesson to perform their prayers because it may disrupt staff, the timetable and other pupils or scheduled activities. However, this is very different from situations where a person has free time at school or at work and observing prayers does not cause any disruption or inconvenience to the wider institution.

89. The School has a strict and highly prescriptive uniform policy from which any departure will result in confiscation of the offending item and/or the pupil being placed in isolation until a parent or guardian brings the correct item to school. The uniform policy permits girls (regardless of religion) to wear headscarves, albeit subject to detailed requirements. They must be black or dark blue, any pins or clips must be small, dark in colour and understated, the headscarf must not have any decorations and the material must not be too long at the front or the back as it must not obscure the uniform or look untidy. The headscarf must also completely cover the hair. Ms Birbalsingh says that compliance with these requirements means that the girls look smart and professional and that there have never been any issues with girls wearing appropriate headscarves.

…

92. Ms Birbalsingh's evidence is that prayer has always been permitted at the School. Until the events of March 2023 prayer rituals had never been prohibited either, but nor had they been actively encouraged or facilitated. The School has never had a designated prayer room and this is made clear to the parents of prospective applicants to the School and pupils, at open days and welcome events.

…

95. Ms Birbalsingh also says that members of the Sixth Form who wish to pray during the lunch period are able to do so at the Brent Civic Centre. This is a reflection of the fact that they are subject to a different, and more permissive, regime to the rest of the School. The Civic Centre is approximately a five-minute walk away from the School and it has at least one prayer room. Many of the Muslim pupils in Years 7–11 who wish to pray at the end of the school day do so there.

96. The Claimant says that by Year 9 she and her friends felt that there was a real problem. They knew that they should be praying at lunchtime but they were not clear how they were going to go about this. Throughout the autumn term of 2022 and at the start of term in 2023 "lots of children were talking amongst themselves

about the possibility of praying at school but, with one possible exception, none of them raised it or acted on this".

97. However, around the start of March 2023 she and her friends spoke with a visitor to the School who was the Headteacher of an Islamic school. He was wearing a thobe (a long white traditional robe worn by male Muslims) and was with a group of women, some of whom were wearing hijabs and others burqas. He spoke to the Claimant and her friends and said that he had heard that they were not encouraged to ask questions. He wanted to know whether this was true, and whether they were able to question the rules. He said that at his school pupils would tell him if they felt that something was wrong.

98. The Claimant says that she understands that the visitor also had a conversation with another group of girls who told him that there was no prayer room, and he suggested that they could just pray in the school yard. After that, she and her friends discussed whether this was a good idea. The problem was that the ground in the yard was dirty and sometimes wet. Whilst she was considering what to do certain other pupils went ahead and began praying in the school yard, using prayer mats.

99. The School's evidence is that, on Friday 17 March 2023, one of the teachers saw a Year 9 pupil (not the Claimant) praying in the yard during the lunch break, using their blazer as a prayer mat. Ms Birbalsingh says she was informed but did not intervene because this was within the School rules at the time.

100. On Monday 20 March, three Year 9 children prayed in the yard using their blazers. On the Tuesday there were six, all from Year 9. It was on one of these days that some of the pupils used prayer mats which they had brought in. These items are not permitted under the School's policies and they were therefore told that they should not be brought into school.

101. On Wednesday 22 March, around 20 children prayed in the yard. They were grouped together, highly visible from the street, and would have been seen by numerous passers-by. Ms Birbalsingh says that there was a high degree of concern and unease amongst teachers and pupils as no one had ever sought to conduct prayer rituals at the School before. A large number of the year 9 girls had coordinated with each other to bring in prayer mats without permission, knowing that this was against the rules. They were using identical travel prayer mats which can be rolled up and put into a pocket. Never before had there been a coordinated attempt to undermine the School's rules. The pupils were told that prayer

mats should not be brought into school. The Claimant denies that the pupils had gone out and bought prayer mats but she accepts that they had discussed that it was not right to use their blazers as prayer mats. She says that they had made their own decisions.

102. On Thursday 23 March, about 25 Year 9 pupils prayed in the yard, again using prayer mats. They included the Claimant. A senior teacher ("Ms A") who, it is relevant to note, is black, told them to put the prayer mats away as they were against school policy. They were, however, allowed to continue praying using their blazers as prayer mats.

103. On the same day, Ms A made a record of what happened. She also says that the bringing in of the prayer mats had clearly been coordinated. When the pupils were told to put them away the majority did this but two, including the Claimant, answered back. The Claimant became very angry and repeatedly interrupted her. Ms A's account relates her surprise at how rude and aggressive the Claimant's tone and facial expression were, and she says that there was a level of contempt towards her which she found shocking despite her extensive experience as a teacher. The Claimant was sent to wait inside and the matter was escalated to Ms Birbalsingh who, having spoken to Ms A, decided that both pupils should be given FTEs for *"extreme rudeness towards a teacher"*. Her decision to impose a 2 day FTE, which would be followed by 4 days of referral (subsequently reduced to 2 days) was communicated to the Claimant's mother by email after school that day. I return to this incident when I consider Ground 4(a) below.

104. Ms Birbalsingh also says that at family lunch on the Thursday, and at the 'break food' stations during morning break, some of the pupils who were conducting prayer rituals in the yard were intimidating other Muslim students who had chosen to eat rather than fast. They would stare at them as they were served food, and pointedly decline to talk to them during the meal or for the rest of the morning break. In addition to this, more children than was usual were given detention for breaching the "*rule of four no more*" by congregating in groups in the yard.

105. On Friday 24 March there were around 30 pupils praying in the yard. The group included pupils from Years 7 and 11 rather than being confined to Year 9s. Ms Birbalsingh says that she was told by a teacher that one of the Muslim pupils who had not previously worn a headscarf had been intimidated into doing so. Around this time she also learned that a Muslim girl had dropped out of the School choir as she had been told by one or more of the other Muslim pupils

that this was "haram," i.e. forbidden, during Ramadan. She says that the intimidation of Muslim pupils who were not fasting at family lunch and during morning break also increased. Some of the Muslim children who were praying had been intimidated into doing so by being told by others that they were bad Muslims if they did not do so. Four of the pupils, two from Year 9 and two from Year 7, were given FTEs for refusing to respond to a teacher when spoken to, on the basis that they should not be interrupted when they were praying.

106. Ms Birbalsingh says that it was also clear that there was a division developing between the Muslim pupils and the non-Muslim pupils. One area in the yard was being exclusively occupied by Muslim children during the lunch period, whether or not they were conducting prayer rituals, while another was occupied by non-Muslim pupils. She says that it was clear that this was undermining of the School's culture of all races and religions mixing and being friends with each other.

107. Also on 24 March 2023, an online petition was started which gave an inaccurate account of the incident between Ms A and the two pupils on the previous day which had led to their FTEs. Ms A was accused of *"disgusting, Islamophobic behaviour"*. The petition was signed by at least 4000 people. Several messages of support for the petition were also posted. Some of these made criticisms of the School in language which was unexceptionable, albeit without knowing the full facts. Others displayed a range of prejudice, including by contrasting the School's supposed favouring of gay people and Jews with its treatment of Muslims. A good deal of abuse was directed at Ms A and Ms Birbalsingh, and the abuse towards the former was particularly shocking. I will not dignify what was said by repeating it, but the comments included references to the Klu Klux Klan, use of the full range of terms which members of the Klu Klux Klan might use to refer to black people, and references to slavery and lynching. There were comparisons with monkeys, there was misogyny and there were threats of violence and death directed at her. There were calls for her and Ms Birbalsingh to be dismissed and for protests outside the School.

108. Two videos which were posted on YouTube and TikTok and a number of blogs also named Ms A and accused the School of Islamophobia. Threatening and abusive emails were sent to the School's general email address which were similar to the comments posted in support of the petition, and the School office received phone calls in which people shouted abuse at staff. The callers accused the School of disrespecting Islam by requiring children to pray outside in dirty and wet conditions rather than allowing them to pray inside in a prayer room. Ms

Birbalsingh says in her evidence that the abuse appeared to stem directly from the fact that the school yard is easily visible to members of the public so that they were reacting to the sight of the children praying outside on their prayer mats or using their blazers as prayer mats.

109. On Saturday 25 March 2023, an email was sent to the School which said that several bombs had been planted in the School building. The abusive and threatening emails and comments continued to arrive on Sunday 26 March. Over the course of the weekend, Ms Birbalsingh spoke repeatedly with the School's senior leadership team to decide what to do. She also discussed various plans of action with the Chair and the Vice Chair of Governors. Their overriding concern was how to keep the School, the teachers and the children safe. They agreed that Ms Birbalsingh should ban the conduct of prayer rituals at the School, with that ban to be reviewed by the Governing Body at its next meeting.

110. The police attended early on Monday 27 March and swept the premises for explosives. Nothing was found. Ms Birbalsingh informed teachers that she had decided to ban prayer rituals and instructed them to inform pupils during Tutor time. Prayers in the yard ceased that day. She met with the Chair and Vice Chair of the Governors in the evening to confirm her decision subject to a full decision being made by the Governing Body in due course.

111. The School felt obliged to engage two security guards, one for Ms A personally, who were present from 27–29 March. Ms Birbalsingh says, and I accept, that there was a very real sense of fear amongst staff and children. She and Ms A no longer felt that they could safely travel to work on public transport.

112. On 29 March, end of term school trips which were due to take place on 30 March were cancelled and the School closed two days early for the Easter holiday. The School term was meant to finish on Friday 31 March with a Reward Day. On 29 March a brick was thrown through the window at the home of one of the teachers. On 30 March 2023, the day after the School had closed, it was found that glass bottles had been thrown into the School yard and smashed. On Tuesday 4 April there was an attempted break in at a teacher's home. Two new videos criticising the School were put up on TikTok.

113. On Friday 14 April, the online petition and the videos on Youtube.com were taken off the internet after lawyers had been instructed. The abusive emails also slowed by around this time.

…

122. Ms Birbalsingh said that she had considered whether the School could take a lesser measure but the nature of the concerns at that stage was such that she could not see a way round this:

> Unacceptable or division, contrary to the whole ethos of the school, was taking place as a result of permitting prayer. An intimidatory atmosphere was developing. Our strict disciplinary policies, on which the ethos and great success of School is based, were at risk of being undermined.

123. She noted that the School had returned to "a peaceful integrated community this summer term" before saying the following:

> My view, as Headmistress with full oversight of how matters have developed, is that the policy to prohibit prayer rituals should be maintained for the time being. If events develop such that it is appropriate to review the policy, then a review can take place at a future Governing Body meeting. In my view the justifications for the policy remain as matters stand. I consider that the policy should be maintained notwithstanding the adverse impacts which I fully appreciate it may have on certain pupils who are religious or who may be disproportionately represented within groups protected under the Equality Act 2010. I believe that the policy is in the interests of at least the great majority of pupils at the School.

…

125. The minutes record the following summary of the reasons that Ms Birbalsingh gave in favour of continuing the PRP:

- "The practicalities of inside prayer, which would require a complete change in the way the school works with regard to staff deployment, pupil bags, coats, etc. and arrangements for Family Lunch. The impact of pupils carrying bags around in the narrow corridors and stairwells and in moving around the school during the lunch break would mean Michaela could not be the very strict school that it is. Instead, it would have corridors and lunchtimes that would be like a normal school.
- The impact of allowing prayer outside would endanger the staff because of the visibility from the street and it would change the attitude of the children and risk another online campaign against the school.
- The ethos of the school, which is that the school community takes precedence over the individual. Other faiths have also had to make concessions, for example there are no special plates provided for Hindus, Year 11 revision sessions take place on a Sunday despite Christians asking for this to change, Macbeth is still taught as a set text despite the beliefs of Jehovah's Witnesses. Muslim families have made the concession for their children to pray at the

end of the day when they return home during Ramadan. The school is proud to be multi-cultural. The ethos is to build friendships across the faiths and not to allow segregation. Where it is possible to accommodate religious practice without undermining this ethos, this is allowed, for example the wearing of the hijab.

– The pupils undertaking formal prayer rituals was undermining the discipline upon which the school is built. If the school made the changes demanded by the court case, there would be a serious risk that it would lose its distinctiveness and become like every other school."

…

127. Ms Birbalsingh says that large numbers of parents were in touch with her about this issue (around 30), as well as with tutors and Heads of Year, between the week of 20 March 2023 and the decision of the Governing Body. Muslim parents, in particular, explained the importance of prayer to them and their children. They generally, although not exclusively, wanted the School to provide a prayer room during the lunch period. Notwithstanding this, her view was and is that the only appropriate response was to prohibit prayer rituals. She gives detailed evidence about her reasons for advocating a continuation of the PRP. In summary, these are:

i) First, permitting prayer rituals had fostered division amongst the pupils and had led to intimidation and an aggressive atmosphere at the School. This was contrary to the School's ethos and undermined the work which had been done over the years to develop this ethos.
"At the School the needs of the community, the team, take precedence over the needs of the individual. The ethos of the School is to build bridges and relationships across the faiths, not to allow them to be divided."

ii) Second, permitting prayer rituals had a significant adverse impact on compliance with the School's behaviour policy. The behaviour of pupils in March 2023, which I have described above, was shocking by the standards of the School and represented a departure from, and an undermining of, the disciplinary ethos. Not only were prayer rituals damaging cohesion; they were "associated with a sense of entitlement which crossed the bounds of acceptable behaviour".

iii) Third, permitting prayer rituals in the yard had resulted in a campaign of abuse, harassment and threats against the School.

iv) Fourth, permitting prayer rituals inside during the lunch period would not be logistically possible without fundamentally changing the operation of the School. Ms Birbalsingh sets out the basis for this view in detail but, in very brief summary, she anticipated that all or nearly all of the 350 pupils would wish to pray during the lunch period. Prayer rituals would have to be conducted in classrooms given that the two larger rooms are in constant use at lunchtime. Several rooms would be needed: she estimates 12. The classrooms are small and it would be necessary for furniture to be moved so that praying could take place, and then put back in time for lessons. There would need to be supervision as there is more generally, but also because of security given that pupils' coats, bags and other valuables are left in their form rooms. There would either need to be a member of staff constantly in each classroom or coats and bags would have to be carried around school during the day, causing very real difficulties and disruption. Staff are already fully deployed in lunchtime supervision and there is no additional capacity so that there would be a need to carry coats and bags around. The fact that the time for Duhr is not fixed throughout the year and the preference for prayer early in the window would add a further layer of complication: for example, would it be necessary to arrange pupils' sittings for family lunch so that they were able to pray during the allotted window? She says that these issues would cause very significant problems even if she is wrong in thinking that there would be substantial take up of the opportunity to pray during the lunch period.

v) Fifth, children would miss important School activities during the lunch period including the "guided socialisation" to which I have referred.

vi) Sixth, once the PRP had been introduced, the operation of the School returned to normal i.e. it had the effect of protecting or promoting the School's ethos etc.

128. Ms Birbalsingh argues that these detrimental consequences have to be considered alongside the point that observant Muslim pupils who miss the Duhr prayer can make up for it later in the day, including by praying at the Brent Civic Centre if they wish. She says that in the aftermath of the events of March and April 2023 she also spoke with the Imam at the London Central Mosque and Islamic Cultural Centre who agreed with this view and offered to speak to any Muslim parents who had doubts on this point.

…

151. In my view, the essence of this aspect of the principle identified at [23] of Lord Bingham's Opinion is that voluntary acceptance of the rules or the regime of an institution may mean that the individual has expressly or impliedly agreed to limitations being placed on their freedom to manifest their religious beliefs and therefore cannot subsequently complain when such limitations become an issue.

This may be so whether or not the precise limitations are known to the claimant at the moment of joining, and whether or not limitations which are known at the time of joining only become an issue later on as a result of decisions which the claimant takes after joining.

152. In any event, the Strasbourg case law, pre Eweida, also demonstrates that the fact that there are other means open to a person to practise their religion—ways to circumvent the limitation placed on their freedom to manifest their religion, as it was put in Eweida—will mean that there has been no interference with that freedom for the purposes of Article 9. This may be the case where they can manifest their beliefs in a modified way whilst remaining at the relevant institution (see *R (Playfoot) v Governing Body of Millais School* [2007] EWHC 1698 (Admin), [2007] HRLR 34 at [30]). It may also be the case where they can choose to leave the particular employer, or can choose to avail themselves of the services of an alternative provider.

153. Ms Hannett placed particular emphasis on the last five words of Lord Bingham's formulation at [23]: "there are other means open to the person to practise or observe his or her religion without undue hardship or inconvenience ..." She also pointed out the different ways in which members of the Judicial Committee expressed their conclusions in *Begum* as part of a submission that it is not difficult for a claimant to establish that they would experience undue hardship or inconvenience if they were obliged to move to a different provider. For example, Lord Bingham said that there was no evidence of "any real difficulty" in the claimant attending a school which permitted her to wear the jilbab [25] and Lord Hoffmann said that there was "nothing" to stop her from doing so [50]. Thus, Ms Hannett's argument was in effect that, if there had been any real difficulty or something to stop Ms Begum from doing so, she would have succeeded in establishing an interference with her Article 9 right.

154. Mr Coppel [counsel for the defendant] relied on Silber J's formulation in the X v Y School case at [30]:

> This issue can be refined to being a question of whether a person's article 9 rights are infringed if a person is prohibited from wearing the article of clothing connected with his or her religion at their present school but that person is permitted to wear the article in another available suitable alternative school. (emphasis added)

155. I respectfully agree with this formulation. The essence of this aspect of the principle identified in Begum is that if the individual has a genuine choice (see

Lord Scott at [87] of Begum, above) to manifest their beliefs elsewhere there will be no interference with their Article 9 rights.

…

Conclusion on interference

175. I do not accept that there has been an interference with the Claimant's Article 9 rights in this case, essentially for the reasons advanced by Mr Coppel. I recognise that this may appear to some to be a surprising conclusion but in my view it is consistent with the pre Eweida case law of the Strasbourg Court, which reflects the fact that Article 9 protects freedom to manifest religious beliefs rather than conferring an absolute right to do so.

176. It seems to me that this is a case, like Karaduman or Kalaç (referred to at [150] above), where the Claimant at the very least impliedly accepted, when she enrolled at the School, that she would be subject to restrictions on her ability to manifest her religion. She knew that the School is secular and her own evidence is that her mother wished her to go there because it was known to be strict. She herself says that, long before the PRP was introduced, she and her friends believed that prayer was not permitted at school and she therefore made up for missed prayers when she got home. Throughout her time at the School the Claimant has accepted restrictions on her ability to pray and she still does, other than during the 25 minutes of the lunch break in the winter months which are in issue in this case. In effect, her case is that the restrictions go too far in one particular respect but, even then, it was not until she was the best part of the way through Year 9 that she indicated any objection.

177. Secondly, the Claimant, who has the burden of proof, has not shown that there would be undue hardship or inconvenience, as that phrase is understood in the relevant Article 9 case law, if she were to move to a different school which permitted her to pray during the school day. She has not adduced any specific evidence about other schools in the area to show, for example, that in fact there is no school within travelling distance which would permit her to do so, or there is no such suitable school, or that it would be impossible for her to secure a place at such a school. Her evidence has focussed on her preferences and what she supposes the position would be elsewhere.

178. I do not suggest that there would be no adverse consequences for the Claimant is she were to choose to move, but it is reasonable to assume that in all of the Article 9 schools cases discussed above the parents and the pupil had a

preference for the school about which they were complaining, and the pupil had no wish to move. They were no doubt keen to be offered a place at the school in question and wished to be able to complete their education there. They would have been able to say very similar things to what is said by the Claimant about why she wishes to stay at the School. In all of those cases there was necessarily a degree of hardship and inconvenience in going to a different school, but that was held not to be sufficient for there to be an interference with their Article 9 rights.

179. I appreciate that the Claimant is now in her first year of GCSEs and it is natural that she would have concerns about moving at this stage. But there is no question of her being required to move: the question is whether, if she were to choose to move in order to be able to pray at school, there would be undue hardship and inconvenience to her. Moreover, the PRP was introduced at the end of the second term of Year 9. This was at a point which would have left her ample time to start Year 10 at a different school and begin her GCSE courses there. She would also have been in good time for the winter months when the issue arises in relation to her ability to pray at lunchtime.

180. Either of these two points is in my view sufficient to lead to the conclusion that the Claimant's case under Article 9 fails. But, in addition to this, whilst accepting that her belief is that she should perform Duhr during the relevant 25 minutes of the lunch break in the winter months, and that this belief falls within Article 9, the evidence indicates that the effect of the PRP is that Qada is available to mitigate the failure to pray within the allotted window. The, at the very least, clear implication of the Claimant's evidence and that of Professor Siddiqui is that Qada is not available where the adherent wilfully or voluntarily chooses not to pray during the allotted time. In any other case, such as where there would be a clash with lessons or family lunch, it is available. As noted above, Ms Hannett's pleaded case at [21] of the Amended Statement of Facts and Grounds, and her position at the hearing, was that the Claimant's "understanding" of Qada is that it is available if there

> Is "good reason" to miss the allotted window. If that is right, it is difficult to see why Qada would not be available in a case where the adherent is in a location, or subject to a regime, where prayer is prohibited. This is not to reject or question the Claimant's belief that Qada is second best to praying at the required time; but it is to point out that the implication of what she says about her beliefs is that she is able to manifest them in accordance with the teachings of Islam notwithstanding the PRP, albeit in a modified and less satisfactory way.

181. Although Ms Hannett suggested that this was circular reasoning when I put this point to her, it is not. She also argued that it amounted to an illegitimate inquiry into the validity of the Claimant's beliefs about Qada but I do not agree that it is. As noted above, the Claimant's belief that Qada is less/unsatisfactory is not in question. The point is that the PRP is a "good reason" for missing Duhr and it is consistent with her beliefs that Qada is therefore available. The Claimant's evidence does not grapple with this point or state that it is her belief that, even with the PRP in place, Qada would not be available. She argues that the PRP ought not to have been introduced because the time in question is "free time" but she does not address her beliefs about the availability of Qada where, notwithstanding this, she is not free to pray during this time because of the PRP. On the contrary, in the passages from her second witness statement which I have summarised at [38]–[40] above, she makes the point that even if Qada is available, being forced to rely on it rather than pray at the allotted time is a significant detriment. In addition to this, the Claimant's own position is that Qada is available where it would cause disruption and inconvenience to others to pray at the allotted time. For reasons which I explain below, I accept Ms Birbalsingh's evidence that this is the case here.

182. In case I am wrong on the issue of interference, and because the issue is also relevant to the question of indirect religious discrimination, I turn to the question of justification under Article 9(2).

…

192. In my judgment the starting point is that the School was right to take the view that the issue was whether to permit and facilitate ritual prayer indoors: in effect, to reverse its longstanding policy of not providing a prayer room. Although Ms Hannett kept her options open, in my view it could not seriously be argued that it would be appropriate for Muslim pupils to pray outside in the yard in the winter months and nor, as I understood her, did Ms Hannett positively argue that it would be. The experience of the public reaction to seeing this in March 2023, is a further reason for taking this view. Even if a screen was put up to shield the yard from public view, as Ms Hannett suggested might be done, it would remain the case that pupils were being required to pray in wet and dirty conditions, that the public would become aware of this, and that there would be a risk of a similar reaction.

193. With this starting point, second, I agree with Ms Hannett that one can and should put aside fears of a repeat of the abuse and threats which occurred in March/April 2023. If prayer indoors were permitted and facilitated, a situation

in which a teacher became involved in a dispute with a pupil connected with praying, and this was then brought to the attention of parents or members of the public, would be less likely to arise. Nor would parents or members of the public have any reason to feel that Islam was being disrespected if pupils were not being required to pray outside, in wet and dirty conditions, using their blazers instead of prayer mats.

194. Third, I also agree with Ms Hannett that an assessment of the implications of pupils being permitted to pray indoors has to be carried out on the assumption that this activity is in accordance with the School rules and regulated by them, and is understood to be by pupils. Part of the reason for aspects of the relevant pupils' apparently defiant behaviour towards the School in March 2023 is likely to have been that they understood that the act of praying at School was prohibited, they were unhappy about this and they had therefore made up their minds to challenge the regime. There would be no need for such an attitude if prayer was permitted indoors.

195. Fourth, however, I do not agree with Ms Hannett that one can therefore discount any possibility that permitting and facilitating prayer at lunchtime would lead to issues in relation to behaviour. It would remain the case that prayer was subject to close supervision by teachers and there would therefore still be scope for differences of view as to whether the presence or behaviour of a given pupil within the School building was or was not appropriate. There would still be the risk of peer pressure or intimidation of Muslim pupils who would not otherwise wish to pray, or who might be regarded as less observant more generally. That was the experience in March 2023. Although Ms Hannett criticises the lack of investigation of these matters, Ms Birbalsingh's evidence about what occurred is based on her own observations and on what teachers saw and heard, no doubt as well as what the teachers were told by pupils. There is no reason for me to do other than accept this evidence and, in any event, this is classically the sort of point on which the court should give weight to the assessment of experienced teachers "on the ground."

196. Again, I accept that part of the reason for what occurred in March 2023 may be that those who had decided to pray in the yard felt that others should show solidarity with what they saw as their defiance of the School and, if so, the risk of peer pressure may be lower if prayer were permitted. But I also consider that, as in *Begum* and the *X v Y School* case, the predictive judgment of Ms Birbalsingh as to the consequences is one which I should accept. It should be remembered that the pressure and intimidation in March 2023 took place despite the strict beha-

vioural regime at the School. It is also entirely plausible that, at the very least, there would be moral pressure placed on Muslim pupils to take part in lunch-time prayer now that it was permitted. The evidence of what happened in the Sixth Form in or around 2021 is not sufficiently cogent to demonstrate that Ms Birbalsingh is wrong on this point and, in any event, the Sixth formers are not a truly comparable case for the reasons which she explains in her evidence. In my view, contrary to Ms Hannett's argument, there therefore is a rational connection between the aim of furthering the behavioural policy of the School and the PRP.

197. Fifth, I also accept Ms Birbalsingh's judgment/prediction that there would be substantial take-up of the opportunity to pray at lunchtime. For nearly 10 years she has been the Headteacher of the School which she founded, working closely with parents and pupils from the local community, half of whom are Muslims. There is also the evidence of the speed of the increase in numbers of pupils joining in prayer in the third week of March 2023 despite their belief that it was forbidden, despite the fact that prayer mats were not permitted and despite the adverse conditions in the yard. And there is the evidence of parents' views expressed to Ms Birbalsingh and staff thereafter. Similarly to Silber J in X v Y School I do not find any contradiction in Ms Birbalsingh saying that, although parents and pupils are willing to accept that there is no prayer room and/or that prayer is not feasible at the School—some may even welcome this—their position would be different if it were permitted and facilitated. Then, even assuming that no one was actually pressuring any pupil to pray during the school day, they would be likely to feel a moral obligation to do so. Indeed, as I have found, the principles governing Qada would be entirely consistent with this prediction: if prayer were permitted in school, there would be no good reason not to pray and Muslim pupils would be likely to feel obligated to do so. Again, Ms Birbalsingh is in a good position to form a judgment on this point.

198. Sixth, this being so, there is in my view a rational connection between the aim of promoting the Team ethos of the School, inclusivity, social cohesion etc and the PRP. What is in effect being proposed by the Claimant is that the School should have introduced a set of special arrangements which facilitated the withdrawal from the secular life of the School by significant numbers of Muslim pupils as such, albeit each individual pupil would do so for a short period of time whilst they went to the relevant classroom, prayed and then returned to the yard. These arrangements would be particular to Muslim pupils and they would serve to emphasise their religious difference, in their minds and in the minds of the rest of the School community. I do not suggest that this would inevitably be a good or a bad thing, as it is not my function to take a view about this. The point

is merely that it is clearly rational for the School to take the view that the permitting and facilitating ritual prayer in school would have these effects, and that the PRP is therefore a way of protecting and promoting the ethos of the School.

199. I take Ms Hannett's point that the School has permitted certain observable signs of religious observance, and that this and permitting prayer in the Sixth Form for a time do not appear to have threatened the ethos of the School. But the question is one of degree. One can see why arrangements for classrooms to be provided and re onfigured, for Muslim pupils (specifically) to be permitted to go in and out of the School building other than for family lunch or one of the clubs or approved activities, for there to be supervision of pupils who wished to pray etc, take the identification of Muslim pupils as such significantly further. This is before one gets to the question whether, on the Claimant's case, family lunch for Muslim pupils should be scheduled taking into account the timing of the allotted window for Duhr on that day and/or the pupil's wishes in relation to prayer.

200. Seventh, I accept the thrust of Ms Birbalsingh's evidence about the complexity of the arrangements which would need to be made to facilitate prayer by Muslim pupils: the logistical difficulties. Although the Claimant gave evidence which suggested that the level of difficulty was exaggerated by Ms Birbalsingh, even on her own assumptions as to take-up, I approached this part of the evidence on the basis that the Headteacher of the School was clearly in a better position than she was to make an assessment. It seems to me that it does not matter precisely how many pupils would wish to pray or precisely how many classrooms would be needed. Ms Birbalsingh predicts, for the purpose of her assessment, that the numbers would be substantial, and that was a judgment which she was best qualified to make, as I have said. Nor does the School have to establish that it would be impossible to facilitate prayer indoors. It might well be possible. But the School is entitled to say that, taken with the other considerations as to the effect on its ethos etc, the level of effort and the cost in terms of use of the School's resources would be such that it would not be proportionate to make the arrangements which would be necessary. Moreover, even if Ms Birbalsingh has overestimated the numbers, there would still be a significant degree of complexity in making special arrangements for a smaller cohort.

201. Eighth, I therefore accept that the aims of the PRP relied on by the School to justify not permitting and facilitating prayer rituals indoors are legitimate aims to which the PRP is rationally connected (Bank Mellatt questions 1 and 2). These were essentially the reasons why there had been no prayer room hitherto. 202.

Ninth, as to the question whether a less intrusive measure could have been introduced without unacceptably compromising these aims, I do not consider that one could. On the basis of Ms Birbalsingh's assessment of the logistical difficulties alone it would not have been feasible to do other than introduce the PRP. The suggestion that permission could be given to some Muslim pupils in Years 7–11, or even 8/9–11, would not be workable. How would the School decide, without entering very difficult territory, who should and should not be permitted to pray? Moreover, the issues in relation to the Team ethos, the behavioural policy and socialisation at lunchtime would still arise.

203. Ms Hannett's argument that the way forward would be to educate pupils to be tolerant of the perspective of others and/or to have strict rules to prevent intimidation and peer pressure does not fully meet the points made above, and particularly the point about separateness versus the Team ethos of the School. Moreover, contrary to her argument, this ethos is not tantamount to preventing pluralism and eradicating difference. Certain outward signs of religious belief are permitted at the School and the PRP does not prevent Muslim pupils from manifesting their religion through prayer altogether, as they are free to do so outside the school day. The Team ethos is also intended to be a means of promoting pluralism, albeit the Claimant argues that it has not had this effect.

204. Tenth, as to the balancing exercise at the fourth stage of the Bank Mellat test, I accept Mr Coppel's submission that in measuring the severity of the effects of the PRP one is entitled to take into account that prayer had not been raised as an issue in relation to Years 7–11 before March 2023. This is not to say that it was of no importance to Muslim pupils or that none wished to pray during the school day—the example of the Sixth formers confirms that that is not the case, as does the Claimant's evidence about how she and her friends came to start praying in the yard—but it does appear that the vast majority of Muslim parents and pupils did not regard the issue as of sufficient concern to wish to raise it. This may well be because they felt that performing Qada was an acceptable compromise, as Ms Birbalsingh suggests.

205. One is also entitled to take account of the fact that the PRP only impacts Muslim pupils in the winter months and that Qada is, on the evidence, available to Muslim pupils at the School when it does. I also agree that it is relevant that the essential nature of the School regime is one which the Claimant and her fellow pupils, or at least their parents, have chosen and, indeed, that they have chosen to remain at the School notwithstanding the PRP. Although the Claimant says that she is aware of resentment of the PRP amongst some Muslim pupils, there is no

evidence that this has affected enrolment or led any of them to choose to leave. Nor, indeed, is there evidence of the issue being raised with the School since the PRP was introduced, other than in the context of this Claim. On the contrary, the evidence is that since the PRP was introduced good relations within the School community have been restored.

206. Eleventh, balancing the adverse effects of the PRP on the rights of Muslim pupils at the School with the aims of the PRP and the extent to which it is likely to achieve those aims, I have concluded that the latter outweighs the former and that the PRP is proportionate.

207. In coming to this conclusion I have had in mind Ms Hannett's criticisms of the decision making process, her argument that whatever Ms Birbalsingh may have thought there is no evidence that the Governing Body took these considerations into account, her argument that the School's case is based on ex post facto rationalisation and her allegations that the Governing Body acted on inaccurate or incomplete information. I deal with these criticisms in greater detail below, in relation to Gound 3 but, in short, in the context of the arguments about proportionality I did not find them persuasive. It is true that further inquiries might have been made but I am confident that the Governing Body considered the matter carefully. Although Ms Birbalsingh may have explained her thinking in greater detail in her evidence than she did at the meeting of the Governing Body on 23 May 2023, her reasoning has been consistent and was explained to Governors. This is not a case of ex post facto rationalisation and, in any event, I have scrutinised the School's case carefully. Nor is it a case in which the Governing Body was labouring under significant factual misapprehensions.

…

Was the PRP "a proportionate means of achieving a legitimate aim"?

232. I have concluded that it was, essentially for the reasons given above in the context of Article 9 ECHR: see [192]–[207]. The disadvantage to Muslim pupils at the School caused by the PRP is in my view outweighed by the aims which it seeks to promote in the interests of the School community as a whole, including Muslim pupils.

…

272. It is clear that the PRP was regarded as an important measure given the issues which there had been in March/April 2023, the ethos of the School and the practicalities. The questions from the Governing Body and the size of the majority

in favour indicate that it very much agreed with the views of Ms Birbalsingh. In my view a greater focus on the specifics of the needs which were required to be considered under section 149(3)(a)–(c), the various inquiries which Ms Hannett advocated, the additional information which she says they should have had available to them, and/or the correction of the inaccuracies in the information provided to them which she says there were, would not have had a material impact on the outcome. I am therefore satisfied that it is highly likely that the decision of the Governing Body would not have been substantially different had the decision making process met the standards which Ms Hannett argues it should have.

273. It follows that, even if I had concluded that Ground 3 was well founded, I would have refused relief.

Conclusion on Ground 3

274. Ground 3 therefore fails.

CHAPTER 6

Burials and Cemeteries

The preference among Muslims to have bodies of the deceased sent back to the country of origin for burial may have declined with a shift to burial in Britain, although it is likely that the demand to return the body to another country may persist. Cities with significant Muslim populations have burial areas set aside with the correct alignment of graves. Problems may still remain because of the preference to have burials within 24 hours of death. There may be issues about whether to bury in a coffin or a shroud; Islamic law permits the former, and local councils tend to insist on coffin burials.[1]

Muslims may often object to autopsies due to various reasons including the notion that the reason for death is God's will, the prospect of the desecration of the body or the need to arrange the burial as soon as possible.[2] Additional delays may occur when a death is reported to a coroner, which may be done by the police, prison officers, the registrar of births and deaths, doctors or a hospital. The coroner determines the cause of death and, if it is due to natural causes, the coroner may not have any further role. The coroner investigates to find out the cause of death when it is not yet known or appears unnatural or violent. This may include a post-mortem (autopsy) and an inquest. An inquest may follow even when a death is natural and the cause known, for example, when a person dies in "state detention" such as in a prison. Funeral arrangements can be made only after the body is released by a coroner. A death cannot be registered until the cause of death is known, although the coroner can provide a "coroner's certificate of the fact of death" or "interim death certificate" to help with administrative matters.

In cases which are the responsibility of the coroner a Ministry of Justice guide informs the bereaved that they ought to report any specific needs for the inquest, including religious needs, to the coroner's office as soon as possible so that reasonable measures to accommodate such needs can be taken.[3]

1 Nielsen, J.S. and Otterbeck, J. (2016), *Muslims in Western Europe*. Edinburgh: Edinburgh University Press. p. 59. See Al-Adnani, M. and Scheimberg, I. (2006), "How can we improve the rate of autopsies among Muslims?", *BMJ*, 332(7536), p. 310 for the view that the demand to return the body to another country persists and can be a reason for expediting an autopsy.

2 Al-Adnani, M. and Scheimberg, I. (2006), "How can we improve the rate of autopsies among Muslims?", *BMJ*, 332(7536), p. 310.

3 Ministry of Justice (2020), *A guide to coroner services for bereaved people*, p. 6.

R (Adath Yisroel Burial Society & Anor) v HM Senior Coroner for Inner North London
[2018] EWHC 969 (Admin)

This case brought in the Administrative Court by a Jewish organisation responsible for managing and facilitating the burials of a large proportion of the orthodox Jewish population in Inner North London challenged the Senior Coroner for Inner North London's policy that no death would be prioritised in any way over any other because of the religion of the deceased or family. The Administrative Court held that the policy was too rigid and failed to strike the right balance required by ECHR, Article 9. Besides the evidence of Jewish burial practices, the court also had evidence regarding Muslim norms for expedited burials. After that case, guidance was issued in 2018 by the Chief Coroner on the making of expedited decisions for religious and other reasons.

> …
>
> 62. The Court also has evidence before it about the impact of the policy on members of the Muslim community in this country. That evidence includes a witness statement by Mufti Abdur-Rahman Mangera, in which he states, at paras. 5–6:
>
> > 5. Under Islamic law there is an important principle that a dead body should be buried as quickly as reasonably possible, and ideally on the same day of death. Hence, our prophetic traditions even show burials taking part on the very night of the death of an individual. This is done to fulfil the rights of the body and allow them to move on to the next stage of their life as quickly as possible. Hence, there is explicit discouragement of delaying a burial that is found within the prophetic tradition.
> >
> > 6. Muslims see this as an important law and people seek to obey it strictly. Where for any reason this cannot be complied with, then the close family with responsibility for ensuring speedy burial will invariably feel very considerable anguish. Not only are they often emotionally vulnerable anyway because of their recent loss, but also they are particularly anxious to do what they can for the body of their loved one and also of course to maintain the tenets of their deeply held religious beliefs.
>
> 63. The Court also has before it a press statement dated 25 January 2018 from the Muslim Council of Britain, which states:
>
> > The Muslim Council of Britain shares the concerns raised by the Mayor of London, Sadiq Khan and the Board of Deputies of British Jews in relation to delays in the release of bodies post mortem.
>
> …

Chief Coroner's Guidance No. 28 Report of Death to the Coroner: Decision Making and Expedited Decisions

HH Judge Mark Lucraft QC, Chief Coroner, 17 May 2018

Introduction

1. This Guidance has been issued following the judgment of the Administrative Court in *R* (*Adath Yisroel Burial Society*) *v Senior Coroner for Inner North London* [2018] EWHC 969 (Admin) ("the AYBS Case").

2. It is intended to be a practical guide to assist coroners in situations where (a) a bereaved family has made a request to the coroner for urgent consideration of the death of a loved one and/or early release of the body or (b) the coroner or coroner's officers otherwise become aware of features of a particular death which may justify treating it as especially urgent.

3. There will be a variety of reasons why a bereaved family may request early release of the body. For example, if the death is that of a young child, the family may ask for the body to be released as soon as possible to a dedicated room in the hospital. Alternatively, a family may have some particular reason for needing the funeral to take place quickly.

4. In other cases, requests for urgent consideration of a particular death may be made on religious grounds, as discussed in more detail below. The Chief Coroner understands and is sensitive to the fact that some faith groups, particularly Jewish and Muslim, have religious and cultural wishes about treatment of a body and burial following a death. Coroners should pay appropriate respect to those wishes, within the framework of their legal duties and in the context of their other responsibilities. Many coroners engage with local community groups to improve mutual understanding.

5. The Chief Coroner also recognises that families generally are concerned to have decisions taken by coroners without unnecessary delay, even if they have no particular wish or need for an early burial or cremation.

6. It should be noted that in many coroner areas, there is no general provision of services outside of office hours. In such areas, most decisions have to be taken during the working day. This guidance document does not address the provision of out-of-hours services, which depend on resources being made available by funding authorities.

Coroners' Decision-Making

7. In a typical day, a coroner's office will receive a number of notifications of deaths. Some will have arrived outside working hours and will usually have to be considered after the office opens, while others will arrive during the working day. It is the practice of most coroners to have coroners' officers prepare short reports of notified deaths. The coroner will consider those reports during the working day and will make decisions. For example, the coroner may decide on the basis of the report that no coroner's investigation is required. Alternatively, the coroner may decide to order further enquiries about the death or a post-mortem examination. At a later stage in a case, the coroner may consider the results of the enquiries or examination and make decisions as to what further work is needed. All these tasks need to be arranged around a coroner's other judicial and administrative workload.

8. A coroner to whom a death has been notified has legal authority over the body for as long as is necessary for enquiries and investigation into the death. The coroner will release the body to the bereaved family for burial or cremation as soon as practicable. The time within which a body can be released will depend upon the time required for enquiries and decisions of the kinds outlined above.

9. Coroners are sometimes made aware of some reason for the consideration of a particular death to be a matter of urgency. For example, in cases of homicide investigations and organ donations, it is commonplace for coroners to take decisions as a matter of great urgency.

10. As noted above, coroners sometimes receive specific requests from bereaved families to treat particular deaths as a matter of urgency. The reasons justifying these requests are many and varied. On occasion, the request will be made on the ground that the family has a religious or cultural belief that the body should be buried on the day of death or as soon as possible thereafter. Jewish and Muslim families, or their representatives, sometimes make such requests. The AYBS Case considered the approach to be taken in this situation. The Divisional Court concluded that it was unlawful for a coroner to adopt a policy ruling out the possibility of prioritising consideration of a death on religious grounds. It is also apparent from the judgment that it would be unlawful for a coroner to adopt a policy ruling out the possibility of prioritising consideration of a death on reasonable non-religious grounds.

Guidance

11. In its judgment at paragraph 160, the Divisional Court made the following general points:

(1) A Coroner cannot lawfully exclude religious reasons for seeking expedition of decisions by that Coroner, including the Coroner's decision whether to release a body for burial.

(2) A Coroner is entitled to prioritise cases, for religious or other reasons, even where the consequence of prioritising one or some cases may be that other cases will have to wait for a decision. It is not necessary that all cases are treated in the same way or in strictly chronological sequence.

(3) Whether to accord one case priority over another or others is for the Coroner to determine. The following further points apply:

   a) It is in principle acceptable for the Coroner to implement a policy to address the circumstances when priority will or may be given, so long as that policy is flexible and enables all relevant considerations to be taken into account.

   b) The availability of resources may be a relevant consideration in drawing up any policy or in making the decision in any individual case but limitations on resources does not justify discrimination.

(4) It would be wrong for a Coroner to impose a rule of automatic priority for cases where there are religious reasons for seeking expedition."

The reference in sub-paragraph (3)(b) to resource limitations not justifying discrimination means that such limitations cannot be used as a reason to rule out giving consideration to proper requests for expedition on religious grounds (see paragraph 124 of the judgment).

12. The Court also stressed that, in making individual decisions on whether to prioritise consideration of particular cases on religious or other grounds, a coroner has a "margin of judgment". In other words, the decision is one for the individual coroner, considering all the circumstances. Such a decision may only ordinarily be challenged if it is unreasonable or if it clearly fails to strike a fair balance between rights of the particular family and the interests of other families who might be affected.

13. Decisions about enquiries to be made (including post-mortem examinations), about concluding investigations and about releasing bodies for burial are judicial decisions. They are made by a coroner under the law, exercising independent judgment and cannot be delegated. They cannot be taken by a coroner's officer or a member of administrative staff. The exercise of that judgment may only be

challenged in the High Court by way of judicial review. The Chief Coroner cannot alter, investigate, comment on or otherwise intervene in the individual judicial decisions of coroners, or in the case management of individual cases. Each judicial decision is a matter entirely for the coroner.

14. The judgment in the AYBS Case reflects two important legal considerations: (i) that a coroner should be open to representations that a particular case should be treated as a matter of urgency (whether for religious or other reasons); and (ii) that proper respect should be given to representations based on religious belief.

15. However, the decision of the Court does not require a coroner to give automatic priority to deaths from particular religious communities, nor does it require coroners to drop other important work to deal with such deaths. The Court also recognised that other deaths may require urgent handling for non-religious reasons.

16. There is no obligation for coroners to adopt formal written policies for dealing with requests for expedition or for dealing with deaths from faith communities. Practices may differ between coronial areas because of the characteristics of the areas. However, any policy or practices adopted by coroners must be sufficiently flexible to allow them to give due consideration to expediting decisions where there is good reason to do so. They should seek to strike a fair balance between the interests of those with a well-founded request for expedition (including on religious grounds) and other families who may be affected.

17. It is essential that each coroner area has sufficient coroner, coroner officer and administrative staff resource to deal with deaths reported within the coroner area. Information technology is also important, and modern case management systems are essential in the majority of coroner areas. In the 'Model Coroner Area' document (revised 30 June 2017) the Chief Coroner has set out parameters for the working arrangements of coroners. In each coroner area, it is the responsibility of the Senior Coroner and the relevant local authority (or authorities) to work together to ensure that adequate resources (of coroners, officers and administrative staff) are available. Nevertheless, even with good co-operation and adequate resources, it is inevitable that some decisions will take time, either because of the complexity of the particular case or because of burdens on the coroner's office.

Abbas Meghjee v BW Foundation

[2020] EWHC 2970 (QB), 2020 WL 03261329, Mr Justice Cavanagh

In this case, the High Court was asked to issue injunctions on account of the defendant's burial practices which involved burying dead bodies in tiers above one another. The claimant argued that he had not consented to this practice and that the practice was against Islamic law. The judgment is also interesting for how the court deals with the claim regarding Islamic law.

> …
>
> 2. The defendant is a charitable non-profit foundation which, amongst other activities, looks after the religious interests for its local religious community. One of its roles is to operate a graveyard for members of the Muslim faith. The defendant holds the relevant area in the graveyard pursuant to a lease with Three Rivers District Council, dated 7 August 2009. There was a later lease in the same terms. It has used this land for Islamic burials since about 2014. The defendant manages and maintains the graveyard, and persons are buried in the plots in the graveyard with the permission of and pursuant to agreements made with the defendant.
>
> 3. These proceedings arise because shortly after the claimant's father's burial, on 8 April 2020, another person was buried above him in the same plot. That person was Mr Fadhil Ghalta. Mr Basheer Meghjee was interred at a depth of three metres. Mr Ghalta was interred above him at a depth of two metres. The claimant claims that the defendant acted unlawfully in interring Mr Ghalta in the same plot without his consent. The claimant seeks two injunctions. The first is an order requiring the defendant to exhume the body of Mr Ghalta and to re-bury him in a separate grave in the same cemetery. The second is an order prohibiting the defendant, its servants, or agents from executing a two-tier burial policy over any grave in the graveyard without the prior knowledge and express consent of the family of the deceased.
>
> …
>
> 29. The next point is breach of Islamic law. The parties disagree about whether the two-tier burial in this way was a breach of the relevant Islamic jurisprudence. I make clear that I am not competent or an appropriate person to rule on Islamic law, but I note that the arguments of the claimant and of Dr Fadhil in this regard are based on the fact that no consent was given by the claimant to the burial of a second body, when, as I have said, the contemporaneous evid-

ence strongly suggests otherwise. In any event, the defendant has put forward evidence that it consulted with an Islamic scholar who advised that this course of action is consistent with Islamic jurisprudence. Before this whole policy was drafted, the defendant sought advice from a leading Islamic scholar, Dr Fazel Milani, as to whether three-tier burials were permissible under Islamic law. The claimant relies upon rules or laws issued by the Grand Ayatollah al-Sistani, specifically rules 612 and 632. However, Dr Melani, when this matter was raised with him, confirmed to the defendant that these rules do not apply to the policy being applied in this graveyard, in particular because the rules are designed for people who are buried in shrouds, not people like the two individuals in this case who were buried in wooden coffins. The claimant says, through Mr Karim, that Dr Milani was not provided with full information when he provided this advice, and that his answers would have been different if he was aware that there had been no consent by the first family, that the two interments had taken place so quickly together, and that there were other single grave plots that had not been used. Nonetheless, in my judgment, this is far short of being a strong *prima facie* case of a breach of Islamic law, and I bear in mind also that the claimant's cousin's evidence referred to the fact that three of the six cemeteries used by Stanmore Mosque have been actively burying on a double interment basis for a while now, without Mr Sakalain Meghjee suggesting that this was in breach of Islamic jurisprudence.

30. In any event, though, there are two points that are worth making finally under this heading. First, religious law, of whatever denomination, does not give a cause of action in these courts, and, secondly, the complaint in relation to Islamic jurisprudence is predicated on the assertion that no consent was given for a two-tier burial, when, as I have said, the preponderance of the evidence before me is that there was consent given by the claimant to a two-tier burial, including the burial of a stranger, before his father was interred.

H (A Child)
[2023] EWCA Civ 995, Court of Appeal

In this case, the court was confronted by conflicting claims for where the burial of a deceased Muslim child should be arranged and according to whose wishes. The mother, who was divorced from the father, claimed that the place of burial should be in England so that the child's maternal family could visit and pay respects. The paternal grandparents wished for the burial to take place in Bangladesh at the plot where the ancestors of the paternal family were buried.

4. This is a most tragic case concerning the death of H who died of natural causes on 29 June 2023. She was 10 years and 1 month old. Her parents, siblings, and paternal grandparents, who were also her Special Guardians, grieve mightily.

5. H was the younger child of three of her mother and father; they married shortly before her birth. H had a neurological developmental disability caused by a genetic disorder encephalopathy. The mother had three other children, one of whom had also suffered from a genetic disorder and unfortunately died in 2013. The mother has subsequently had two other children, one of whom also died in 2019.

6. The mother and father separated in 2014. The children remained in the care of the father and, initially his new partner, although the paternal grandmother, who had travelled to London from Singapore to assist following H's premature birth, remained actively involved in H's care. From 2016, the paternal grandmother became her sole carer, and in 2017 she and her husband, the paternal grandfather, were appointed Special Guardians for all five children of the family (that is, including H's two half siblings). They were their primary carers and assumed financial responsibility for all of them.

...

9. In June 2022, the family returned to England with a view to selling their home and wholesale removal to Singapore. Unfortunately, soon after arrival H became ill and was admitted to hospital where she remained, often placed in intensive care and high dependency units, for 12 months. She was discharged home in June 2023, but after a few days was re-admitted to hospital and died a few days later. Her paternal grandmother had been constantly at her side during the periods of her critical illness.

...

15. The ... mother objected to the proposal to remove H's body from the jurisdiction, she wished H to be cremated and for her ashes to be buried in the United Kingdom in order that her maternal family would be able to visit her grave and pay their respects. Consequently, she sought an injunction preventing the release of the body to the paternal family, pending the hearing to consider a declaration as to who should have the authority to deal with the funeral.

...

17. The judge was satisfied, and found as a fact, that H had been raised in the Muslim faith and that, for the best part of her life, she had been cared for by her

paternal grandparents and given an excellent quality of care. The judge commented on the devotion of the paternal grandmother and noted she had attended upon H throughout her time in hospital over the past 12 months.

18. The judge was pleased that the mother had been able to visit H before her death but stated that he could not ignore the fact that she had not cared for H, or seen her, since 2014. The mother's wish for cremation was wholly contrary to the Muslim faith and, whilst appreciating that the mother and other members of the maternal family in the United Kingdom would have difficulties to pay their respects at the place of her interment if in Bangladesh, it would be "wholly wrong and wholly inappropriate" for him to make any order regarding the funeral arrangements against the wishes of the paternal grandmother.

19. The judge granted letters of administration to the paternal grandparents, who he joined as parties to the proceedings, in order that they and the father, could arrange for the transportation of H's body to Bangladesh for burial in the paternal family plot where her mortal remains would be laid to rest with her paternal great grandfather.

…

30. The options are for H to be buried in the United Kingdom, specifically in London in a plot in which, or near to which, her paternal great-grandmother is buried, or in Bangladesh, a family plot which contains many of her ancestors. The mother wishes for H to be buried in the United Kingdom to enable her and the maternal family to pay their respects to a marked grave within the jurisdiction. The father and paternal grandparents seek that H be removed to Bangladesh in order that all due rights and customs, not only at the time of burial and interment, but thereafter, may be observed by members of her immediate and extended family. H cannot be buried in Singapore.

…

32. This court must address the balance of interests which is fact specific to H's circumstances during her life and those aspects of the religion and tenets of her faith that regard the individual's afterlife to be of equal importance to their time on earth. As indicated above, the mother accepts that H was a Muslim and was raised by her paternal grandparents in accordance with that faith. At this time, her body has been cleansed in accordance with the attendant Muslim rites whilst the place of her interment awaits this decision.

…

38. However, it is a matter of undisputed fact that the greatest personal connection that H had to another human being was to her paternal grandmother. The evidence before us bears out the devotion of the paternal grandmother to H's physical and emotional care. At all relevant times of H's sentient life, she would have known her paternal grandmother as her primary caregiver. I would give great weight in the circumstances of H's congenital disabilities to the undoubted singular emotional attachment she would have formed with the paternal grandmother, and obviously vice versa. I find that the strength of this attachment informs the verity of the proposals the paternal grandmother advances for H's burial and which she believes will benefit H's afterlife. I find them to be made in good faith, without animus to the mother or other ulterior motive.

...

40. I have found considerable assistance in the paternal grandfather's statement which details the necessary religious funeral rites and observances dictated by the Muslim faith, but also why the paternal family wish for the interment to be in Bangladesh rather than in Singapore, assuming all necessary permissions could be obtained, which is currently the main residence of the paternal grandparents and father, and their 'centre of interest'.

41. That is, the paternal grandfather describes the important connotations of the divine family plot in Bangladesh. The plot is the resting place of H's paternal great-grandfather who was of great standing in the community; his piety and devotion were recognised by the Viceroy of India. The Islamic faith requires that those who are respected for their piety in this life should be afforded great respect in their afterlife. His ancestors pay their due respects at his grave, as they would equally pay all due respect to H if she was to be interred within. H's full siblings reside in Singapore. The paternal family will also have to travel to pay their respects to H.

...

43. Weighing all these matters in the balance, I am satisfied that it is right that the paternal grandparents should be granted letters of administration and thereby permitted to arrange the burial of H. Their claim is strengthened by the special personal relationship that they, and particularly the paternal grandmother, had with H. The long-standing Special Guardianship order in their favour elevates their position above the normal grandparental role. These 'rights' do not automatically trump those of the mother so as to enable any court to peremptorily dismiss them, but I find that the predominant force is the well-articulated and genuinely held devout religious views of those with the real closest relationship to H, and their wish to best support what they believe will be her afterlife.

CHAPTER 7

Education

The Education Act 1944 set the tone for how the legal framework for primary and secondary education in England and Wales would be pursued henceforth. It was part of a compromise between the state and the churches whereby the latter ceded control over education on the former's undertaking that schools run by the churches would be offered an infusion of state funding for running costs, including for staff; that religious education and worship would be maintained not only in church schools, but extended to schools with a secular ethos; and that schools with a religious character would retain control over school admissions. Secular schools (then called "county schools") would be controlled by local authorities, with religious education being the only statutorily mandated core curriculum, and an act of worship was stipulated but was to be delivered in a manner that was not denominational. The 1944 Act is remarkable for taking the Christian background for granted but without mentioning it explicitly.

The state-church compromise also accommodated religious schools mainly of the Christian churches in differing legal and funding models, resulting in the creation of voluntary aided schools (mainly Catholic) and voluntary controlled schools (Anglican). The former had greater autonomy over matters of employment of teachers and the religious requirements teachers had to follow. From the late 1990s, schools with a Muslim religious character began to come within this framework, whereas they had previously existed only as independent schools. It should be noted that, while they may have greater autonomy than other schools, independent schools also have to work within statutory constraints.

This settlement came under pressure with increased scepticism towards matters such as religious education and worship, a changing attitude to the purpose of religious education away from an instructional and towards a world religions model, a changing political questioning of local authorities' role in education, and the increasing diversity of society as a result of immigration which also brought in more people who did not follow the Christian faith, including a large number of Muslim immigrants and their descendants. However, many Christians were also part of this post-Second World War immigration, often holding on to Christianity more than the native British population.[1]

1 These might include the Black churches frequented by Afro-Caribbean and African immi-

Reforms from the 1980s saw several developments. For secular schools, local authorities' control was reduced and the powers of school governing bodies increased, allowing the central government directly to fund schools, especially the newly created "grant-maintained schools." The choice of school was increased further at the expense of local authorities allocating school places in county schools. New school models emerged, bringing further diversification in the form of the so-called "foundation schools," which could also acquire a "religious character." This partly explains the complicated set of rules laid out in successive legislation that had to cater for the variety of schools and their being either of a religious character or not.

The religious education syllabi and religious worship were, under the Education Act 1988, supposed to reflect that "the religious traditions in Great Britain are in the main Christian whilst taking account of the teaching and practices of the other principal religions represented in Great Britain." Despite the several statutes on education that have been passed since the 1990s, this formula has essentially been retained. Accordingly, Standing Advisory Councils on Religious Education (SACREs) are constituted in each local education authority. SACREs are required to have representatives of all the religious traditions present in a local area, which requirement secures a Muslim voice in their activities. SACREs have to devise school opt-outs from the statutory religious worship and religious education obligations or tailor them to the ages of pupils.

Apart from contingent Muslim representation on SACREs, local demographic factors can also influence schools pursuing their worship and religious education obligations, and to decide whether schools with a religious character are to be viably established. Indirectly, the responsiveness of local authorities to Muslim demands might also be relevant. Although the role of local authorities in the governance of schools is reduced, they remain employers of schoolteachers in all schools other than voluntary aided and independent schools.

Schools also have to manage potential conflicts between the Equality Act and the autonomy allowed to them under the education legislation, which makes distinctions according to the different school models. The main distinction here concerns schools with or without a religious character.[2] Those

grants or the increase in Catholic church attendance by Polish, Filipino or South American immigrants.

2 Sandberg, R. (2011), *Law and religion*. Cambridge: Cambridge University Press. pp. 151–168 provides a clear account of the salience of this religious-non-religious character distinction with a table at p. 167 setting out the different types of schools, and their rights and obligations with respect to admissions, religious education, religious worship and the treatment of teachers.

without a religious character may not discriminate on grounds of religion. Those with such character can discriminate for admissions and, to varying degrees (depending on whether they are voluntary aided, voluntary controlled, foundation or independent), in decisions about the employment and the religious attitudes of teachers. Since the Human Rights Act 1998, human rights law has offered an additional means of scrutiny, beyond the restricted sphere of discrimination, although that remains a relevant factor.[3]

1 Human Rights and Non-discrimination Provisions Applicable to Schooling

1.1 *Human Rights Obligations*

As noted in the introduction, adherence to the ECHR and most of its protocols is obligatory for domestic public authorities, courts and tribunals. Most obviously relevant in the educational context is Article 2 of the First Protocol to the ECHR which is reproduced in the extracts from the case of *R (on the application of K) v Newham LBC* (at ch. 7, section 2, para. 7). The obligations undertaken by Article 2 are qualified by a reservation entered by the United Kingdom government, also extracted in the *Newham* judgment (at para. 8).[4] That reservation limits the obligations under Article 2 to those compatible with the provision of efficient instruction training and the avoidance of unreasonable public expenditure. Additionally, Article 9 is often relevant to issues such as prayer (covered in at ch. 5, section 2) and Islamic dress (covered in ch. 13).

1.2 *Anti-discrimination Law*

The main relevant provisions of anti-discrimination law are those now contained in the Equality Act 2010, section 85. They provide for rules relating to the admission of pupils and their treatment after admission in terms of discrimination, harassment and victimisation. This reflects a specific tailoring of the general rules on non-discrimination in the Equality Act to the schooling context. These rules apply to the range of responsible bodies and persons as specified. It will be noted that other provisions of anti-discrimination law are also raised in the context of schooling, including rules against sex dis-

3 For an excellent discussion of both anti-discrimination law and human rights law as it applies to education see Knights, S. (2021), *Law, rights, and religion*. Oxford: Oxford University Press, pp. 119–157.

4 The reservation is also reproduced in the Human Rights Act 1998, Schedule 3.

crimination (see ch. 7, section 2). These rules may not only support claims made by Muslims but can also be invoked against them because of discrimination on religious or sex grounds or on other grounds. Within the Equality Act 2010, specific exemptions are available in Schedule 11 for single sex schools and schools with a religious ethos, and also for anything done in connection to acts of worship. Then, on the one hand, there are more specific provisions elsewhere in the law, such as the permission given to schools that have a religious character to deal with teachers differently depending on their religious views (ch. 7, section 6.1). On the other hand, there are very specific provisions such as the obligation not to discriminate against teachers because of their religious opinions or practices of worship (ch. 7, section 6.2).

Equality Act 2010

85 Pupils: admission and treatment, etc.

(1) The responsible body of a school to which this section applies must not discriminate against a person—
   (a) in the arrangements it makes for deciding who is offered admission as a pupil;
   (b) as to the terms on which it offers to admit the person as a pupil;
   (c) by not admitting the person as a pupil.

(2) The responsible body of such a school must not discriminate against a pupil—
   (a) in the way it provides education for the pupil;
   (b) in the way it affords the pupil access to a benefit, facility or service;
   (c) by not providing education for the pupil;
   (d) by not affording the pupil access to a benefit, facility or service;
   (e) by excluding the pupil from the school;
   (f) by subjecting the pupil to any other detriment.

(3) The responsible body of such a school must not harass—
   (a) a pupil;
   (b) a person who has applied for admission as a pupil.

(4) The responsible body of such a school must not victimise a person—
   (a) in the arrangements it makes for deciding who is offered admission as a pupil;
   (b) as to the terms on which it offers to admit the person as a pupil;
   (c) by not admitting the person as a pupil.

(5) The responsible body of such a school must not victimise a pupil—
 (a) in the way it provides education for the pupil;
 (b) in the way it affords the pupil access to a benefit, facility or service;
 (c) by not providing education for the pupil;
 (d) by not affording the pupil access to a benefit, facility or service;
 (e) by excluding the pupil from the school;
 (f) by subjecting the pupil to any other detriment.

(6) A duty to make reasonable adjustments applies to the responsible body of such a school.

(7) In relation to England and Wales, this section applies to—
 (a) a school maintained by a local authority;
 (b) an independent educational institution (other than a special school);
  (ba) an alternative provision Academy that is not an independent educational institution;
 (c) a special school (not maintained by a local authority).

(8) In relation to Scotland, this section applies to—
 (a) a school managed by an education authority;
 (b) an independent school;
 (c) a school in respect of which the managers are for the time being receiving grants under section 73(c) or (d) of the Education (Scotland) Act 1980.

(9) The responsible body of a school to which this section applies is—
 (a) if the school is within subsection (7)(a), the local authority or governing body;
 (b) if it is within subsection (7)(b), (ba) or (c), the proprietor;
 (c) if it is within subsection (8)(a), the education authority;
 (d) if it is within subsection (8)(b), the proprietor;
 (e) if it is within subsection (8)(c), the managers.

(10) In the application of section 26 [on harassment] for the purposes of subsection (3), none of the following is a relevant protected characteristic—
 (a) gender reassignment;
 (b) religion or belief;
 (c) sexual orientation.

89 Interpretation and exceptions

…

(2) Nothing in this Chapter applies to anything done in connection with the content of the curriculum.

2 Separate Provision for the Sexes

A major concern of many Muslim parents is for their children, especially girls, to receive an education apart from male strangers. This is part of a wider pattern of limiting exposure and interaction between males and females that results in other behaviours such as face and head coverings, separate worshipping in mosques, and other forms of segregation, all of which are broadly tolerated in Britain. The Casey Review commissioned by the British government reported in 2016 that the "segregation of women and men in mosques is common but has also been found by Office of Standards in Education (Ofsted) in independent Muslim and Orthodox Jewish faith schools and reported in wider non-religious community meetings, including meetings of political parties and in universities."[5] The so-called "Operation Trojan Horse" affair led to an official scrutiny of practices at 14 non-faith schools in Birmingham. The investigation that took place in 2013–2014 found a sustained and coordinated agenda to impose upon children in a number of Birmingham schools the segregationist attitudes and practices of a hard-line and politicised strand of Sunni Islam. One of the observations made in the ensuing report was that schools had taken measures to ensure boys and girls do not mix.[6]

In principle, schools offering education to either sex are permitted and even funded by the state. As a result, specific exemptions are made in the Equality Act 2010 with respect to the prohibition of discrimination and the ability of the state to fund single sex schools.[7] Challenges have been made successfully under the Education Act 1944 and the Sex Discrimination Act 1975, which predates and is superseded by the Equality Act 2010, where there is inadequate provision for single sex schooling.[8] However, these may be fact-specific. In one case of a Muslim pupil, it was held not to be unlawful for the Secretary of State

5 Casey, L. (2016), *The Casey Review: A review into opportunity and integration*. London: Her Majesty's Stationery Office, p. 107. Ofsted is the Office for Standards in Education, Children's Services and Skills and has competence over standards in education and children's social care in England, which includes conducting school inspections.

6 Clarke, P. (2014), *Report into allegations concerning Birmingham schools arising from the 'Trojan Horse' letter*. London: Her Majesty's Stationery Office, pp. 45–46. For a more detailed analysis of the affair, taking into account other reports that were written after investigations into the same and other schools see Nash, P. (2022), *British Islam and English law: A classical pluralist perspective*. Cambridge: Cambridge University Press, pp. 185–218.

7 Respectively, see the Equality Act 2010, Sch. 3, paras 6(a) and 8, and Sch. 11, para. 1.

8 *R. v BirminghamCity Council Ex p. Equal Opportunities Commission (No. 1)* [1989] A.C. 1155 where the challenge to close down a school was upheld; and *R. v Birmingham City Council Ex*

to approve a decision by a local authority to close a single-sex school despite a lack of single-sex schools in the area.[9]

As the case below against Newham Borough Council in East London indicates, preference for single sex schooling becomes quite an important one raising questions about the extent to which Local Education Authorities should have regard to or accede to such demands. In other instances, when co-educational Islamic schools are established, they may still make efforts to separate girls and boys within school activities and this has been a cause of concern for Ofsted and led to court action in which sex segregation was regarded as unlawful, as shown in the *Al-Hijrah* case below. Despite legal action, schools may continue to perpetrate such segregation, showing that the law is often ignored because priority is given to religious precepts and that attitudes that support sex segregation are common among Muslims.

***R. (on the application of K) v Newham* LBC**
[2002] EWHC 405 (Admin), Collins J

K, a Muslim, had indicated a preference for a place in a single sex school for his daughter, Z. The local authority had issued a leaflet to parents outlining its school selection policy and a single sex school preference was stated to be one of the criteria for selection. The local authority had concluded that the allocation of Z to K's preferred choice of school would not have been an efficient use of its resources. There had been no indication whether K's religious beliefs had been considered in reaching that decision. K then applied for judicial review of the decisions of the local authority and its education appeal panel that Z would not be given a place at the preferred school. The case is especially relevant for the way in which Article 2 of the First Protocol to the ECHR was considered applicable. Although the court found that there was an error of law committed by the Local Education Authority [LEA] and its education appeal panel, the decision obliges LEAs only to take into account the choice made on grounds of religion, not to follow it.

p. Equal Opportunities Commission (No. 2) [1993] 1 F.C.R. 753 where the same local authority was found to have acted unlawfully in relying on the fact that a boys school had changed its status to grant-maintained (and therefore outside the local authority's control) to assess the number of places available in girls-only schools and whether there were a sufficient number of schools to provide education of a suitable kind under the Education Act 1944 and whether it complied with the Sex Discrimination Act.

9 *R. v Secretary of State for Education and Science, ex p. Parveen Malik* [1994] E.L.R. 121.

4. The relevant statutory provisions which are in issue in this case are contained in the School Standards and Framework Act 1998 Part III which deals with admission arrangements. Section 86(1) reads:

> A local education authority [LEA] shall make arrangements for enabling the parent of a child in the area of the authority-
> (a) to express a preference as to the school at which he wishes education to be provided for his child in the exercise of the authority's functions, and
> (b) to give reasons for his preference.
> (2) Subject to subsection (3) and (6) in section 87 (children excluded from two or more schools), the local education authority and the governing body of a maintained school shall comply with any preference expressed in accordance with arrangements made under subsection (1).
> (3) The duty imposed by subsection (2) does not apply-
> (a) if compliance with the preference would prejudice the provision of efficient education or the efficient use of resources.

…

7. I was referred to the Human Rights Act and Article 2 of the First Protocol which deals with the right to education and which reads:

> No person shall be denied the right to education. In the exercise of any functions which it assumes in relation to education and to teaching, the State shall respect the right of parents to ensure such education and teaching in conformity with their own religious and philosophical convictions.

8. The United Kingdom, when signing the First Protocol, issued a reservation in respect of that Article which is in these terms:

> At the time of signing the present (First) Protocol, I declare that, in view of certain provisions of the Education Acts in the United Kingdom, the principle affirmed in the second sentence of Article 2 is accepted by the United Kingdom only so far as it is compatible with the provision of efficient instruction and training, and the avoidance of unreasonable public expenditure.

…

29. It seems to me … that since the coming into effect of the Human Rights Act, the religious conviction of a parent is something to which due weight must be given in considering admission to a particular school. It may be that it is unusual that religious conviction should play a part in a decision whether a single sex or a mixed sex school should be chosen. But there is no question but that in the case

of this claimant, and it may be, one suspects, that there are others who will be in the same position, that is an important consideration.

…

38. … As the court has made clear in the passage I have read from *Valsamis v Greece*, it is necessary, in order to comply with Article 2, for there to be some positive action on the part of the State.[10] That must mean, in the context of an admission case such as this, that the LEA, initially, and the Appeal Panel on appeal must give weight to such conviction. Indeed, as it seems to me, it is necessary that the LEA and, indeed, all LEAs, take that on board in their admissions policies.

…

43. Mr Glover [Counsel for the Local Education Authority] has submitted that the question of religion was clearly before the Appeals Panel. It was not raised earlier because the claimant had not mentioned it, albeit he had not had drawn to his attention its potential importance, as in my view he should have had. But it seems to me to be clear, looking at the notes of the hearing and of the decision that no one appreciated its potential importance. If they had, I do not doubt that it would have been and should have been referred to, whether in the reasons letter or at the hearing or both. Nothing has been done in the context of this case by the defendants to take the positive steps required to fulfil the requirements of Article 2 of the First Protocol and that failure in my view, does amount to an error of law.

Regina (Interim Executive Board of Al-Hijrah School) v HM Chief Inspector of Education, Children's Services and Skills (Secretary of State for Education and others intervening)
[2017] EWCA Civ 1426, Court of Appeal

The governors of a co-educational voluntary aided Muslim school had a policy of segregating pupils by gender from the age of nine for all purposes, including lessons, breaks, school clubs and trips. Following an inspection, the school was assessed as inadequate. Although the gender segregation policy had not been the subject of adverse comments in previous inspectors' reports, the school inspectors criticised it as having adverse educational consequences and a directly discriminatory effect in breach of sections 13 and 85 of the Equality Act

10 The court here is referring to its own citation from the case of *Valsamis v Greece* 24 EHRR 294, para. 27.

2010. Section 85 of the 2010 Act prohibited discrimination by a school against a pupil in the way it afforded the pupil access to a benefit, facility or service. Section 13 discrimination included less favourable treatment because of a person's sex. The claimant sought judicial review of the report. The judge allowed the claim on the basis that each sex was to be viewed as a group and a comparison made between the groups, and that, since the treatment of each group was equivalent in nature and character with equivalent consequences for both sexes, neither sex was treated less favourably than the other and so the segregation of male and female pupils did not in itself constitute discrimination contrary to the 2010 Act. The chief inspector [here cited interchangeably with Ofsted] appealed on five grounds as follows: (1) the girls lost an opportunity to learn and socialise with boys or individual boys, which boys at the school enjoyed; (2) the boys lost an opportunity to learn and socialise with girls or individual girls, which girls at the school enjoyed; (3) the girls lost the opportunity to socialise confidently with the boys and the boys similarly lost the opportunity to socialise confidently with the girls and/or to learn to socialise confidently in preparation for personal, educational and work-related contexts on leaving school; (4) each loss of opportunity imposed a particular detriment on girls because the female sex was the group with the minority power in society, so that the restrictions on interaction between the sexes had adverse social implications for women which outweighed the adverse social implications for men, as those with the minority of power were socialised to be regarded by themselves and by those with the majority of power as relevantly different in contexts where gender ought to be treated as irrelevant; and (5) the very fact of segregation constituted less favourable treatment of girls because it amounted to an expressive harm caused by the necessary implication that girls were inferior to or otherwise relevantly different from boys in day to day social and working contexts. Sir Terence Etherton, MR, Beatson LJ and Gloster LJ all agreed on grounds 1, 2, and 3 of the appeal, finding in favour of Ofsted. Gloster J dissented with respect to grounds 4 and 5. The other two judges said that it was not necessary to make findings on those questions but did express the view that they would not have allowed the appeal on those grounds. Gloster J, meanwhile, said that she would have allowed the appeal on those grounds also. Since the Court of Appeal delivered its judgment in the *Al-Hijrah* case, more inspections by the schools' inspection body, Ofsted, brought to light the kind of practices which the case involved.[11] This would indicate that such practices are

11 See "Islamic schools 'in breach of law' over segregation of boys and girls," *Birmingham Mail*, 3 November 2018, https://www.birminghammail.co.uk/news/midlands-news/islamic-schools-in-breach-law-15357775; "Birmingham Islamic school unlawfully segregates

potentially widespread in schools with an Islamic religious character, and that the school authorities tended not to act on legal judgments, although they did appear to say that they would reform their practices in light of the reports by Ofsted.

Sir Terence Etherton, MR and Lord Justice Beatson

45. Ms Helen Mountfield QC, for Ofsted, presents Ofsted's case on this part of the appeal very simply. She submitted that a girl pupil who wishes to mix or socialise with a boy pupil is precluded from doing so because of her sex, a protected characteristic; whereas, if she did not have that characteristic, and was a boy pupil, she would be able to mix or socialise with all the other boys. Equally, if a boy pupil wishes to mix or socialise with a girl pupil, he is precluded from doing so because of his sex; and if he did not have that characteristic, and was a girl pupil, he would be able to mix or socialise with all the other girls. Ofsted's view was that this restriction on the freedom of a girl pupil to mix or socialise with boy pupils and on a boy pupil to mix or socialise with girl pupils was detrimental to their education. The Judge appears to have accepted the existence of such a detriment in principle when he said (at para [118]):

> I would hold that, at least in principle, the denial of the choice to seek the society of and interaction with the opposite sex, and of the educational benefits which might flow from the exercise of that choice, is capable of amounting to the denial of a 'benefit' or 'facility' for the purposes of section 85(2)(b), read in conjunction with section 212(4); and, as a possibly better fit, the subjection of the pupils to a 'detriment' for the purposes of sub-paragraph (f).

46. It was submitted that the point can be put on the basis of a comparator, namely (in the case of discrimination against a girl pupil) a boy pupil who can mix with other boy pupils, and (in the case of discrimination against a boy pupil) a girl pupil who can mix with other girl pupils, or it can be advanced without any comparator by simply asking what would have been the position if the girl pupil or the boy pupil did not have the protected characteristic of their sex. It is said that, either way, there is discrimination contrary to any one or all of EA 2010

pupils by sex—and boys are given 'more privileges'," *The Sun*, 7 January 2020, https://www.thesun.co.uk/news/10692009/islamic-headteacher-unlawfully-segregating-birmingham/, both accessed on 12 February 2025. Meanwhile, the Al-Hijrah school, although not under investigation, was linked to the non-faith based schools in the "Operation Trojan Horse" investigation. See Clarke, P. (2014), *Report into allegations concerning Birmingham schools arising from the 'Trojan Horse' letter*. London: Her Majesty's Stationery Office.

s. 85(2)(a)(b)(d) and (f). Viewed from the perspective of an individual pupil, in that way, both the girl pupil and the boy pupil are treated less favourably than the other.

47. We agree with those submissions of Ofsted.

48. There is no doubt that the restriction on a girl pupil socialising with boy pupils, and on a boy pupil socialising with girl pupils, is by reason of their respective sex. There is no doubt that Ofsted could reasonably take the view, which it did, that the differential treatment, as Ofsted portrays it, was detrimental to both the girl pupil and the boy pupil. As it happens, there was direct evidence from some, albeit a small number, of the pupils in the present case that they regarded the complete separation of the sexes as detrimental to their social awareness and development, and there is equally no doubt that that view was a reasonable one to hold, reasonableness of perception of adverse detriment being the touchstone of detriment in this context: compare *St Helens Metropolitan Borough Council v Derbyshire* [2007] UKHL 16, [2007] IRLH 16 at [37]; *Birmingham City Council v Equal Opportunities Commission* [1989] 1 AC 1155 at p. 1193H. The Judge reached the same conclusion on detriment in paragraph [118] of his judgment.

…

50. We agree with Ofsted that the Judge was wrong to approach the matter in that way. The starting point is that EA 2010 s.13 specifies what is direct discrimination by reference to a "person". There is no reference to "group" discrimination or comparison. Each girl pupil and each boy pupil is entitled to freedom from direct discrimination looking at the matter from her or his individual perspective. That is consistent with the following observation by Lord Mance in R(E) v Governing Body of JFS [2009] UKSC 15, [2010] 2 AC 728 at [90]:

> Finally, I also consider it to be consistent with the underlying policy of section 1(1)(a) of [the Race Relations Act 1976] that it should apply in the present circumstances. The policy is that individuals should be treated as individuals, and not assumed to be like other members of a group: R (European Roma Rights Centre) v Immigration Officer at Prague Airport (United Nations High Comr for Refugees intervening) [2005] 2 AC 1, paras 82 and 90, per Baroness Hale of Richmond and R (Gillan) v Comr of Police of the Metropolis [2006] 2 AC 307, paras 44 and 90, per Lord Hope of Craighead and Lord Brown of Eaton-under-Heywood. To treat individual applicants to a school less favourably than others, because of the happenstance of their respective ancestries, is not to treat them as individuals, but as members in a group defined in a manner unrelated to their individual attributes.

51. Viewed in that way, Ofsted's analysis of "less favourable treatment" is correct. An individual girl pupil cannot socialise and intermix with a boy pupil because, and only because, of her sex; and an individual boy pupil cannot socialise and intermix with a girl pupil because, and only because, of his sex. Each is, therefore, treated less favourably than would be the case if their sex was different.

…

56. Furthermore, we do not accept the School's argument that, whether looked at from an individual or group perspective, separate but equal treatment by reason of gender cannot be unlawful discrimination even if it is detrimental. The way Mr Oldham put it in the course of his submission was there cannot be unlawful discrimination if both the complainant and the comparator suffer the same detriment even if they would have been treated differently if they were a different sex. The following cases support the rejection of that argument, as does the general principle that the discrimination legislation should be given a wide and purposive interpretation rather than a narrow one: see, for example, Jones v Tower Boot Co Ltd [1997] IRCR 168 at [31].

…

62. The statutory scheme embodied in EA 2010 also supports the conclusion that separate but equal treatment may constitute unlawful discrimination, and it will do so (subject to statutory exceptions) if such treatment is based on gender and is more detrimental than it would have been but for that gender. Part 7 of Schedule 3 sets out exceptions to Part 3 of EA 2010, which deals with "Services and Public Functions". That Part does not apply in the present case (see s.28(2)(a)) but it is relevant that the exceptions in paragraph 26 of Part 7 show that Parliament did have in mind that both separate but equal treatment as well as separate but different treatment could constitute unlawful discrimination.

…

[Paragraph 26 is reproduced above at ch. 4, section 1]

…

71. Schedule 11 specifies exceptions to the provisions of chapter 1 of Part 6, which deals with schools and includes section 85: section 89(12). Schedule 11 does not contain an equivalent provision to paragraph 26 of Part 7. The clear inference, however, from the provisions of Schedule 11 is that Parliament did not envisage the kind of strict gender separation in a notionally co-educational school that is practised in the present case.

…

80. We do not consider that EA 2010 s.13(5) is of any material assistance in the present case. We do not find that there is discrimination in the present case merely because of the fact of segregation. So far as concerns the School, in the context of section 85(2), we find that the strict segregation by gender is a detriment which involves less favourable treatment because it diminishes the quality of education that the girl pupils and the boy pupils would receive but for their respective sex. It is not the mere fact of segregation which gives rise to discrimination, as would be the situation under section 13(5) in the case of race, but rather it is the impact on the quality of education which the pupils would receive but for their respective sex.

81. It is common ground, and well-established by authority, that the motive for discrimination is irrelevant: the JFS case at [20], [35], [65]. There are certain exemptions from section 85(1) and (2) in Part 2 of Schedule 11 of EA 2010 relating to religion but they are not relied upon by the School in the present case. It is irrelevant, therefore, that in adhering to its strict policy of segregation of sexes the School is motivated by conscientious adherence to what it regards as the applicable tenets of Islam.

82. The same is also true of parental satisfaction with the School's policy and indeed the decision of parents to choose the school precisely because of its segregation policy. Mr Oldham drew attention to section 9 of the Education Act 1996, which provides that, in exercising or performing their respective powers and duties under the Education Acts, the Secretary of State and local authorities shall have regard to the general principle that pupils are to be educated in accordance with the wishes of their parents. He also referred to section 86 of the School Standards and Framework Act 1998, which provides that a local authority shall make arrangements for enabling the parent of a child in the area of the authority to express a preference as to the school at which he wishes education to be provided for his child in the exercise of the authority's functions. Those provisions, however, and parental choice more generally plainly cannot negate the statutory right of a child to be educated in a non-discriminatory manner as required by EA 2010 …

3 Religious Education

The legal requirement for schools to provide religious education (and an act of worship) has been present since the Education Act 1944, but with changes made in the Education Reform Act 1988 which have been retained since then and are currently reflected in the Education Act 1998, section 69, and Schedule 19 (with respect to the duty itself), the Education Act 1996, sections 375, 390–392 (with respect to the content and methodology of devising a syllabus) and the Education Act 2002, section 80 (which specifies religious education as well as relationships, sex and health education as part of the basic curriculum). The basic formula is that every agreed syllabus which is devised at local (significantly, not national) level "shall reflect the fact that the religious traditions in Great Britain are in the main Christian whilst taking account of the teaching and practices of the other principal religions represented in Great Britain".[12] The devising is done by a local authority after advice by a SACRE, which is itself constituted by a local authority. The composition of SACREs is supposed to be done in accordance with section 390 of the 1996 Act so that, broadly speaking, it proportionately reflects the religious traditions or denominations in that area. This means that Muslim representation is bound to be reflected where they compose a significant size of the local population. Although legal actions or controversies have not yet arisen with respect to it, the wording of the legislation is not consistent given that section 390(4)(a) of the Education Act 1996 refers to "religious traditions", section 390(6) refers to "denomination or religion", and section 392(1) and (2) refer to "religion, denomination or associations". Opt-outs are possible depending on the type of schools, which means a great deal of diversity can take place on the ground. Withdrawal of pupils from religious education in schools that do not have a religious character is also possible. In schools with a religious character, it is the character that determines the sort of religious education provided. Although it is stated that in schools without a religious character the syllabus should not favour any particular religious denomination,[13] it remains a question whether such a syllabus, when it includes reference to Islam, would be able to successfully provide a religious education curriculum which is not distinctive of denominational Islamic doctrines.[14]

Education Act 2002

80 Basic curriculum for every maintained school in England

(1) The curriculum for every maintained school in England shall comprise a basic curriculum which includes—

12 Education Act 1996, section 375(3).

13 School Standards and Framework Act 1998, Sch. 19, para. 2(5).

14 This point is raised by Jamal, A. and Panjwani, F. (2016), "Having faith in our schools: Struggling with definitions of religion," in Hunter-Henin, M. (ed.), *Law, religious freedoms and education in Europe*. Milton Park, Abingdon: Routledge, pp. 69–86.

(a) provision for religious education for all registered pupils at the school (in accordance with such of the provisions of Schedule 19 to the School Standards and Framework Act 1998 (c. 31) as apply in relation to the school),
(b) a curriculum for all registered pupils at the school who have ceased to be young children for the purposes of Part 1 of the Childcare Act 2006] but are not over compulsory school age (known as "the National Curriculum for England"),
(c) provision for relationships education for all registered pupils at the school who are provided with primary education,
(d) provision for relationships and sex education for all registered pupils at the school who are provided with secondary education, and
(e) provision for health education for all registered pupils at the school.

(2) Subsection (1)(a) does not apply—
(a) in relation to pupils who are under compulsory school age, or
(b) in the case of a maintained special school (provision as to religious education in special schools being made by regulations under section 71(7) of the School Standards and Framework Act 1998).

Education Act 1996

RELIGIOUS EDUCATION AND WORSHIP
Agreed syllabuses

375 Agreed syllabuses of religious education.
(1) Subject to the provisions of Schedule 31, any agreed syllabus in force immediately before the commencement of this Act shall continue to have effect.
(2) In this Act "agreed syllabus" means a syllabus of religious education—
(a) prepared before the commencement of this Act in accordance with Schedule 5 to the Education Act 1944 or after commencement in accordance with Schedule 31, and
(b) adopted by a local authority under that Schedule,
whether it is for use in all the schools maintained by them or for use in particular such schools or in relation to any particular class or description of pupils in such schools.

(3) Every agreed syllabus shall reflect the fact that the religious traditions in Great Britain are in the main Christian whilst taking account of the teaching and practices of the other principal religions represented in Great Britain.

(4) Any reference in this Act to an agreed syllabus adopted by a local authority includes a reference to an agreed syllabus deemed to be adopted by such an authority by virtue of paragraph 11 of Schedule 5 to the Education Act 1944 or paragraph 14 of Schedule 31; and accordingly, in relation to an agreed syllabus deemed to be so adopted, any reference to the date on which an agreed syllabus was adopted is a reference to the date of deemed adoption specified by the Secretary of State in a direction under that paragraph.

(5) Subsection (3) does not apply to any agreed syllabus adopted before 29th September 1988.

…

Constitution of standing advisory councils on religious education

390 Constitution of advisory councils.

(1) A local authority shall constitute a standing advisory council on religious education for the purposes mentioned in section 391(1).

(2) The council shall consist of such groups of persons appointed by the authority as representative members ("representative groups") as are required by subsection (4).]

(3) The council may also include co-opted members (that is, persons co-opted as members of the council by members of the council who have not themselves been so co-opted).

(4) The representative groups required by this subsection are –

(a) a group of persons to represent such Christian denominations and other religions and denominations of such religions as, in the opinion of the authority, will appropriately reflect the principal religious traditions in the area;

(b) except in the case of an area in Wales, a group of persons to represent the Church of England;

(c) a group of persons to represent such associations representing teachers as, in the opinion of the authority, ought to be represented, having regard to the circumstances of the area; and

(d) a group of persons to represent the authority.

(5) Where a representative group is required by subsection (4)(b), the representative group required by subsection (4)(a) shall not include persons appointed to represent the Church of England.

(6) The number of representative members appointed to any representative group under subsection (4)(a) to represent each denomination or religion required to be represented shall, so far as consistent with the efficient discharge of the group's functions, reflect broadly the proportionate strength of that denomination or religion in the area.

(7) On any question to be decided by the council only the representative groups on the council shall be entitled to vote, and each representative group shall have a single vote.

391 Functions of advisory councils.

(1) The purposes referred to in section 390(1) are—

(a) to advise the local authority on such matters connected with—

(i) religious worship in community schools or in foundation schools which (within the meaning of Part II of the School Standards and Framework Act 1998) do not have a religious character, and

(ii) the religious education to be given in accordance with an agreed or other syllabus in accordance with Schedule 19 to that Act,

as the authority may refer to the council or as the council may see fit, and

(b) to carry out the functions conferred on them by section 394.

(2) The matters referred to in subsection (1)(a) include, in particular, methods of teaching, the choice of materials and the provision of training for teachers.

(3) The representative groups on the council required by section 390(4), other than the group consisting of persons appointed to represent the authority, may at any time require a review of any agreed syllabus for the time being adopted by the authority.

(4) Each representative group concerned shall have a single vote on the question of whether to require such a review.

(5) Paragraph 3 of Schedule 31 has effect to require the authority, on receiving written notification of any such requirement, to cause a conference constituted in accordance with that Schedule to be convened for the purpose of reconsidering any agreed syllabus to which the requirement relates.

(6) The council shall in each year publish a report as to the exercise of their functions and any action taken by representative groups on the council under subsection (3) during the last preceding year.

(7) The council's report shall in particular—

(a) specify any matters in respect of which the council have given advice to the authority,

(b) broadly describe the nature of the advice given, and

(c) where any such matter was not referred to the council by the authority, give the council's reasons for offering advice on that matter.

(10) A council for an area in Wales must send a copy of each report published by them under subsection (6) to the Welsh Ministers.

392 Advisory councils: supplementary provisions.

(1) In this section "the council" means the standing advisory council on religious education constituted by a local authority under section 390.

(2) Before appointing a person to represent any religion, denomination or associations as a member of the council, the authority shall take all reasonable steps to assure themselves that he is representative of the religion, denomination or associations in question.

(3) A member of the council who was appointed by the authority may be removed from membership by the authority if, in their opinion, he ceases to be representative of the religion, denomination or associations which he was appointed to represent or (as the case may be) he ceases to be representative of the authority.

...

School Standards and Framework Act 1998

69 Duty to secure due provision of religious education: England.

(1) Subject to section 71, in relation to any community, foundation or voluntary school in England—

(a) the local authority and the governing body shall exercise their functions with a view to securing, and

(b) the head teacher shall secure,

that religious education is given in accordance with the provision for such education included in the school's basic curriculum by virtue of section 80(1)(a) of the Education Act 2002.

(2) Schedule 19 has effect for determining the provision for religious

education which is required by section 80(1)(a) of that Act to be included in the basic curriculum of schools within each of the following categories, namely—

(a) community schools and foundation and voluntary schools in England which do not have a religious character,

(b) foundation and voluntary controlled schools in England which have a religious character, and

(c) voluntary aided schools in England which have a religious character.

(3) For the purposes of this Part a foundation or voluntary school in England has a religious character if it is designated as a school having such a character by an order made by the Secretary of State.

(4) An order under subsection (3) shall state, in relation to each school designated by the order, the religion or religious denomination in accordance with whose tenets religious education is, or may be, required to be provided at the school in accordance with Schedule 19 (or, as the case may be, each such religion or religious denomination).

(5) The procedure to be followed in connection with—

(a) the designation of a school in an order under subsection (3), and

(b) the inclusion in such an order, in relation to a school, of the statement required by subsection (4), shall be specified in regulations.

...

SCHEDULE 19 REQUIRED PROVISION FOR RELIGIOUS EDUCATION

...

Community schools and foundation and voluntary schools without a religious character

2(1) This paragraph applies to—

(a) any community school in England; and

(b) any foundation or voluntary school in England which does not have a religious character.

(2) Subject to sub-paragraph (4), the required provision for religious education in the case of pupils at the school is provision for religious education in accordance with an agreed syllabus adopted for the school or for those pupils.

(3) If the school is a secondary school so situated that arrangements

cannot conveniently be made for the withdrawal of pupils from it in accordance with section 71 to receive religious education elsewhere and the local authority are satisfied—

(a) that the parents of any pupils at the school desire them to receive religious education in the school in accordance with the tenets of a particular religion or religious denomination, and

(b) that satisfactory arrangements have been made for the provision of such education to those pupils in the school, and for securing that the cost of providing such education to those pupils in the school will not fall to be met from the school's budget share or otherwise by the authority,

the authority shall (unless they are satisfied that because of any special circumstances it would be unreasonable to do so) provide facilities for the carrying out of those arrangements.

...

(5) No agreed syllabus shall provide for religious education to be given to pupils at a school to which this paragraph applies by means of any catechism or formulary which is distinctive of a particular religious denomination (but this is not to be taken as prohibiting provision in such a syllabus for the study of such catechisms or formularies).

Foundation and voluntary controlled schools with a religious character

3(1) This paragraph applies to any foundation or voluntary controlled school in England which has a religious character.

(2) Subject to sub-paragraph (4), the required provision for religious education in the case of pupils at the school is provision for religious education—

(a) in accordance with any arrangements made under sub-paragraph (3), or

(b) subject to any such arrangements, in accordance with an agreed syllabus adopted for the school or for those pupils.

(3) Where the parents of any pupils at the school request that they may receive religious education—

(a) in accordance with any provisions of the trust deed relating to the school, or

(b) where provision for that purpose is not made by such a deed, in accordance with the tenets of the religion or religious denomination specified in relation to the school under section 69(4), the foundation governors shall (unless they are satisfied that because of any special circumstances it would be unreasonable to do so) make arrangements for securing that such religious education is given to those pupils in the school during not more than two periods in each week.

(4) If immediately before the appointed day the school was a grant-maintained school (within the meaning of the Education Act 1996), and in relation to the school or any pupils at the school the appropriate agreed syllabus as defined by section 382 of that Act was a syllabus falling within subsection (1)(c) of that section, then until—
(a) the end of such period as the Secretary of State may by order prescribe, or
(b) such earlier date as the governing body may determine,
that syllabus shall be treated for the purposes of sub-paragraph (2)(b) as an agreed syllabus adopted for the school or (as the case may be) those pupils.

Voluntary aided schools with a religious character

4(1) This paragraph applies to any voluntary aided school in England which has a religious character.

(2) The required provision for religious education in the case of pupils at the school is provision for religious education—
(a) in accordance with any provisions of the trust deed relating to the school, or
(b) where provision for that purpose is not made by such a deed, in accordance with the tenets of the religion or religious denomination specified in relation to the school under section 69(4), or
(c) in accordance with any arrangements made under sub-paragraph (3).

(3) Where the parents of any pupils at the school—
(a) desire them to receive religious education in accordance with any agreed syllabus adopted by the local authority, and
(b) cannot with reasonable convenience cause those pupils to attend a school at which that syllabus is in use,
the governing body shall (unless they are satisfied that because of any special circumstances it would be unreasonable to do so) make arrangements for religious education in accordance with that syllabus to be given to those pupils in the school.

(4) Religious education under any such arrangements shall be given during the times set apart for the giving of religious education in

the school in accordance with the provision for that purpose included in the school's basic curriculum by virtue of section 80(1)(a) or 101(1)(a) of the Education Act 2002.

(5) Any arrangements under sub-paragraph (3) shall be made by the governing body, unless the local authority are satisfied that the governing body are unwilling to make them, in which case they shall be made by the authority.

(6) Subject to sub-paragraph (3), the religious education given to pupils at the school shall be under the control of the governing body.

4 Religious Worship

The formula for the observance of an act of religious worship derives from the Education Act 1988, and its essence has been restated in subsequent legislation. The current provisions in relation to schools without a religious character are contained in the School Standards and Framework Act 1998, Schedule 20, para. 3(2), which states that "the required collective worship shall be wholly or mainly of a broadly Christian character." Schools must hold a daily act of collective worship, normally on school premises. It does not have to be held at the beginning of the day. Separate acts of worship may be held for pupils in different age or school groups. Not every required act of collective worship need be of a broadly Christian character, "provided that, taking any school term as a whole, most such acts which take place in the school do comply." A relevant factor in deciding whether some acts of worship that do not comply with the general expectation is "the family backgrounds of the pupils" (Schedule 20, para. 3(6)). The Standing Advisory Councils on Religious Education (SACREs) advise the local education authorities on matters connected with religious worship in community schools or in foundation schools. Under the Education Act 1996, section 394, after consulting the Governing Body, which should take appropriate steps to consult parents, a head teacher may apply to the SACRE for worship requirements in prescribed schools to be disapplied for particular classes or for particular descriptions of pupils. In making its decision, the SACRE should "have regard to any circumstances relating to the family backgrounds of the pupils at the school, or of the pupils of the particular class or description in question, which are relevant for determining the character of the collective worship appropriate in their case" (section 394(2)). In the case of the schools that came under the "Operation Trojan Horse" investigation,[15] some practices

15 See ch. 2 and ch. 7, section 2, this volume.

were identified that may amount to coercion into taking part in Islamic acts of worship. The investigation report found that Friday prayers had been introduced at several schools and there was pressure on students and staff to attend them.[16]

School Standards and Framework Act 1998

SCHEDULE 20

Collective worship

Introductory

1 In this Schedule "the required collective worship", in relation to a school, means the collective worship in that school which is required by section 70.

General provisions as to collective worship

2(1) This paragraph applies to any community, foundation or voluntary school.

(2) The arrangements for the required collective worship may, in respect of each school day, provide for a single act of worship for all pupils or for separate acts of worship for pupils in different age groups or in different school groups.

(3) For the purposes of sub-paragraph (2) a "school group" is any group in which pupils are taught or take part in other school activities.

(4) Subject to sub-paragraph (6), the arrangements for the required collective worship shall be made—

(a) if the school is a community school or a foundation school which does not have a religious character, by the head teacher after consulting the governing body;

(b) if the school is a foundation school which has a religious character or a voluntary school, by the governing body after consulting the head teacher.

(5) Subject to sub-paragraph (6), the required collective worship shall take place on the school premises.

(6) If the governing body of a community, foundation or voluntary school are of the opinion that it is desirable that any act of collective worship in the school required by section 70 should, on a special

16 Clarke, P. (2014), *Report into allegations concerning Birmingham schools arising from the 'Trojan Horse' letter*. London: Her Majesty's Stationery Office, p. 42.

occasion, take place elsewhere than on the school premises, they may, after consultation with the head teacher, make such arrangements for that purpose as they think appropriate.

(7) The powers of a governing body under sub-paragraph (6) shall not be exercised so as to derogate from the rule that the required collective worship must normally take place on the school premises.

Nature of collective worship in community schools and foundation schools without a religious character

3(1) This paragraph applies to—
  (a) any community school; and
  (b) any foundation school which does not have a religious character.

(2) Subject to paragraph 4, the required collective worship shall be wholly or mainly of a broadly Christian character.

(3) For the purposes of sub-paragraph (2), collective worship is of a broadly Christian character if it reflects the broad traditions of Christian belief without being distinctive of any particular Christian denomination.

(4) Not every act of collective worship in the school required by section 70 need comply with sub-paragraph (2) provided that, taking any school term as a whole, most such acts which take place in the school do comply with that sub-paragraph.

(5) Subject to sub-paragraphs (2) and (4)—
  (a) the extent to which (if at all) any acts of collective worship required by section 70 which do not comply with sub-paragraph (2) take place in the school,
  (b) the extent to which any act of collective worship in the school which complies with sub-paragraph (2) reflects the broad traditions of Christian belief, and
  (c) the ways in which those traditions are reflected in any such act of collective worship,

shall be such as may be appropriate having regard to any relevant considerations relating to the pupils concerned which fall to be taken into account in accordance with sub-paragraph (6).

(6) Those considerations are—
  (a) any circumstances relating to the family backgrounds of the pupils which are relevant for determining the character of the collective worship which is appropriate in their case, and
  (b) their ages and aptitudes.

(7) In this paragraph references to acts of collective worship in the school include such acts which by virtue of paragraph 2(6) take place otherwise than on the school premises.

Disapplication of requirement under paragraph 3(2)

4(1) This paragraph applies where a standing advisory council on religious education constituted under section 390 of the Education Act 1996 have determined (under section 394 of the Education Act 1996) that it is not appropriate for the requirement imposed by paragraph 3(2) to apply in the case of any school to which paragraph 3 applies or in the case of any class or description of pupils at any such school.

(2) While the determination has effect—

(a) paragraph 3 shall not apply in relation to the school or (as the case may be) the pupils in question, and

(b) the collective worship required by section 70 in the case of the school or pupils shall not be distinctive of any particular Christian or other religious denomination;

but paragraph (b) shall not be taken as preventing that worship from being distinctive of any particular faith.

Nature of collective worship in foundation schools with a religious character and voluntary schools

5 In the case of a foundation school which has a religious character or a voluntary school, the required collective worship shall be—

(a) in accordance with any provisions of the trust deed relating to the school, or

(b) where—

(i) provision for that purpose is not made by such a deed, and

(ii) the school has a religious character,

in accordance with the tenets and practices of the religion or religious denomination specified in relation to the school under section 68A or 69(4).

Education Act 1996

394 Determination of cases in which requirement for Christian collective worship is not to apply.

(1) The council constituted by a local authority under section 390 shall, on an application made by the head teacher of—

(a) any community school maintained by the authority, or
(b) any foundation school which has not been designated under section 69(3) of the School Standards and Framework Act 1998 by the Secretary of State as having a religious character,

consider whether it is appropriate for the requirement imposed by paragraph 3(2) of Schedule 20 to the School Standards and Framework Act 1998 (requirement for Christian collective worship) to apply in the case of the school or in the case of any class or description of pupils at the school.

(2) In determining whether it is appropriate for that requirement to apply as mentioned in subsection (1), the council shall have regard to any circumstances relating to the family backgrounds of the pupils at the school, or of the pupils of the particular class or description in question, which are relevant for determining the character of the collective worship appropriate in their case.

(3) The council shall give the head teacher written notification of their decision on the application.

(4) Where the council determine that it is not appropriate for the requirement to apply as mentioned in subsection (1), the determination shall take effect for the purposes of paragraph 4 of Schedule 20 to the School Standards and Framework Act 1998 (disapplication of requirement for Christian collective worship) on such date as may be specified in the notification of the council's decision under subsection (3).

(5) Before making an application under subsection (1), the head teacher of a school shall consult the governing body.

(6) On being consulted by the head teacher, the governing body may if they think fit take such steps as they consider appropriate for consulting all persons appearing to them to be parents of registered pupils at the school.

…

5 Withdrawal from Religious Education and Worship

The School Standards and Framework Act 1998, section 71 provides parents of pupils with a right to withdraw pupils from either religious education or religious worship, while sixth formers, who will normally be above 16 years of age, have a right to request withdrawal themselves. A withdrawn pupil may receive alternative religious education in accordance with parental wishes, but the school or local authority is not obliged to provide that alternative. In the case of boarding schools, however, the governing body of the school is obliged to also provide that alternative religious education.

School Standards and Framework Act 1998

71. Exceptions and special arrangements; provision for special schools.

(1) If the parent of a pupil at a community, foundation or voluntary school in England requests that he may be wholly or partly excused from receiving religious education given at the school in accordance with the school's basic curriculum, the pupil shall be so excused until the request is withdrawn.

(1A) If the parent of any pupil at a community, foundation or voluntary school other than a sixth-form pupil requests that he may be wholly or partly excused from attendance at religious worship at the school, the pupil shall be so excused until the request is withdrawn.

(1B) If a sixth-form pupil requests that he may be wholly or partly excused from attendance at religious worship at a community, foundation or voluntary school, the pupil shall be so excused.

(2) In subsections (1) to (1B)—

  (a) the reference to religious education given in accordance with the school's basic curriculum is to such education given in accordance with the provision included in the school's basic curriculum by virtue of section 80(1)(a) of the Education Act 2002, and

  (b) the reference to religious worship in the school includes religious worship which by virtue of paragraph 2(6) of Schedule 20 takes place otherwise than on the school premises.

(3) Where in accordance with subsection (1) or (1A) a pupil has been wholly or partly excused from receiving religious education or from attendance at religious worship and the local authority are satisfied—

  (a) that the parent of the pupil desires him to receive religious education of a kind which is not provided in the school during the periods of time during which he is so excused,

  (b) that the pupil cannot with reasonable convenience be sent to another community, foundation or voluntary school where religious education of the kind desired by the parent is provided, and

(c) that arrangements have been made for him to receive religious education of that kind during school hours elsewhere, the pupil may be withdrawn from the school during such periods of time as are reasonably necessary for the purpose of enabling him to receive religious education in accordance with the arrangements.

(4) A pupil may not be withdrawn from school under subsection (3) unless the local authority are satisfied that the arrangements there mentioned are such as will not interfere with the attendance of the pupil at school on any day except at the beginning or end of a school session (or, if there is only one, the school session) on that day.

(5) Where the parent of a pupil who is a boarder at a community, foundation or voluntary school and is not a sixth-form pupil requests that the pupil be permitted—

(a) to receive religious education in accordance with the tenets of a particular religion or religious denomination outside school hours, or

(b) to attend worship in accordance with such tenets on Sundays or other days exclusively set apart for religious observance by the religious body to which his parent belongs, the governing body shall make arrangements for giving the pupil reasonable opportunities for doing so.

(5A) Where a sixth-form pupil who is a boarder at a community, foundation or voluntary school requests that he be permitted—

(a) to receive religious education in accordance with the tenets of a particular religion or religious denomination outside school hours, or

(b) to attend worship in accordance with such tenets on Sundays or other days exclusively set apart for religious observance by the religious body to which the pupil belongs, the governing body shall make arrangements for giving the pupil reasonable opportunities for doing so.

(6) Arrangements under subsection (5) or (5A) may provide for making facilities for such education or worship available on the school premises, but any expenditure entailed by the arrangements shall not be met from the school's budget share or otherwise by the local authority.

(7) Regulations shall make provision for ensuring that, so far as practicable, every pupil attending a community or foundation special school in England—

(a) receives religious education unless withdrawn from receiving such education in accordance with the wishes of his parent, and
(b) attends religious worship unless withdrawn from attendance at such worship—
(i) in the case of a sixth-form pupil, in accordance with his own wishes, and
(ii) in any other case, in accordance with the wishes of his parent.

(7A) Regulations made by the Welsh Ministers shall make provision for ensuring that, so far as practicable, every pupil attending a community or foundation special school in Wales attends religious worship unless withdrawn from attendance at such worship—
(a) in the case of a sixth-form pupil, in accordance with the pupil's own wishes, and
(b) in any other case, in accordance with the wishes of the pupil's parent.

(8) In this section "sixth-form pupil" means any pupil who—
(a) has ceased to be of compulsory school age, and
(b) is receiving education suitable to the requirements of pupils over compulsory school age.

6 Teachers

As with the provisions relevant to expectations about religious worship and religious education, the main divide in the rules applicable to teachers also depends on the religious and non-religious character distinction.

6.1 *Teachers of Religious Education at Schools with a Religious Character*

There are provisions in the education legislation for schools which allow those with a religious character to appoint a reserved number of teachers to deliver religious education, and special rules apply to them with respect to their fitness, competence and dismissal. For England and Wales, these rules are contained in the School Standards and Framework Act 1998, sections 58 and 58A. In addition, schools with a religious character may have regard to religious opinions, attendance at worship and willingness to provide religious education in accordance with the tenets of a religion or a religious denomination when it comes to the appointment, remuneration, promotion, termination or engagement of teachers: see sections 60, 124A and 124AA.

School Standards and Framework Act 1998

Appointment and dismissal of teachers of religious education

58 Appointment and dismissal of certain teachers at schools with a religious character.

(1) In this section—
  (a) subsections (2) to (6) apply to a foundation or voluntary controlled school in England which has a religious character; and
  (b) subsection (7) applies (subject to subsection (8)) to a voluntary aided school in England which has a religious character;

and references in this Chapter to a school which has (or does not have) a religious character shall be construed in relation to a school in England, in accordance with section 68A and section 69(3).

(2) Where the number of teachers at a school to which this subsection applies is more than two, the teachers shall include persons who—
  (a) are selected for their fitness and competence to give such religious education as is required in accordance with arrangements under paragraph 3(3) of Schedule 19 (arrangements for religious education in accordance with the school's trust deed or with the tenets of the school's specified religion or religious denomination), and
  (b) are specifically appointed to do so.

(3) The number of reserved teachers in such a school shall not exceed one-fifth of the total number of teachers, including the head teacher (and for this purpose, where the total number of teachers is not a multiple of five, it shall be treated as if it were the next higher multiple of five).

(5) Where the appropriate body propose to appoint a person to be a reserved teacher in such a school, that body—
  (a) shall consult the foundation governors, and
  (b) shall not so appoint that person unless the foundation governors are satisfied as to his fitness and competence to give such religious education as is mentioned in subsection (2)(a).

(6) If the foundation governors of such a school consider that a reserved teacher has failed to give such religious education efficiently and suitably, they may—
  (a) in the case of a teacher who is an employee, require the appropriate body to dismiss him from employment as a reserved teacher at the school, and

(b) in the case of a teacher who is engaged otherwise than under a contract of employment, require the governing body to terminate his engagement.

(7) If a teacher appointed to give religious education in a school to which this subsection applies fails to give such education efficiently and suitably, he may be dismissed on that ground by the governing body without the consent of the local authority.

(8) Subsection (7) does not apply—

(a) where the school has a delegated budget, or

(b) to religious education in accordance with an agreed syllabus.

(9) In this section—

"the appropriate body" means—

(a) in relation to a foundation school, the governing body, and

(b) in relation to a voluntary controlled school, the local authority;

"reserved teacher", in relation to a foundation or voluntary controlled school, means a person employed or engaged at the school in pursuance of subsection (2).

58A Appointment and dismissal of certain teachers at schools with a religious character: Wales

(1) In this section—

(a) subsections (3) to (7) apply to a foundation or voluntary controlled school in Wales that has a religious character, and

(b) subsections (8) and (9) apply (subject to subsection (10)) to a voluntary aided school in Wales that has a religious character.

(2) References in this Chapter to a school which has (or does not have) a religious character are to be construed, in relation to a school in Wales, in accordance with section 68A(1).

(3) Where the number of teachers at a school to which this subsection applies is more than two, the teachers must include persons ("reserved teachers") who—

(a) are selected for their fitness and competence to provide teaching and learning within subsection (11), and

(b) are specifically appointed to provide that teaching and learning.

(4) The number of reserved teachers at a school must not exceed one fifth of the total number of teachers, including the head teacher; and for this purpose where the total number of teachers is not a multiple of five, it is to be treated as if it were the next higher multiple of five.

(5) Where the appropriate body propose to appoint a person as a reserved teacher in a school, that body—

(a) must consult the foundation governors, and

(b) must not appoint that person unless the foundation governors are satisfied as to the person's fitness and competence to provide teaching and learning within subsection (11).

(6) Subsection (7) applies if the foundation governors of a school to which subsection (3) applies consider that a person appointed as a reserved teacher at the school has failed to provide teaching and learning within subsection (11) efficiently and suitably.

(7) The foundation governors may—

(a) in the case of a teacher who is an employee, require the appropriate body to dismiss the teacher from employment as a teacher appointed under subsection (3);

(b) in the case of a teacher who is engaged otherwise than under a contract of employment, require the governing body to terminate that engagement.

(8) Subsection (9) applies if a teacher appointed to provide teaching and learning within subsection (11), in a school to which this subsection applies, fails to provide that teaching and learning efficiently and suitably.

(9) The teacher may be dismissed by the governing body, without the consent of the local authority, on the ground of failure to provide the teaching and learning efficiently and suitably.

(10) Subsection (9) does not apply where the school has a delegated budget.

(11) Teaching and learning within this section is teaching and learning in Religion, Values and Ethics that accords with—

(a) any provisions of the school's trust deed that relate to teaching and learning in Religion, Values and Ethics, or

(b) if there are no such provisions, the tenets of the religion or religious denomination specified in relation to the school under section 68A.

(12) In this section—

"the appropriate body" means—

(a) in relation to a foundation school, the governing body, and

(b) in relation to a voluntary controlled school, the local authority;

"Religion, Values and Ethics" has the same meaning as in the Curriculum and Assessment (Wales) Act 2021.

…

60 Staff at foundation or voluntary school with religious character.

(1) This section applies to a foundation or voluntary school which has a religious character.

(2) If the school is a foundation or voluntary controlled school, then (subject to subsections (3) and (4) below) section 59(2) to (4) shall apply to the school as they apply to a foundation or voluntary controlled school which does not have a religious character.

(3) Section 59(2) to (4) shall not so apply in relation to a reserved teacher at the school; and instead subsection (5) below shall apply in relation to such a teacher as it applies in relation to a teacher at a voluntary aided school.

(4) In connection with the appointment of a person to be head teacher of the school (whether foundation or voluntary controlled) in a case where the head teacher is not to be a reserved teacher regard may be had to that person's ability and fitness to preserve and develop the religious character of the school.

(5) If the school is a voluntary aided school—

(a) preference may be given, in connection with the appointment, remuneration or promotion of teachers at the school, to persons—

(i) whose religious opinions are in accordance with the tenets of the religion or religious denomination specified in relation to the school under section 68A or section 69(4), or

(ii) who attend religious worship in accordance with those tenets, or

(iii) who give, or are willing to give, religious education at the school in accordance with those tenets (in the case of a school in England) or to provide teaching and learning in Religion, Values and Ethics in accordance with those tenets (in the case of a school in Wales); and

(b) regard may be had, in connection with the termination of the employment or engagement of any teacher at the school, to any conduct on his part which is incompatible with the precepts, or with the upholding of the tenets, of the religion or religious denomination so specified.

(6) If the school is a voluntary aided school in Wales, no person shall be disqualified by reason of his religious opinions, or of his attending or omitting to attend religious worship, from being employed or engaged for the purposes of the school otherwise than as a teacher.

(7) Where immediately before the appointed day a teacher at a school which on that day becomes a school to which this section applies enjoyed, by virtue of section 304 or 305 of the Education Act 1996 (religious opinions of staff etc.), any rights not conferred on him by this section as a teacher at a school to which it applies, he shall continue to enjoy those rights (in addition to those conferred by this section) until he ceases to be employed as a teacher at the school.

(8) In this section "reserved teacher", in relation to a foundation or voluntary controlled school, means a person employed at the school in pursuance of section 58(2).

...

124A. Employment of teachers at independent schools having a religious character

(1) This section applies to an independent school which has a religious character, other than an Academy to which section 124AA applies.

(2) Preference may be given, in connection with the appointment, promotion or remuneration of teachers at the school, to persons—
   (a) whose religious opinions are in accordance with the tenets of the religion or the religious denomination specified in relation to the school under section 124B(2), or
   (b) who attend religious worship in accordance with those tenets, or
   (c) who give, or are willing to give, religious education at the school in accordance with those tenets.

(3) Regard may be had, in connection with the termination of the employment or engagement of any teacher at the school, to any conduct on his part which is incompatible with the precepts, or with the upholding of the tenets, of the religion or religious denomination so specified.

124AA Staff at certain Academies with religious character

(1) This section applies if—
   (a) an Academy order has been made in respect of a foundation or voluntary controlled school which is designated by order under section 69(3) as a school having a religious character,
   (b) the school has been converted into an Academy (see section 4(3) of the Academies Act 2010), and
   (c) the Secretary of State has not made an order in respect of the school under subsection (2).

(2) The Secretary of State may by order provide that this section does not apply to a school specified in the order.

(3) Where there are more than two teachers at the Academy, the teachers must include persons who—

(a) are selected for their fitness and competence to give religious education in accordance with the tenets of the religion or the religious denomination specified in relation to the Academy in the order under section 69(3) (as applied by section 6(8) of the Academies Act 2010), and

(b) are specifically appointed to do so.

A teacher employed or engaged at the Academy in pursuance of this subsection is a "reserved teacher", and any other teacher at the Academy is a "non-reserved teacher".

(4) The number of reserved teachers in the Academy must not exceed one-fifth of the total number of teachers, including the principal (and for this purpose, where the total number of teachers is not a multiple of five, it is to be treated as if it were the next higher multiple of five).

(5) In connection with the appointment of a person to be the principal of the Academy, in a case where the principal is not to be a reserved teacher, regard may be had to that person's ability and fitness to preserve and develop the religious character of the Academy.

(6) Preference may be given, in connection with the appointment, promotion or remuneration of reserved teachers at the Academy, to persons—

(a) whose religious opinions are in accordance with the tenets of the religion or the religious denomination specified in relation to the Academy in the order under section 69(3) (as applied by section 6(8) of the Academies Act 2010), or

(b) who attend religious worship in accordance with those tenets, or

(c) who give, or are willing to give, religious education at the Academy in accordance with those tenets.

(7) Regard may be had, in connection with the termination of employment or engagement of any reserved teacher at the Academy, to any conduct on the part of the teacher which is incompatible with the precepts, or with the upholding of the tenets, of the religion or religious denomination specified in the order under section 69(3) (as applied by section 6(8) of the Academies Act 2010).

(8) No person, other than a reserved teacher, is to be disqualified by reason of their religious opinions, or of their attending or omitting to attend religious worship—
   (a) from being a teacher at the Academy, or
   (b) from being employed or engaged for the purposes of the Academy otherwise than as a teacher.

(9) A non-reserved teacher must not be required to give religious education.

(10) A non-reserved teacher must not receive any less remuneration than any other non-reserved teacher, or be deprived of, or disqualified for, any promotion or other advantage available to other non-reserved teachers—
   (a) for the reason that the teacher gives, or does not give, religious education, or
   (b) for reasons related to the teacher's religious opinions or to the teacher's attending or omitting to attend religious worship.]

6.2 *Religious Opinions of and Acts of Worship by Teachers in Schools without a Religious Character*

The original provision in the Education Act 1944, section 30 (reproduced at ch. 5, section 2), on employment has seen several adjustments in the light of the changing statutory framework for the organisation of school education and the variety of schools for which standards have to be set. The provisions below contained in the School Standards and Framework Act 1998 are those currently applicable and they take into account the changes that have been made since the 1998 Act was enacted. Although they relate to a specific area of employment, they are set out in this chapter because of their relevance to schooling. The 1998 Act (as amended) makes provision for a variety of schools which now exist that have a religious character. It ought to be noted that while the 1998 Act, section 59, prohibits schools from remunerating, disqualifying or depriving of a promotion or other advantage on religious grounds, the variety of schools with an Islamic religious character would be able to rely on the other relevant statutory provisions (ch. 7, section 6.1) in order to show preferences for teachers on religious grounds. It is possible that in cases such as Operation Trojan Horse in Birmingham, where there were some moves to remove a headteacher, or the suspension of a religious studies teacher from the Batley Grammar School for showing an image of the prophet Mohamed, can amount to a breach of section 59(2), which prohibits disqualification on account of a teacher's religious opinions, although other legal grounds such as straightforward discrimination, harassment or victimisation under the Equality Act 2010 might also be potentially invoked in such cases.[17]

School Standards and Framework Act 1998

Religious opinions etc. of staff

59. Staff at community, secular foundation or voluntary, or special school.
(1) This section applies to—
  (a) a community school or a community or foundation special school, or
  (b) a foundation or voluntary school which does not have a religious character.
(2) No person shall be disqualified by reason of his religious opinions, or of his attending or omitting to attend religious worship—
  (a) from being a teacher at the school, or
  (b) from being employed or engaged for the purposes of the school otherwise than as a teacher.
(3) No teacher at the school shall be required to give religious education (in the case of a school in England) or to provide teaching and learning in Religion, Values and Ethics (in the case of a school in Wales).
(4) No teacher at the school shall receive any less remuneration or be deprived of, or disqualified for, any promotion or other advantage—
  (a) by reason of the fact that he does or does not give religious education or (as the case may be) provide teaching and learning in Religion, Values and Ethics, or
  (b) by reason of his religious opinions or of his attending or omitting to attend religious worship.

7 Relationships and Sex Education

Relationships and sex education (RSE) are a part of the statutory guidance which the British government has to issue. The current document, which was

17 On the Trojan Horse affair, and specifically the treatment of a Sikh headteacher, Balwant Bains, see ibid., and more generally on the affair Nash, P. (2022), *British Islam and English law: A classical pluralist perspective*. Cambridge: Cambridge University Press, esp. at pp. 192–218. On the Batley case see "Batley Grammar School protest report 'deeply disturbing'—MP," 26 March 2021, https://www.bbc.co.uk/news/uk-england-leeds-68659435, accessed on 12 February 2025.

issued in 2019, is entitled *Relationships Education, Relationships and Sex Education (RSE) and Health Education*.[18] It is worded in a generic manner and refers to religion and faith without specifying any issues of specific concern to Islam or Muslims. It states that all schools may teach about faith perspectives which pertain to relationships and sex. It envisages that schools with a religious character may teach a distinctive faith perspective on relationships, and that balanced debate may take place about issues that are seen as contentious. As an example, it states that such schools may wish to reflect on faith teachings about certain topics as well as on how their faith institutions may support people in matters of relationships and sex. It goes on to say that the teaching in all schools should reflect the law (including the Equality Act 2010) as it applies to relationships, so that young people clearly understand what the law does and does not allow, and the wider legal implications of decisions they may make.

As the guidance relates to the expectations to be met at the end of primary schooling, it states that schools must also ensure that their teaching and materials on sex education are appropriate, having regard to the age and religious backgrounds of their pupils. This is left quite unspecific and it is unclear what appropriateness to religious background would mean in practice. It is presumably what schools must work out for themselves. Under the heading "Families and those who care for me" the guidance states that primary school pupils must leave knowing that marriage and civil partnerships represent a formal and legally recognised commitment of two people to each other which is intended to be lifelong. It refers to the fact that marriage in England and Wales is available to both opposite-sex and same-sex couples. The Marriage (Same Sex Couples) Act 2013 extended marriage to same-sex couples in England and Wales.

RSE may come into conflict with Muslim religious beliefs and expectations in a number of ways. Opinion surveys and studies of Muslims in Britain have consistently indicated their opposition to homosexuality and include the desire for its criminalisation at rates which are much higher than those coming from other segments of the population.[19] Gay Muslims therefore face isola-

18 Relationships Education, Relationships and Sex Education (RSE) and Health Education Statutory guidance for governing bodies, proprietors, head teachers, principals, senior leadership teams, teachers. https://assets.publishing.service.gov.uk/media/62cea352e90e071e789ea9bf/Relationships_Education_RSE_and_Health_Education.pdf.

19 Taher, A., "A third of Muslims students back killings," in *The Sunday Times*, 27 July 2008, citing a YouGov poll used for a report produced by the Centre for Social Cohesion. "Muslims in Britain have zero tolerance of homosexuality, says poll," *The Guardian*, 7 May 2009, https://www.theguardian.com/uk/2009/may/07/muslims-britain-france-germany-homosexuality, accessed on 12 February 2025, which compares Muslims in France and Germany to British Muslims who have less favourable views of homosexuality; Casey, L. (2016), *The*

tion and other difficulties such as being forced into marriages.[20] Many Muslims might therefore disagree with RSE in schools, and protests of the kind seen in the *Birmingham City Council v Afshar* case (below) should not be surprising, notwithstanding the fact that the protestors may not have an accurate grasp of the contents of RSE, as the facts of the same case show. It was in Birmingham that a number of schools came under scrutiny after the so-called "Operation Trojan Horse" letter. The report into the investigation into 14 schools found that school governors and staff openly displayed homophobic behaviour.[21]

The RSE guidance further states that the ceremony in which a couple gets married may be civil or religious. This is an interesting reference, since it is ambiguously worded and links to the situation of many unregistered marriages among Muslims in Britain, although any causal effect can be doubted. This is especially so considering that the section stipulates that by the end of secondary school pupils should know what marriage is, including its legal status, for example, "that marriage carries legal rights and protections not available to couples who are cohabiting or who have married, for example, in an unregistered religious ceremony."[22]

Birmingham City Council v Afsar
[2019] EWHC 3217 (QB)

Although it was not a direct party, this case concerned a mixed-sex primary school with approximately 700 children, a majority of whom were of British Pakistani heritage. The local authority ("the council") sought the continuation of interim injunctions which had been granted to restrict street protests near the school and to prohibit the online abuse of its teachers. In February 2019, some parents asked the school to stop teaching "LGBT" issues. Protests took

---

Casey Review: A review into opportunity and integration. Her Majesty's Stationery Office, p. 111, citing an ICM poll of April 2016; and see the studies cited by Hlaimi, S. and Littlewood, C. (2023), "Too Muslim to be homosexual or too homosexual to be Muslim: Belonging experiences of British homosexual Muslims," *Journal of Muslims in Europe*, 13(2), pp. 162–192.

20 "More men being forced into marriage," 1 July 2010, https://www.gov.uk/government/news/more-men-being-forced-into-marriage, accessed on 12 February 2025.

21 Clarke, P. (2014), *Report into allegations concerning Birmingham schools arising from the 'Trojan Horse' letter*. London: Her Majesty's Stationery Office, pp. 45–46.

22 Relationships Education, Relationships and Sex Education (RSE) and Health Education Statutory guidance for governing bodies, proprietors, head teachers, principals, senior leadership teams, teachers, p. 27. https://assets.publishing.service.gov.uk/media/62cea352e90e071e789ea9bf/Relationships_Education_RSE_and_Health_Education.pdf.

place outside the school nearly every school day from the middle of March to June 2019. The usual number of protestors was around 10 to 30. They chanted slogans using a microphone or megaphone. Speakers alleged that the school was pursuing "a paedophile agenda" and teaching children how to masturbate. Leaflets alleged that the school was providing LGBT sexual education, and videos accused it, for example, of bringing in gay teachers to teach children about anal sex. The court accepted that these claims about teaching at the school were false. On several occasions, police concluded that the gathering posed a danger to those involved in the protest and to those wanting to park and use the road. On one day at least 60 people were present and a police riot van attended because of the perceived risk of violence. The local authority had obtained the interim injunctions to curtail the way in which some of the objections were expressed. Of the five defendants, the first three were individual protestors who were family members of children at the school; the fourth was a group of unidentified protestors and the fifth was an individual who had been joined on his own application to resist a part of the claim that sought to prohibit the online abuse of teachers. The injunctions prohibited: (a) entry into a designated area around the school (the exclusion zone); (b) conduct which harassed, alarmed or caused distress to others; (c) the approaching of school staff or witnesses in the case; (d) the use of social media to offend or abuse teachers; and (e) otherwise engaging in or encouraging others to protest within the exclusion zone against the "teaching of equalities" at the school. Among the claims made by the defendants was that the teaching and conduct of the school amounted to unlawful discrimination against Pakistani Muslim children contrary to the Equality Act 2010 and the Human Rights Act 1998. The judgment of Warby J. is useful in examining the extent to which the Equality Act 2010 and the Human Rights Act, and, effectively, Article 2, Protocol 1 to the ECHR, permit objections to the syllabus as taught by schools and whether interferences against protests (such as with injunctions to limit protests) about policies that are claimed to be unlawful violate the same statutes. The judge also considered the effect of ECHR, Articles 8, 9, 10 and 11, and did not find any violation of them.

…

> 18. Each of the four individual defendants made a witness statement, gave oral evidence confirming the statement, and was cross-examined—in the case of Mr Allman, very briefly (he was not challenged on most of what he said). The first three defendants called additional factual evidence from Rosina Akhtar ("Mrs Akhtar"), and expert evidence from two witnesses. One of these was Ajmal Masroor ("Imam Masroor"), an Imam and broadcaster, who offered opinions on a

range of religious, ethical and social issues. The other was John Holmwood, Professor of Sociology in the School of Sociology and Social Policy at the University of Nottingham. Prof. Holmwood addressed regulatory frameworks; their interrelationship with the EA; the professional expectations of senior managers in relation to the implementation of those frameworks; and the impact on children with regard to social integration and welfare. All these additional witnesses gave oral evidence and were cross-examined.

...

38. It was in support of this part of their case that the defendants called from Imam Masroor. The Imam expressed a number of opinions about aspects of the School's conduct, all of which were based on hearsay and which, in my judgment, are issues for me to determine. His principal remit was to provide expert evidence as to Islamic doctrine and teaching. His report did however correctly identify the nature of the issue at the centre of the debate as whether schools should be teaching young children of primary school age about the different types of relationship that exist in the UK today, including homosexuality as a valid form of family relationship. He said, "there is no simple answer to this question". He set out to identify the Islamic approach to sex and sexuality, and its inter-relationship with teaching. The following aspects of the Imam's evidence on those issues were not disputed. "A Muslim can have homosexual, bisexual or transsexual thoughts or tendencies" but they commit grave sins if they translate their thoughts into sexual acts. There is "no room for ... kinds of sexual relationship" other than the heterosexual, which is "the moral absolute in Islam." In Islam, "standing up against wrong is a religious obligation". His evidence was that "equality should not be confused with sexuality" and "certainly should not be taught as only a sexual act and the promotion of casual sexual behaviour". The principle that, in his opinion, "should form the bedrock for teaching human relationship" is one that he identifies as clearly stated in the Quran: "everyone is born with inalienable right to dignity, honour and respect regardless of their background."

...

42. The Council submits that the defence case proceeds from a number of inaccurate factual premises, set out in the defendants' witness statements and repeated in the skeleton argument filed by their Counsel. The Council's factual case is that it is teaching children about all aspects of equality, after conducting appropriate consultations; it has made every effort to engage with parents in relation to this teaching. And the Council maintains that it has not acted in any way that can properly be said to involve unlawful discrimination against any of the defendants, or any member of the group relied on. But the Council has two more

fundamental answers to this part of the defence case: (1) allegations of discrimination cannot be an answer to the Council's claim for an injunction; (2) in any event, the conduct to which objection has been taken is outside the scope of the EA [Equality Act].

43. In the Interim Judgment … I observed that it might be open to the protestors to seek judicial review of the educational policy that has been adopted and applied at the School, but it was "not easy to see how the merits of that policy can figure large in this case". That remains my view, despite the submissions of [counsel for the defendants] Mr de Mello. …

44. The EA does not outlaw all discrimination based on any protected characteristic. It covers specific territory, carefully mapped out in the Act. Conduct is only unlawful discrimination if it relates to an activity falling within one or more of Parts 3 to 7 of the Act, which cover, respectively, Services and Public Functions, Premises, Work, Education, and Associations. … The application is for an order curtailing what is said to be anti-social behaviour, public nuisance, and obstruction of the highway. The application pursues inherently legitimate aims, concerned with upholding the rights of others. The Council's conduct in seeking such injunctions does not fall within the ambit of the EA.

45. Even if that is wrong, the acts complained of appear to me to fall outside the scope of the EA. Education in schools is covered by Part 6, Chapter 1 of the EA. The relevant provisions for present purposes are contained in ss 85 and 89.

…

[The court then sets out the relevant parts of the Equality Act, sections 85 and 89]

…

46. The proscribed conduct is, therefore, discrimination by the local authority or governing body against a pupil "in the way it provides education for the pupil", and in the other ways identified above; but not in "anything done in connection with the content of the curriculum." It is not easy to see how the conduct complained of, as regards the pupils, can fall within s 85(2)(b), (d) or (f). Although all those sub-paragraphs have been mentioned in the defendants' written materials, the defendants have nowhere pleaded, nor have they set out in writing or orally any detailed case in relation to those provisions. The argument has focused on s 85(2)(a) and its relationship with s 89.

47. Mr Manning [counsel for the claimants] submits that the term "curriculum", in its context within s 89(2), embraces all learning and other experiences that

a school plans for its pupils, and that the national curriculum forms only part of this. Mr de Mello counters that s 85(2)(a) should be given an expansive interpretation, and that the term "curriculum" in s 89 has a narrow meaning, denoting the national curriculum, and not any other aspect of what is taught in schools. Since the teaching of "LGBT issues" and equality in the School is not required or covered by the national curriculum, the argument goes, the discrimination complained of is proscribed by s 85(2)(a). In my judgment, Mr Manning's submissions are clearly to be preferred.

48. As is common knowledge, the national curriculum is a prescribed sub-set of what is taught in schools. It is one element of the picture, albeit an important one. The national curriculum is not new. It has been a feature of the education landscape for over thirty years, first prescribed by the Education Reform Act 1988. It would be odd, to say the least, if Parliament had meant EA s 89(2) to exempt only things done in respect of the "national curriculum", for it to use the single word "curriculum". It is not plausible, in any event, to ascribe to Parliament an intention to afford local authorities and governing bodies protection against allegations of discrimination in connection with things done in relation to the content of the "national curriculum". The content of the national curriculum is not the responsibility of a local authority or school governing body. Even if such limited protection had an identifiable purpose, it would leave the responsible bodies open to attack in relation to the content of other, more peripheral, aspects of what is taught in schools. No rational ground for such a policy has been identified. Furthermore, the language of s 85(2)(a) supports Mr Manning's submissions. The distinction may sometimes be blurred in practice, but in principle there is a clear distinction between the content of the curriculum at a School, and "the way it provides education".

49. Mr Manning has helpfully referred me to the Explanatory Notes to the EA, and to paragraph 2.2 of the National Curriculum in England: Key Stages 1 and 2 Framework Document (September 2013). I am not sure that the latter is a legitimate aid to construction, but the Explanatory Notes certainly are, and they support the Council's argument.[23] The Notes say this:

> "**Effect**
> 302. This section … makes it clear that the prohibitions in the Chapter do not apply to anything done in relation to the content of the school curriculum. …

23 As this passage suggests, the explanatory notes to legislation are treated in British legal systems as aids to its interpretation.

The way in which the curriculum is taught is, however, covered by the reference to education in section 85(2)(a), so as to ensure issues are taught in a way which does not subject pupils to discrimination. ....

Background

303. This section is designed to replicate the effect of an exception relating to discrimination because of religion or belief in the Equality Act 2006, and extends it to other protected characteristics.

Examples

- A school curriculum includes teaching of evolution in science lessons. This would not be religious discrimination against a pupil whose religious beliefs include creationism.
- A school curriculum includes *The Taming of the Shrew* on the syllabus. This would not be discrimination against a girl."

The second example is very much in point, given the defendants' reliance on specific books, as part of their PCP [provision, criterion or practice].[24] It indicates, rightly in my judgment, that a decision to use a particular text as part of a programme of instruction is likely to be something done in relation to "curriculum content".

50. I cannot accept Mr de Mello's invitation to give the wording of s 89(2) the narrow interpretation for which he contends, on the grounds that giving the words their natural meaning would militate against the purpose of the Act. This seems to me to be circular reasoning, as it presumes a legislative intention to do something other than that which the statutory wording indicates. To adopt this approach would deprive the sub-section of all or most of the effect it is evidently intended to have. It is easy to understand the rationale for the exemption. The purpose of s 89(2) is to enable a school to teach controversial material without being accused of contravening the EA. Paragraph 302 of the Explanatory Notes makes this clear:-

> This ensures that the Act does not inhibit the ability of schools to include a full range of issues, ideas and materials in their syllabus and to expose pupils to thoughts and ideas of all kinds.

51. The exemption is cast in broad terms; it does not just apply to decisions about the curriculum content, but to "anything done in connection with" that content.

24 This wording, "provision, criterion or practice", refers to the Equality Act 2010, section 19, which defines indirect discrimination. See ch. 4, section 1 for the extract.

This is consistent with an intention to protect against collateral attack. In my judgment, the PCP alleged by the defendants is entirely concerned with the "content of the curriculum" within the meaning of s 89(2). None of it is about the "way education is delivered" so as to fall with s 85(2)(a), and outside the scope of that sub-section.

52. The defendants' pleaded case on this issue goes beyond complaint about discrimination against pupils in relation to the content of the curriculum. Paragraphs 7, 8 and 9 of the Amended Defence allege discrimination against parents, and those in parental roles, including Mrs and Mr Afsar. Paragraph 9.1 contains 13 sub-paragraphs alleging conduct said to be direct discrimination, and to demonstrate "expressive harm and detriment suffered by" a group of "parents/pupils/protestors/close associates". It is unnecessary to list all the complaints. It is enough to say that they include the language used by the Head Teacher towards and about parents and protestors opposing the School's policy; decisions to invite an MP and others onto the school premises; failures or deficiencies in consultation; the inclusion of a rainbow colour on the School's letterhead; and various other collateral matters. These aspects of the claim face several difficulties. First, these are not complaints about "the way in which education is delivered" by the School. Secondly, as I have noted, the conduct proscribed by EA s 85 is discrimination against pupils, not parents, still less discrimination against third parties who hold views about the content of the curriculum or, indeed, the way in which education is delivered. Aggrieved parents and interested third parties have no standing to complain of a contravention of Part 6 of the EA.

...

[The court also considered whether the complainant had breached the duty in the Equality Act, section 29 not to discriminate in the provision of services.]

58. No doubt education authorities are public authorities for the purposes of s 29. Schools may provide services to members of the public, for instance by making their facilities available out of hours to parents, or others, for non-educational purposes. I am unable to see how s 29 could be relied on in relation to any alleged discrimination against protestors who are not parents of pupils at the school, or "close associates" (if such a contention is pursued). Those are not people to whom the school is providing any relevant service, or persons requesting a service from the school. Nor is the delivery of teaching by a state school to a child pursuant to a statutory duty the provision of a service to parents. Nor can it realistically be said that Ms Afsar was a person "requesting a service" from the Head Teacher, such that (for instance) permitting third parties to tie ribbons to the school gates

(at a weekend) represented a "detriment" to which the Head Teacher subjected Mrs Afsar "in the course of providing a service".

…

60. In these circumstances, it is unnecessary for me to address in detail the further factual and legal submissions advanced by the parties in relation to the pleaded case of discrimination. I will however say that at the end of the evidence and argument I was left unpersuaded that the School had engaged in any illegitimate direct or indirect discrimination against any of the defendants, on the grounds of race, religion or belief.

61. It is necessary to have in mind the legal and policy context, which includes the following key features. A2P1 [Article 2, Protocol 1 to the ECHR] has two aspects. One is the right to education, possessed by all pupils at the School. The other is the right of parents "to ensure … education and training in conformity with their own religious and philosophical convictions", a right which the State must "respect." That second right is, in comparison with most other Convention guarantees, "a weak one", which is principally aimed at ensuring fair and non-discriminatory access to the state education system: *A v Head Teacher and Governors of Lord Grey School* [2006] UKHL 14 [2006] 2 AC 363 [24]. A2P1 does not prevent the State from imparting unwelcome information or knowledge: "It is not possible to deduce from the Convention a right not to be exposed to convictions contrary to one's own": *Appel-Irrgang v Germany* (Application No. 45216/07) [12]. A2P1 "does not even permit parents to object to the integration of such teaching in the school curriculum": *Kjeldsen v Denmark* (1979–1980) 1 EHRR 711 [53]. The key requirement is for the State to avoid indoctrination, confining itself to instruction that is "objective, critical and pluralistic": *Kjeldsen* (ibid.)

62. Domestic law requires the state, including local education authorities to "have regard to the general principle that pupils are to be educated in accordance with the wishes of their parents, so far as that is compatible with the provision of efficient instruction and training …": Education Act 1996, s 9. But the duty to "have regard" to parental wishes is not a duty to comply with those wishes. An authority can have regard to other things as well, and can make exceptions to the general principle …. An authority must, in addition, comply with the duties imposed by s 11 of the Children Act 2004 (to safeguard and promote the welfare of children), s 78 of the Education Act 2002 (to promote fundamental British values so as to ensure that pupils are able to understand the norms of modern British society), and s 149 of the EA (to have due regard to the need to achieve the equality objectives set out in that section). The equality objectives include the elimina-

tion of discrimination prohibited by the EA, and fostering good relations between people with a protected characteristic and those who do not share it: s 149(1)(a) and (c). Sexual orientation is a protected characteristic: s 149(7).

63. The defendants' case involves much criticism of the School's approach to consultation, including a complaint that parents have not been permitted to "vet" the books their children will be given or allowed to read. The defendants have however failed to identify any legal duty to consult. There was in fact engagement, as I shall explain. I do not consider the School's conduct in this respect is open to objection, as a matter of law. I do not accept Mr de Mello's contention, that the School failed to take account of racial or religious considerations, in breach of s 149 of the EA. Nor am I persuaded that the School's decision to provide its pupils with the limited instruction in relation to sexual orientation … notwithstanding objection from some parents on cultural, religious or philosophical grounds, involves direct or indirect discrimination against the pupils or their parents on grounds of race, religion or belief. I find it hard to detect any real conflict between what the school is teaching, and the beliefs identified by Imam Masroor, which I have set out above. If, contrary to my views, the limited instruction provided does represent indirect discrimination, it is justified by the need to comply with the legal requirements I have identified.

64. With respect to Prof Holmwood his views, trenchant as they were, did not assist me. The topics on which he had been asked to provide his opinions were somewhat diffuse, and their relationship with the legal issues I have had to decide was tangential. He expressed opinions, for instance, on whether, under the Ofsted inspection criteria, fault might be found with the School because relationships with the parents had broken down, without more. I have not been able to see how an opinion on that question can help me resolve the issues defined above. His conclusion, that an injunction would not address the underlying causes of the protest, may well be right. But that is not the aim and purpose of the injunction. He is clearly right to say that if the causes of the protest are removed the need for an injunction disappears. But his assessment of the causes is not the same as mine. Much of what he said was founded upon an account of events provided to him by the defendants, which does not correspond with what, after a 5-day trial, I find to be the facts. It seems to me, moreover, that while the causes of the protest have not been removed, it is legitimate to protect innocent third parties from unwarranted intrusion into their private and family lives, and homes.

CHAPTER 8

Further and Higher (Tertiary) Education

Some of the background to and dimensions of the Prevent programme have been discussed in chapter 2 above. The Prevent programme was placed on a statutory footing under the Counter-Terrorism and Security Act 2015, under which "specified authorities" came under a duty to "prevent people from being drawn into terrorism" (section 26(1)). The Act empowered the Secretary of State to issue guidance to the specified authorities, which include institutions of further and higher education. In addition, local authorities, prisons or offenders' institutions, schools, health providers and police bodies are also classed as specified authorities by Schedule 6 of the Act. Institutions of further and higher education and the Secretary of State, when issuing the relevant guidance, must have particular regard to "the duty to ensure freedom of speech" and "to the importance of academic freedom" (section 31). Although universities, higher education trade unions and individual academics have been critical of the Prevent duty, the 2015 Act does address the importance of both free speech and academic freedom, alongside the Human Rights Act 1998.[1]

The provisions on universities in the Counter-Terrorism and Security Act 2015 are of particular interest for this chapter. In 2008, a study showed that a third of British Muslim students believed that killing in the name of Islam can be justified, two in five students supported the incorporation of *Shari'a* codes into British law, and substantial proportions of Muslim students were against free mixing between men and women, had little or no respect for gays, and supported the creation of a world-wide caliphate.[2] Universities were also the site for extremist preachers who supported or advocated such positions and were described as sites for radicalisation. There have been several incidents of speak-

1 These duties may have become subject to revision in the light of the Higher Education (Freedom of Speech) Act 2023 which introduced consequential amendments to the 2015 Act, especially because the 2023 Act contained a more active duty to "take steps to secure freedom of speech". Although the new government at Westminster postponed the coming into force of the Act until 1 August 2025, one year after the originally planned commencement, and it does not intend to bring the entirety of the legislation into force, it is not thought that the duty will be affected.

2 Taher, A. (2008), "A third of Muslim students back killings," *The Sunday Times*, 27 July 2008, citing a YouGov poll used for a report produced by the Centre for Social Cohesion. In *R v Zafar and others* [2008] EWCA Crim 184 4 of the 5 defendants were students at Bradford University and planned to travel to Pakistan to receive training and thereafter commit a terrorist act or acts in Afghanistan.

ers at universities being "cancelled" or disrupted because of accusations that speakers have Islamophobic views.[3] Additionally, university academics have been threatened by students or student societies that adopt extreme Islamic attitudes, while universities may accede to the demands for curtailment of academic freedom through changes in curricula or penalties imposed on academics.[4]

Counter-Terrorism and Security Act 2015

26 General duty on specified authorities

(1) A specified authority must, in the exercise of its functions, have due regard to the need to prevent people from being drawn into terrorism.

(2) A specified authority is a person or body that is listed in Schedule 6.

(3) In the case of a specified authority listed in Schedule 6 in terms that refer to the exercise of particular functions or to a particular capacity that it has, the reference in subsection (1) to the authority's functions is to those functions or its functions when acting in that capacity.

29 Power to issue guidance

(1) The Secretary of State may issue guidance to specified authorities about the exercise of their duty under section 26(1).

(2) A specified authority must have regard to any such guidance in carrying out that duty.

(3) The Secretary of State—

   (a) may issue separate guidance in relation to different matters;

   (b) may issue guidance to all specified authorities, to particular specified authorities or to specified authorities of a particular description.

(4) Before issuing guidance under subsection (1) the Secretary of State must (whether before or after this Act is passed) consult—

3 Khan, S. and McMahon, T. (2016), *The battle for British Islam: Reclaiming Muslim identity from extremism*. London: Saqi, pp. 119–128.

4 For one such case that involved the targeting of Prof. Steven Greer, a specialist in terrorism research, initiated by a student Islamic society at Bristol university on grounds of Islamophobia, see Greer, S. (2023), *Falsely accused of Islamophobia: My struggle against academic cancellation*. Washington: Academica Press. The University of Bristol commissioned a Queen's Counsel's report clearing Prof. Greer of Islamophobia but a freedom of information request by the present writer for that report was rejected.

(a) the Welsh Ministers so far as the guidance relates to the devolved Welsh functions of a Welsh authority;
(b) the Scottish Ministers so far as the guidance relates to the devolved Scottish functions of a Scottish authority;
(c) any person whom the Secretary of State considers appropriate.

(5) Guidance issued under subsection (1) takes effect on whatever day the Secretary of State appoints by regulations made by statutory instrument.
A statutory instrument containing regulations under this subsection may not be made unless a draft of the instrument has been laid before each House of Parliament and approved by a resolution of each House.

(6) The Secretary of State may from time to time revise any guidance issued under this section.

(7) Subsections (2), (3) and (5) have effect in relation to any revised guidance.

(8) Subsection (4) has effect in relation to any revised guidance unless the Secretary of State considers that the proposed revisions to the guidance are insubstantial.

(9) The Secretary of State must publish the current version of any guidance issued under this section.

30 Power to give directions: general

(1) Where the Secretary of State is satisfied that a specified authority has failed to discharge the duty imposed on it by section 26(1), the Secretary of State may give directions to the authority for the purpose of enforcing the performance of that duty.

(2) A direction given under this section may be enforced, on an application made on behalf of the Secretary of State, by a mandatory order.

(3) The Secretary of State must consult the Welsh Ministers before giving directions under subsection (1) so far as relating to the devolved Welsh functions of a Welsh authority.

(4) The Secretary of State must consult the Scottish Ministers before giving directions under subsection (1) so far as relating to the devolved Scottish functions of a Scottish authority.

31 Freedom of expression in universities etc

(1) This section applies to a specified authority if it is the proprietor or governing body of—

(a) an institution that provides further education (within the meaning given by section 2(3) of the Education Act 1996), or
(b) an institution that provides courses of a description mentioned in Schedule 6 to the Education Reform Act 1988 (higher education courses).

(2) When carrying out the duty imposed by section 26(1), a specified authority to which this section applies—
(a) must have particular regard to the duty to ensure freedom of speech, if it is subject to that duty;
(b) must have particular regard to the importance of academic freedom, if it is the proprietor or governing body of a qualifying institution.

(3) When issuing guidance under section 29 to specified authorities to which this section applies, the Secretary of State—
(a) must have particular regard to the duty to ensure freedom of speech, in the case of authorities that are subject to that duty;
(b) must have particular regard to the importance of academic freedom, in the case of authorities that are proprietors or governing bodies of qualifying institutions.

(4) When considering whether to give directions under section 30 to a specified authority to which this section applies, the Secretary of State—
(a) must have particular regard to the duty to ensure freedom of speech, in the case of an authority that is subject to that duty;
(b) must have particular regard to the importance of academic freedom, in the case of an authority that is the proprietor or governing body of a qualifying institution.

(5) In this section—
"the duty to ensure freedom of speech" means the duty imposed by section 43(1) of the Education (No. 2) Act 1986;
"academic freedom" means the freedom referred to in section 202(2)(a) of the Education Reform Act 1988;
"qualifying institution" has the meaning given by section 202(3) of that Act.

Regina (Butt) v Secretary of State for the Home Department
[2019] EWCA Civ 256, [2019] 1 WLR, Court of Appeal

In September 2015 the Prime Minister's Office and the Home Office issued a press release announcing the coming into force of statutory guidance, the July

2015 revised Prevent Duty Guidance ("PDG"), whose purpose, together with the associated Higher Education Prevent Duty Guidance ("HEPDG"), was to explain how universities and other further educational institutions should give effect to their duty under section 26(1) of the Counter-Terrorism and Security Act 2015. The guidance advised that where a visiting speaker was likely to express extremist views, a higher education body should not allow him to speak unless it was entirely convinced that there was no risk of people being drawn into terrorism thereby. The press release stated, among other things, that the claimant, a British citizen and a practising Muslim who had spoken at universities at the invitation of student societies, had been identified as an extremist on the basis of research carried out by the Extremism Analysis Unit (EAU) of the Home Office. The claimant sought judicial review on a number of grounds. The relevant ones for present purposes are that the guidance was *ultra vires* the Secretary of State's power to issue guidance under section 29 of the 2015 Act in that it required universities to take steps to prevent people being drawn into non-violent extremism, which was not the same as terrorism (on which see the extract from the judgment below). The Administrative Court held, and the Court of Appeal agreed, that the claimant did not show that the guidance had any concrete impact on him. The Court of Appeal did agree with the claim, as against the decision of the Administrative Court, that the guidance to universities did not clarify, in line with the relevant legislation (section 43(1) of the Education (No. 2) Act 1986), that the free speech obligations of universities to "visiting speakers" extended not merely to invited speakers but also to those who would in future be invited to visit and speak.

> 79. There were three occasions on which the EAU obtained information about Dr Butt. …
>
> …
>
> 81. The third occasion followed the publication of the press release on 17 September 2015, which led to Dr Butt's MP, Fiona McTaggart, writing a letter to the Home Office Minister, Lord Tariq Ahmad, asking why Dr Butt was on the list, and also putting down a parliamentary question (PQ) on 9 October 2015 asking what evidence was used to identify the six hate preachers named in the press release and whether the evidence would be published which demonstrated that Dr Butt had expressed views at a university contrary to British values. In order to brief ministers, the EAU carried out a search of Home Office databases, including a search of the EAU's own databases. Nothing new was thrown up by that search. In addition, a search was made of Facebook, Twitter, Google and Islam21C. Those searches

resulted in the following answer to the PQ by Karen Bradley MP on 1 December 2015. In relation to Dr Butt, she said that he:

> is the chief editor of Islam21c, a publication that hosts material contrary to British values, and has himself expressed views of concern in this publication and on social media, appearing to compare homosexuality to paedophilia as a sin and supporting FGM. He has spoken alongside CAGE and used social media to support CAGE's position on Mohammed Emwazi ('Jihadi John'), which has been to try to justify his resort to violence.

154. As below, the Secretary of State submits that the Judge's analysis was correct when he considered the section 26 duty: it was to prevent a process occurring which would be likely to draw individuals into terrorism. The PDG does not equate or treat as synonymous "terrorism", "extremism", and "active or vocal opposition to fundamental British values". That equation is expressed by Mr Bowen [counsel for the claimant] to be one of his "core" submissions. The PDG recognises explicitly (see paragraph 8) that "extremism" as defined may be legal. However, it is also true that extremists may draw people into terrorism by radicalising them, creating an atmosphere which conduces to terrorism: see PDG paragraphs 7/8, HEPDG paragraphs 11, 19, 22 and 29. The Judge was right to reject the submission that the Guidance equates the terms in the way suggested.

155. In our view this aspect of Dr Butt's challenge cannot succeed. The Judge was correct in his conclusions. It is not in issue that preventing people from being drawn into terrorism is a legitimate aim: see the judgment below [*Regina (Butt) v Secretary of State for the Home Department* [2017] EWHC 1930 (Admin)] at [40]. The Guidance concerns the section 26 duty: it is directed to preventing people being drawn into terrorism through non-violent extremism. As the Judge put it:

> Non-violent extremism which carries no risk of drawing people into terrorism is not subject to the guidance. [129]

156. It cannot be a part of this challenge to assert that there is no such thing as non-violent extremism which carries the relevant risk. Firstly, that is not a point of law. Secondly, the Judge expressed rather cogently how this might arise: see [136] to [139]. The Judge's conclusion is expressed in [140]:

> 140. I regard it as plain that if non-violent extremism does risk drawing people into terrorism, then a degree of consideration, which may lead to RHEBs countering, mitigating or restricting that effect on its students towards whom they owe some safeguarding duty, (and ultimately that effect on the wider society

of which they form part) is a legitimate objective for government to set for achievement through guidance. I am far from clear that Mr Bowen submitted otherwise.

157. Provided that the "extremism" in question is understood as subject to the additional requirement that it must be of a kind such as to risk drawing people into terrorism, then the aim is legitimate and the Guidance *intra vires*.

CHAPTER 9

Islamic Chaplaincy in Public Institutions

The conception of chaplaincy has its roots in Christianity and its role in the context of non-Christian religions represents an expansion of that institution. Legislation and practice in different public institutions have allowed for chaplaincy to be gradually extended to ministers beyond those of the Church of England. Chaplaincies are to be found in the armed forces, prisons, hospitals, universities, schools, and in certain professions and industries. In the armed forces chaplains are appointed and carry out their duties not under statute, but under the Royal Prerogative, with the basic provisions set out in King's Regulations. Muslim chaplains alongside Buddhist, Hindu, and Sikh chaplains have been appointed as fully integrated members of the armed services chaplaincy, albeit as civil servants.[1]

In the prison service the institution of chaplaincy was formalised and provision made for its extension to non-Church of England ministers, as demonstrated in the Prison Act 1952, section 10, by amendment in 1963. The Prison Rules 1999 (SI 1999/728) provide more specific detail as to what is expected of chaplains in prisons. Both instruments refer to "denomination" rather than "religion". Prior to 2002 there were insufficient numbers of Muslim prisoners to warrant their employment, and they were engaged on a sessional basis. However, since then, Muslim chaplains have been employed by the Prison Service. The case of *Naeem v Secretary of State for Justice* (not extracted here) is an interesting one in this regard because it concerns a claim for discrimination in the salaries that were paid to the claimant as compared to those paid to other ministers.[2] The justification for this difference in salary, accepted by the Court of Appeal, was that Muslim chaplains had only recently begun to be engaged because of the change in the need for their service as the proportion of Muslim prisoners grew.

1 Rivers, J. (2010), *The law of organized religions: Between establishment and secularism*. Oxford: Oxford University Press, p. 209.

2 *Naeem v Secretary of State for Justice* [2015] EWCA Civ 1264, [2016] I.C.R. 289.

Prison Act 1952

10 Appointment of prison ministers.

(1) Where in any prison the number of prisoners who belong to a religious denomination other than the Church of England is such as in the opinion of the Secretary of State to require the appointment of a minister of that denomination, the Secretary of State may appoint such a minister to that prison.

(2) The Secretary of State may pay a minister appointed under the preceding subsection such remuneration as he thinks reasonable.

(3) The Secretary of State may allow a minister of any denomination other than the Church of England to visit prisoners of his denomination in a prison to which no minister of that denomination has been appointed under this section.

(4) No prisoner shall be visited against his will by such a minister as is mentioned in the last preceding subsection; but every prisoner not belonging to the Church of England shall be allowed, in accordance with the arrangements in force in the prison in which he is confined, to attend chapel or to be visited by the chaplain.

(5) The governor of a prison shall on the reception of each prisoner record the religious denomination to which the prisoner declares himself to belong, and shall give to any minister who under this section is appointed to the prison or permitted to visit prisoners therein a list of the prisoners who have declared themselves to belong to his denomination; and the minister shall not be permitted to visit any other prisoners.

The Prison Rules 1999

Regular visits by ministers of religion

15.—(1) The chaplain shall visit the prisoners belonging to the Church of England.

(2) A prison minister shall visit the prisoners of his denomination as regularly as he reasonably can.

(3) Where a prisoner belongs to a denomination for which no prison minister has been appointed, the governor shall do what he reasonably can, if so requested by the prisoner, to arrange for him to be visited regularly by a minister of that denomination.

CHAPTER 10

Employment and Social Law

Although the foundations of employment law lie in the common law, which is judge-made, there is a large amount of British employment-related legislation which includes that which implemented the EU rules on employment. However, until the Employment Equality (Religion or Belief) Regulations 2003, which reflected the United Kingdom's domestic implementation of European Union Council Directive 2000/78/EC, specific mention of religion within employment-related legislation was the exception.[1] One such exception occurs in the rules that relate to the employment of teachers and is discussed further below together with the case of *Ahmad*. The 2003 Regulations were the start of a greater recognition of religion within anti-discrimination law, which also includes employment within its scope. The 2003 regulations were later superseded by the Equality Act 2006 and then by the Equality Act 2010 (see ch. 4). Because of the relevance of the ECHR (especially Article 9), as well as anti-discrimination law, many cases occur in an employment context but are discussed elsewhere in this volume because of their closer relationship to the topics covered in the relevant chapters. In this chapter, a focus is maintained on employment-related law which may be regarded as peculiarly restricted or particularly relevant to the bounds of the employment context, and regarding the case law, because of the factual context in which it arises.[2]

1 Anti-discrimination Provisions on Employment

Besides the general principles contained in the Equality Act 2010 (see chapter 4), the same legislation makes specific reference to principles to be applied to employment- or work-related situations. These provisions in sections 39–41 flesh out the variety of situations in which discrimination may be claimed to arise. In addition, sections 44 and 45 (not extracted here) apply to partnerships and limited liability partnerships.

1 See Knights, S. (2021), *Law, rights, and religion*. Oxford: Oxford University Press. pp. 160–161.

2 See ch. 12, section 1 for the parts of the Equality Act 2010 that relate to the provision of goods, services and facilities.

Equality Act 2010

39 Employees and applicants

(1) An employer (A) must not discriminate against a person (B)—
  (a) in the arrangements A makes for deciding to whom to offer employment;
  (b) as to the terms on which A offers B employment;
  (c) by not offering B employment.

(2) An employer (A) must not discriminate against an employee of A's (B)—
  (a) as to B's terms of employment;
  (b) in the way A affords B access, or by not affording B access, to opportunities for promotion, transfer or training or for receiving any other benefit, facility or service;
  (c) by dismissing B;
  (d) by subjecting B to any other detriment.

(3) An employer (A) must not victimise a person (B)—
  (a) in the arrangements A makes for deciding to whom to offer employment;
  (b) as to the terms on which A offers B employment;
  (c) by not offering B employment.

(4) An employer (A) must not victimise an employee of A's (B)—
  (a) as to B's terms of employment;
  (b) in the way A affords B access, or by not affording B access, to opportunities for promotion, transfer or training or for any other benefit, facility or service;
  (c) by dismissing B;
  (d) by subjecting B to any other detriment.

(5) A duty to make reasonable adjustments applies to an employer.

(6) Subsection (1)(b), so far as relating to sex or pregnancy and maternity, does not apply to a term that relates to pay—
  (a) unless, were B to accept the offer, an equality clause or rule would have effect in relation to the term, or
  (b) if paragraph (a) does not apply, except in so far as making an offer on terms including that term amounts to a contravention of subsection (1)(b) by virtue of section 13, 14 or 18.

(7) In subsections (2)(c) and (4)(c), the reference to dismissing B includes a reference to the termination of B's employment—
  (a) by the expiry of a period (including a period expiring by reference to an event or circumstance);

(b) by an act of B's (including giving notice) in circumstances such that B is entitled, because of A's conduct, to terminate the employment without notice.

(8) Subsection (7)(a) does not apply if, immediately after the termination, the employment is renewed on the same terms.

40 Employees and applicants: harassment

(1) An employer (A) must not, in relation to employment by A, harass a person (B)—

(a) who is an employee of A's;

(b) who has applied to A for employment.

41 Contract workers

(1) A principal must not discriminate against a contract worker—

(a) as to the terms on which the principal allows the worker to do the work;

(b) by not allowing the worker to do, or to continue to do, the work;

(c) in the way the principal affords the worker access, or by not affording the worker access, to opportunities for receiving a benefit, facility or service;

(d) by subjecting the worker to any other detriment.

(2) A principal must not, in relation to contract work, harass a contract worker.

(3) A principal must not victimise a contract worker—

(a) as to the terms on which the principal allows the worker to do the work;

(b) by not allowing the worker to do, or to continue to do, the work;

(c) in the way the principal affords the worker access, or by not affording the worker access, to opportunities for receiving a benefit, facility or service;

(d) by subjecting the worker to any other detriment.

(4) A duty to make reasonable adjustments applies to a principal (as well as to the employer of a contract worker).

(5) A "principal" is a person who makes work available for an individual who is—

(a) employed by another person, and

(b) supplied by that other person in furtherance of a contract to which the principal is a party (whether or not that other person is a party to it).

(6) "Contract work" is work such as is mentioned in subsection (5).

(7) A "contract worker" is an individual supplied to a principal in furtherance of a contract such as is mentioned in subsection (5)(b).

2 Exceptions to the Reach of Anti-discrimination Law

Muslims can avail themselves of some exceptions made to the application of the Equality Act 2010. Those apply to religious organisations, religious charities, faith schools, the membership of charities, education and training, welfare, and care within the family. There are also particular situations in which an occupational requirement may be used to restrict liability under the Equality Act 2010. This is when a particular requirement as to sex, marital or other status, or sexual orientation is used in order to comply with the doctrines of the religion (the "compliance principle") or when it is used to avoid conflict with the strongly held religious convictions of a significant number of the religion's followers (the "non-conflict principle"). A requirement as to religion may also be used where the work in question is regarding a particular religious ethos. Special provisions are available for schools of a religious character within the legislation on education (discussed in chapter 7).

Equality Act 2010

SCHEDULE 9

WORK: EXCEPTIONS

PART 1
OCCUPATIONAL REQUIREMENTS

General

1 (1) A person (A) does not contravene a provision mentioned in sub-paragraph (2) by applying in relation to work a requirement to have a particular protected characteristic, if A shows that, having regard to the nature or context of the work—

(a) it is an occupational requirement,

(b) the application of the requirement is a proportionate means of achieving a legitimate aim, and

(c) the person to whom A applies the requirement does not meet it (or A has reasonable grounds for not being satisfied that the person meets it).

…

Religious requirements relating to sex, marriage etc., sexual orientation

2 (1) A person (A) does not contravene a provision mentioned in sub-paragraph (2) by applying in relation to employment a requirement to which sub-paragraph (4) applies if A shows that—

(a) the employment is for the purposes of an organised religion,

(b) the application of the requirement engages the compliance or non-conflict principle, and

(c) the person to whom A applies the requirement does not meet it (or A has reasonable grounds for not being satisfied that the person meets it).

…

(3) A person does not contravene section 53(1) or (2)(a) or (b) by applying in relation to a relevant qualification (within the meaning of that section) a requirement to which sub-paragraph (4) applies if the person shows that—

(a) the qualification is for the purposes of employment mentioned in sub-paragraph (1)(a), and

(b) the application of the requirement engages the compliance or non-conflict principle.

(4) This sub-paragraph applies to—

(a) a requirement to be of a particular sex;

(b) a requirement not to be a transsexual person;

(c) a requirement not to be married or a civil partner;

(ca) a requirement not to be married to or the civil partner of, a person of the same sex;

(cb) a requirement not to be the civil partner of a person of the opposite sex;

(d) a requirement not to be married to, or the civil partner of, a person who has a living former spouse or civil partner;

(e) a requirement relating to circumstances in which a marriage or civil partnership came to an end;

(f) a requirement related to sexual orientation.

(5) The application of a requirement engages the compliance principle if the requirement is applied so as to comply with the doctrines of the religion.

(6) The application of a requirement engages the non-conflict principle if, because of the nature or context of the employment, the requirement is applied so as to avoid conflicting with the strongly held religious convictions of a significant number of the religion's followers.

(7) A reference to employment includes a reference to an appointment to a personal or public office.
(8) In the case of a requirement within sub-paragraph (4)(a), sub-paragraph (1) has effect as if in paragraph (c) the words from "(or" to the end were omitted.

Other requirements relating to religion or belief

3 A person (A) with an ethos based on religion or belief does not contravene a provision mentioned in paragraph 1(2) by applying in relation to work a requirement to be of a particular religion or belief if A shows that, having regard to that ethos and to the nature or context of the work—
(a) it is an occupational requirement,
(b) the application of the requirement is a proportionate means of achieving a legitimate aim, and
(c) the person to whom A applies the requirement does not meet it (or A has reasonable grounds for not being satisfied that the person meets it).

3 Proselytism in the Workplace

Wasteney v East London NHS Foundation Trust [2016] ICR, EAT

This case concerns a claimant who was a born-again Christian and member of an evangelical church. She was employed in a senior role by a trust within the National Health Service that provided community-based mental health services. A junior Muslim employee of Pakistani heritage complained that the claimant had tried to impose her religious views on her by inviting her to church services, praying over her and giving her a book concerning a Muslim's conversion to Christianity. Although the claimant was a Christian, it is conceivable that suggestions to convert to another religion may be made by a Muslim employee too. Therefore this case may be important generally for acts in the workplace related to proselytising and conversion, particularly where the proselytising employee holds a position of relative seniority or authority. This is yet another case in which a complaint of discrimination and harassment under the Equality Act 2010 and Article 9 of the ECHR are run together.

The claimant was disciplined and given a written warning, and she then made a complaint to an Employment Tribunal (ET) that the warning was an oppressive sanction amounting to harassment on the ground of her religion or belief, under section 26 of the Equality Act 2010, and that she had been directly discriminated against by being subjected to less favourable treatment than a colleague of no faith or of a different faith would have been, under section 13 of the Act. She also complained that the employing trust's actions amounted to a breach of her right to manifest her belief, contrary to Article 9 of the ECHR. The tribunal dismissed her complaints, deciding that Article 9 did not give the claimant an unfettered right to discuss her religious beliefs, and that, while the context of the disciplinary process was religious acts, the reason the claimant was disciplined was not because of her religion, but because she had subjected a junior employee to unwanted and inappropriate treatment. The claimant then appealed to the Employment Appeal Tribunal (EAT) against the ET's decision.

> 48. It is common ground that, whilst the employment tribunal did not have jurisdiction (as it correctly recognised) to determine self-standing claims under it, the Convention can be relevant in that the employment tribunal (and this court) has a duty under section 3 of the Human Rights Act 1998 to interpret and give effect to domestic legislation in a way which, so far as possible, is compatible with Convention rights.
>
> …
>
> 54. In domestic law, the expression of right and limitation as allowed by article 9 of the Convention is most easily discernible when addressing cases of indirect discrimination under section 19 of the Equality Act 2010 (which may be the more obvious route of challenge in most cases involving the manifestation of a religious belief). Whilst there is no statutory means of justifying direct discrimination or harassment, however, the claimant accepts that the limitations permitted by article 9.2 are relevant to the approach to be adopted to claims brought under sections 13 (direct discrimination) and 26 (harassment). Although the claimant relies on the protection of the right to manifest religious belief in the workplace, as recognised by the European Court of Human Rights in *Eweida* [*v United Kingdom* (2013) 57 EHRR 8], she (correctly) does not seek to suggest that right cannot be subject to limitation.
>
> 55. The concession is in some senses easier to state than apply, but the task will always be made easier by having a clear understanding of the nature of the claim and how it is being put. If the case is one of direct discrimination then the focus on the reason why the less favourable treatment occurred should permit an employment tribunal to identify those cases where the treatment is not because of the manifestation of the religion or belief but because of the inappro-

priate manner of the manifestation (where what is inappropriate may be tested by reference to article 9.2 and the case law in that respect) .... Similarly, whilst the definition of harassment permits the looser test of related to, a clear sense of what the conduct did in fact relate to should permit the employment tribunal to reach a conclusion as to whether it is the manifestation of religion or belief that is in issue or whether it is in fact the complainant's own inappropriate conduct (and that must be right, otherwise an employer's attempt to discipline an employee for the harassment of a co-worker related to, e g, the co-worker's religion or belief could itself be characterised as harassment related to that protected characteristic).

...

62. That characterisation of the claimant's case exposes, however, the real difficulty that she faces on this appeal: it assumes a factual basis that the tribunal's findings reject. The tribunal did not find that the trust had pursued disciplinary action against the claimant and imposed a warning on her because of or for reasons related to her sharing of her faith with a consenting colleague. It expressly found that the trust took the actions it did because the colleague in question had made serious complaints about acts which blurred professional boundaries and placed improper pressure on that colleague.

...

65. In oral argument, Mr Diamond [counsel for the claimant] cautioned against courts or tribunals seeking to form a view as to whether a person might be too vulnerable to be a proper recipient of the sharing of religious faith. That is, however, not what the tribunal purported to do in this case. The evidence was that EN (who, the claimant had accepted, might properly be described as vulnerable) had herself complained about the claimant's conduct, characterising it as inappropriate; something the claimant had accepted might have been so in certain respects. Keeping its focus firmly on the reasons why the trust had taken disciplinary action against the claimant, the tribunal was clear that it did so because of, or for reasons related to, the claimant's blurring of professional boundaries and placing of improper pressure on a junior colleague. The claimant was not subjected to disciplinary process or sanction because she manifested her religious belief in voluntary and consensual exchanges with a colleague but because as the tribunal expressly found she subjected a subordinate to unwanted and unwelcome conduct, going substantially beyond religious discussion, without regard to her own influential position. The treatment of which the claimant complained was because of, and related to, those inappropriate actions; not any legitimate manifestation of her belief.

CHAPTER 11

Islamic Slaughter, Food Regulation, Diet and Fasting

1 Ritual Slaughter

Ritual slaughter for the production of *halal* (and kosher) meat is governed by the Welfare of Animals (Slaughter or Killing) Regulations 1995, which are based on Directive 93/119/EEC. The earlier Council of Europe Convention for the Protection of Animals for Slaughter 1979 also allows for derogations for slaughtering in accordance with religious concerns (Article 17). In the Welfare of Animals (Slaughter or Killing) Regulations 1995, Regulation 22 removes the requirement to stun an animal before slaughter in the case of slaughter by a religious method in accordance with Schedule 12. Schedule 12 covers slaughter "without the infliction of unnecessary suffering" by Jews or Muslims who must be licensed as slaughtermen. Although Jewish slaughtermen in England and Wales must be licensed by the Rabbinical Commission, there is no further formal religious licensing for Muslims. Part II of Schedule 12 sets out the specific requirements of slaughtering by a religious method. The exemption for religious slaughter methods to the general requirement of stunning was maintained in the Council Regulation on the protection of animals at the time of killing ((EC) 1099/2009), Article 4(4).

Under the Slaughterhouses Act 1974, section 16(2), a local authority is prevented from using its powers to deny religious communities reasonable facilities for obtaining food slaughtered by the method required by their religion, when the authority itself operates a public slaughterhouse.

There may be differences regarding what is considered "*halal*" (Arabic for "permissible") according to Islamic *Shari'a*. The issue emerged in litigation in *Halal Meat Sellers Committee Limited, Nimat Halal Food Limited v HMC (UK) Limited.*[1] The Commercial Court was asked to declare that a charity engaged in certification for *halal* meat was acting against its charitable objects, in restraint of trade and against natural justice. The defendant charity successfully argued that the claim be struck out. The judgment is nevertheless interesting as an illustration of the disputed nature of what sort of slaughter is accepted as

1 [2020] EWHC 2190 (Comm).

"*halal.*" The charity, which provided *halal* certification, held that it is not permissible to use pre-stunned animals to produce *halal* meat. The witness statements showed and the court recognised that the issue of stunning has long divided Islamic scholarly opinion, but the practice is becoming common in both Muslim majority and minority countries. Similarly, Muslims in the United Kingdom are not agreed upon a single set of criteria for the *halal* slaughter process, and the differentiating factors include whether stunning was used, the method of stunning, and whether the animal was stunned to kill it or render it unconscious. The evidence showed that some 80 per cent of the *halal* market involved meat sourced from stunned animals.

It will be noted that Schedule 12, para. 2, of the 1995 Regulations provides that slaughter by religious method includes slaughter "by the Muslim method for the food of Muslims by a Muslim …" Identical wording was previously used in an exemption provided in the Slaughter of Poultry Act 1967, section 2. The criteria came to the attention of a court in the earlier case of *Malins v Cole & Attard*, which heard an appeal against conviction because of a breach of that provision.[2] The specific point was that no inquiry was made of a purchaser, who was wearing a crucifix, which type of slaughter he required to be carried out on the bird. He had no intention of using the bird "for the food of Muslims" and would have said so if he had been asked. The court did not accept that "local knowledge" of the premises was that it was used only for *halal* slaughter since the premises were in the Petticoat Lane market area which is renowned for tourist interest and teaming with people with no local knowledge.

Interestingly, the owner of a poultry slaughterhouse did not appear to be a Muslim, but his slaughtermen were Muslims and so that criterion had not been breached. Because that part of the provision appears to require that the activity be carried out by Muslims only, it seems to provide an exemption from the anti-discrimination law. In any case, the Equality Act 2010, Schedule 9, recognises religious exemptions for employment purposes, while Schedule 3, para. 30, recognises exemptions for services provided for persons who share a protected characteristic.

The Welfare of Animals (Slaughter or Killing) Regulations 1995

…

PART IV

SLAUGHTER BY A RELIGIOUS METHOD

2 [1986] 1 WLUK 272, [1986] C.L.Y. 89, Crown Court (Knightsbridge).

Additional requirements relating to slaughter by a religious method

21. Schedule 12 shall have effect in relation to the slaughter of any animal by a religious method.

Exemption for slaughter by a religious method

22. Schedule 5 (which relates to the stunning and killing of animals) shall not apply to any animal which is slaughtered in accordance with Schedule 12 (which relates to slaughter by a religious method).

SCHEDULE 12

ADDITIONAL PROVISIONS FOR SLAUGHTER BY A RELIGIOUS METHOD

PART I

GENERAL

Interpretation

1. In this Schedule—
   (a) "animal" means any sheep, goat or bovine animal;
   (b) "bovine animal" means—
      (i) in sub-paragraph (a) above and paragraph 7(b) below, any ox, bullock, cow, heifer, steer or calf; and
      (ii) elsewhere, any ox, bullock, cow, heifer or steer or any calf which is too large to be restrained manually for slaughter on a cradle or table; and
   (c) "bird" means any turkey, domestic fowl, guinea-fowl, duck, goose or quail.

Slaughter by a religious method

2. In this Schedule references to slaughter by a religious method are references to slaughter without the infliction of unnecessary suffering—
   (a) by the Jewish method for the food of Jews by a Jew who holds a licence in accordance with Schedule 1 (which relates to the licensing of slaughtermen) and who is duly licensed—
      (i) in England and Wales by the Rabbinical Commission referred to in Part IV of this Schedule; or
      (ii) in Scotland by the Chief Rabbi; or
   (b) by the Muslim method for the food of Muslims by a Muslim who holds a licence in accordance with Schedule 1.

PART II
PROVISIONS RELATING TO THE SLAUGHTER OF ANIMALS BY A RELIGIOUS METHOD

Slaughter of bovine animals by a religious method

3.—(1) Subject to sub-paragraph (3) below, no person shall slaughter, or cause or permit to be slaughtered, any bovine animal in a slaughterhouse by a religious method unless the animal is in an upright position in a restraining pen which has been approved by the Minister and which the Minister is satisfied has been installed in such a manner as to ensure that it will operate efficiently.

(2) The Minister may, for the purposes of sub-paragraph (1) above, give his approval to a restraining pen, but he shall not give any such approval unless he is satisfied that the pen is of such a size and design, and is able to be so operated, as to protect a bovine animal from any avoidable pain, suffering, agitation, injuries or contusions while confined in it or while entering it and, in particular, unless he is satisfied that the pen—

- (a) contains an effective means of restraining any bovine animal confined in it (including a suitable head restraint for that purpose); and
- (b) contains means of support which will take the weight of the animal during and following slaughter in it.

(3) Sub-paragraphs (1) and (2) above shall not apply where the bovine animal is stunned, or stunned and pithed, before slaughter, but in such cases any bovine animal shall be restrained before stunning in accordance with paragraph 3(a) of Schedule 4.

Use and maintenance of restraining pens

4. The occupier of a slaughterhouse in which there is a restraining pen shall ensure that—

- (a) the means of restraining and supporting a bovine animal confined in such a pen described in paragraph 3(2)(a) and (b) above are used in respect of any bovine animal confined in it;
- (b) the pen is kept in good working order; and
- (c) if it has been modified after it has been approved by the Minister, the pen is not used again until a fresh approval is given by the Minister.

Handling of animals during slaughter

5. The occupier of a slaughterhouse where animals are slaughtered by a religious method and any person engaged in the slaughter of any animal by a religious method shall ensure that—
   (a) no bovine animal is placed in a restraining pen unless the person who is to carry out the slaughter is ready to make the incision immediately the bovine animal is placed in the pen;
   (b) no animal is shackled or hoisted until the appropriate period referred to in paragraph 7 below has elapsed and unless the animal is unconscious;
   (c) any sheep or goat, or any calf which is small enough to be restrained manually on a cradle or table, is slaughtered only on a cradle or table and that only one such animal is placed on the cradle or table at any one time; and
   (d) where the slaughter is carried out in a slaughterhouse, a captive bolt instrument is kept close to the restraining pen, cradle or table for use in case of emergency and is immediately used where the animal is subjected to any avoidable pain, suffering or agitation or has any injuries or contusions.

Method of slaughter

6. Any person who slaughters by a religious method any animal which has not been stunned before bleeding shall—
   (a) before each animal is slaughtered, inspect the knife to be used and ensure that it is not used unless it is undamaged and of sufficient size and sharpness to be capable of being used to slaughter the animal in the manner described in sub-paragraph (b) below; and
   (b) ensure that each animal is slaughtered by the severance, by rapid, uninterrupted movements of a knife, of both its carotid arteries and both its jugular veins.

Handling animals after slaughter by a religious method

7. The occupier of a slaughterhouse in which animals are slaughtered by a religious method and any person engaged in the slaughter by a religious method of any animal shall ensure that where the animal has not been stunned, or stunned and pithed, before bleeding it is not moved until it is unconscious and in any event not before the expiry of—

(a) in the case of any sheep or any goat, a period of not less than 20 seconds; and
(b) in the case of any bovine animal, a period of not less than 30 seconds, after it has been slaughtered in the manner described in paragraph 6 above.

Slaughter by a religious method elsewhere than in a slaughterhouse

8. No person shall slaughter any animal by a religious method, or cause or permit any animal to be so slaughtered, elsewhere than in a slaughterhouse unless the slaughter is carried out in the presence of an authorised person.

PART III

PROVISIONS RELATING TO THE SLAUGHTER OF BIRDS BY A RELIGIOUS METHOD

Slaughter of birds by a religious method

9. Any person who slaughters by a religious method any bird which has not been stunned before slaughter shall ensure that—
(a) each bird is slaughtered by the severance, by rapid and uninterrupted movements of a knife, of its carotid arteries; and
(b) the knife to be used for the slaughtering of the birds is undamaged and of sufficient size and sharpness to enable each bird to be slaughtered in the manner described in sub-paragraph (a) above.

Handling birds after slaughter by a religious method

10. The occupier of a slaughterhouse in which birds are slaughtered by a religious method and any person engaged in the slaughter of any bird by a religious method shall ensure that, where the bird has not been stunned before bleeding, no further dressing procedure or any electrical stimulation is performed on the bird before it is unconscious and in any event not before the expiry of—
(a) in the case of a turkey or goose, a period of not less than 2 minutes; and
(b) in the case of any other bird, a period of not less than 90 seconds, after it has been slaughtered in the manner described in paragraph 9 above.

2 Diet and Fasting

Questions of diet and fasting come up incidentally in litigation in various contexts, and often arise in care proceedings for children and matters to do with children upon separation or divorce. One such arose in *P (Circumcision: Child in Care), Re* [2021] EWHC 1616 (Fam), which concerned care proceedings for children and entailed questions of the children's education in Islam including their access to a *halal* diet. Another such instance came up in the Scottish case of *KS v TS* (F307/10 Sheriffdom of Tayside, Central and Fife at Dunfermline 2012 WL 4888757) concerning contact with children upon the breakdown of a marriage between a Muslim man and a Christian woman. Again, the question came up in the context of the father, who was a Muslim claiming that the children ought to be brought up as Muslims, it being his duty as the father to ensure that that happened and, consequently, the children ought to be eating only *halal* food. In the event the Sheriff reached the conclusion that it was not in the best interests of the children that a specific issue order be made that they be brought up in the Muslim faith. The case of *Re: IH* below sets out some clarifications on when it may not be reasonable to expect fasting during Ramadan by a person who lacks capacity under both Islamic and English law.

***Re: IH* (*Observance of Muslim Practice*)**
[2017] EWCOP 9, Mr Justice Cobb, Court of Protection

Although fasting is considered one of the pillars of Islam there may be questions as to when Muslims are exempt from the duty to fast. The following case concerned applications before the Court of Protection concerning a 39-year-old man ("IH") who suffered from a profound learning disability, functioning intellectually at the developmental level of a 1–3-year-old, and who had atypical autism. Born in Pakistan, from a Punjabi family, IH then lived in West Yorkshire all his life. IH had been raised by his family throughout his life as a Sunni Muslim and cared for at home until recently when his living environment started being provided by the Local Authority and funded by the local Clinical Commissioning Group. Part of the application for IH, brought on his behalf by the Official Solicitor, was for a declaration that it was not in his best interests for him to fast during the daylight hours of Ramadan.

> 14. TH [IH's father] is anxious that his adult son should adhere as fully as possible to the tenets of the Islamic faith, and follow to the extent that this is possible religious observance and custom. TH and DH [IH's mother] would expect IH to celebrate Eid with his family, and generally to eat *Halal* food, but they recognise

that IH should not be expected to fast during Ramadan, given that IH would not understand the withholding of food and liquid during daylight hours. TH initially deposed to the fact that "the removal of underarm and pubic hair is a very essential part of" (emphasis added) being brought up in the Muslim faith; he added that it was "compulsory". In the final analysis, TH's case has been modified in line with Dr. Ali's [Dr. Mansur Ali, lecturer in Arabic and Islamic Studies at Cardiff University, a witness] evidence below.

…

20. There is no dispute that IH lacks capacity to make the decisions which are the focus of these applications; the diagnostic and functional criteria contained in, respectively, sections 2 and section 3 MCA 2005 [Mental Capacity Act 2005] are clearly established on the evidence. Specifically, to have capacity to make the decision to fast for Ramadan, a person would be expected to understand (section 3(1)(a)):

i) What fasting is; the lack of food and liquid, eating and drinking;
ii) The length of the fast;
iii) If for religion, for custom (family or otherwise), for health-associated reasons, or for other reasons;
iv) If for religion reasons, which religion and why;
v) The effect of fasting on the body;
vi) What the consequences would be of making a choice to fast and the risks of choosing to not fast or of postponing the decision.

21. Dr. Carpenter [Honorary Consultant Psychiatrist in Learning Disabilities, a witness] is clear that IH is not able to understand any of the six points listed in [20] above. It is further agreed between the parties, having received Dr. Carpenter's advice, that, given the nature of his disability, IH will not ever acquire capacity to make such decisions (section 4(3)).

…

27. Significantly for present purposes, Islam stipulates different arrangements for those who lack "legal competence." "Legal competence" in Islamic terms is defined by Dr. Ali as "a capacity or a potential for mental functioning, required in a decision specific manner, to understand and carry out decision-making. Competence is always presumed; its absence or inactivity has to be affirmed by a court." It is normal (per Dr. Ali) to defer to medical practitioners or experts on the issue of legal (mental) competence; their opinion would be likely to be deemed valid and authoritative in the *Shari'a*. The evidence filed in these proceedings, most notably from Dr. Carpenter, would be sufficient, I was advised, to form the

basis in Islamic law to declare IH to be "legally incompetent"; all parties agree that IH is not legally competent under Islamic law.

28. Dr. Ali advises that the legally incompetent person (along with the terminally ill, the disabled and minors) is perpetually in a heightened state of spirituality, hence he or she is exempt from practising the major rituals of Islam including adherence to the Five Pillars.

29. On the specific issues engaged in this application, Dr. Ali advises as follows:

> …
>
> i) Fasting during the daylight hours of Ramadan is one of the Qur'anically mandated obligations for all Muslims who are legally competent, and who are not exempt. Certain groups are exempt from fasting; they include the incapacitous, minors, the ill, pregnant women, those who are travelling. Those who are exempt are not morally culpable for not keeping the daylight fast.
>
> …
>
> Is it in IH's best interests to be relieved of his obligation to fast during Ramadan?

30. As indicated above ([29](i)) there is no Islamic obligation on IH to fast given his lack of capacity. IH has never been required to fast by his family, and has not fasted while in their care. He has not, thus far, fasted while in the care of the Local Authority.

31. If this had been a case in which IH had some appreciation of the religious significance of fasting in Ramadan (as a means to attaining *taqwa*, i.e. the essence of piety, protecting one's self from evil) there may be said to be some benefit in him doing so. But he has no such appreciation.

32. IH, I am satisfied, would not in fact understand why food and water was being withheld for the daylight hours in the month of Ramadan; the absence of food/water would be likely to cause him stress, or distress; this may cause him to become irritable and/or aggressive in the ways described above ([13]) increasing the risks to staff and himself. There is some minor anxiety that fasting and/or mild dehydration would increase the side effects of any one of his multiple medications. It is plainly not in his interests that he should fast, and the declaration will be granted.

CHAPTER 12

Islamic Goods and Services

1 Equality Legislation on the Provision of Services

While the Race Relations At 1976 catered for the provision of goods, facilities or services, it made no specific provision for discrimination on religious grounds. As with other parts of the 1976 Act the ethnic group provision could indirectly cater for those religious groups when they were represented disproportionately in one ethnic group. For example, a claim of indirect discrimination would have to be made on grounds that persons of Pakistani heritage are disproportionately impacted on by a particular requirement or condition that meant that a smaller proportion of Muslims could comply. The EU Council Directive 2000/78/EC (the so-called "employment directive") skipped non-employment situations and so left the gap open in so far as the provision of goods, services and facilities was concerned. The issue of the religious gap in UK law was addressed first by the Equality Act 2006, section 46, which catered for discrimination in the provision of goods, facilities or services. Not only was religious discrimination covered but a claim of direct discrimination could be made in appropriate circumstances where there was less favourable treatment, alongside claims for indirect discrimination where a particular provision, criterion or practice impacted disproportionately and unjustifiably on members of a religious group (Equality Act 2006, section 45, covering both direct and indirect discrimination). The 2006 Act was repealed by the Equality Act 2010 which now acts as a single general reference point for UK anti-discrimination law and specific provision for goods, facilities or services is made by section 29. Although section 29 looks as though it refers to services only, it actually extends to good and facilities too (section 31 on interpretation). Although section 29 extends to acts of discrimination and victimisation, it does not extend to harassment when it comes to matters related to the religion of the person requiring the services, etc. (see subsection (8)), although conduct that would otherwise have amounted to harassment may still amount to direct discrimination.

Equality Act 2010

29 Provision of services, etc.

(1) A person (a "service-provider") concerned with the provision of a service to the public or a section of the public (for payment or not)

must not discriminate against a person requiring the service by not providing the person with the service.

(2) A service-provider (A) must not, in providing the service, discriminate against a person (B)—
  (a) as to the terms on which A provides the service to B;
  (b) by terminating the provision of the service to B;
  (c) by subjecting B to any other detriment.

(3) A service-provider must not, in relation to the provision of the service, harass—
  (a) a person requiring the service, or
  (b) a person to whom the service-provider provides the service.

(4) A service-provider must not victimise a person requiring the service by not providing the person with the service.

(5) A service-provider (A) must not, in providing the service, victimise a person (B)—
  (a) as to the terms on which A provides the service to B;
  (b) by terminating the provision of the service to B;
  (c) by subjecting B to any other detriment.

(6) A person must not, in the exercise of a public function that is not the provision of a service to the public or a section of the public, do anything that constitutes discrimination, harassment or victimisation.

(7) A duty to make reasonable adjustments applies to—
  (a) a service-provider (and see also section 55(7));
  (b) a person who exercises a public function that is not the provision of a service to the public or a section of the public.

(8) In the application of section 26 for the purposes of subsection (3), and subsection (6) as it relates to harassment, neither of the following is a relevant protected characteristic—
  (a) religion or belief;
  (b) sexual orientation.

(9) In the application of this section, so far as relating to race or religion or belief, to the granting of entry clearance (within the meaning of the Immigration Act 1971), it does not matter whether an act is done within or outside the United Kingdom.

(10) Subsection (9) does not affect the application of any other provision of this Act to conduct outside England and Wales or Scotland.

2 Islamic Finance

The tax and regulatory framework was changed from the early 2000s to allow for the development of Islamic finance products. There was reform of the applicable stamp duty to facilitate the market in Islamic mortgages in 2003, specifically *morabaha* (purchase) and *ijara* (lease) based mortgages. The Finance Act 2003, sections 71 and 73 (as amended) eased the development of Islamic mortgages which work on the basis not of a single transfer of title but of two transactions which had previously attracted a double application of stamp duty. The extract below is of sections 71A and 73 as they have been subsequently amended several times. Islamic banks are licensed to operate as UK institutions and the transactions they enter into are ultimately governed by English law even when they are designated as *Sharīʿa* transactions.

Finance Act 2003

…

71A Alternative property finance: land sold to financial institution and leased to person

(1) This section applies where arrangements are entered into between a person and a financial institution under which—
   (a) the institution purchases a major interest in land or an undivided share of a major interest in land ("the first transaction"),
   (b) where the interest purchased is an undivided share, the major interest is held on trust for the institution and the person as beneficial tenants in common,
   (c) the institution (or the person holding the land on trust as mentioned in paragraph (b)) grants to the person out of the major interest a lease (if the major interest is freehold) or a sub-lease (if the major interest is leasehold) ("the second transaction"), and
   (d) the institution and the person enter into an agreement under which the person has a right to require the institution or its successor in title to transfer to the person (in one transaction or a series of transactions) the whole interest purchased by the institution under the first transaction.

(2) The first transaction is exempt from charge if the vendor is—
   (a) the person, or
   (b) another financial institution by whom the interest was acquired under arrangements of the kind mentioned in subsection (1) entered into between it and the person.

(3) The second transaction is exempt from charge if the provisions of this Part relating to the first transaction are complied with (including the payment of any tax chargeable).

(4) Any transfer to the person that results from the exercise of the right mentioned in subsection (1)(d) ("a further transaction") is exempt from charge if—
   (a) the provisions of this Part relating to the first and second transactions are complied with, and
   (b) at all times between the second transaction and the further transaction—
      (i) the interest purchased under the first transaction is held by a financial institution so far as not transferred by a previous further transaction, and
      (ii) the lease or sub-lease granted under the second transaction is held by the person.

(5) The agreement mentioned in subsection (1)(d) is not to be treated—
   (a) as substantially performed unless and until the whole interest purchased by the institution under the first transaction has been transferred (and accordingly section 44(5) does not apply), or
   (b) as a distinct land transaction by virtue of section 46 (options and rights of pre-emption).

(6) The requirements of subsection (1), or (4)(b)(ii), are not met if—
   (a) the person enters into the arrangement, or holds the lease or sub-lease, as trustee and any beneficiary of the trust is not a person, or
   (b) the person enters into the arrangements, or holds the lease or sub-lease, as partner and any of the other partners is not a person.

(7) A further transaction that is exempt from charge by virtue of subsection (4) is not a notifiable transaction unless the transaction involves the transfer to the person of the whole interest purchased by the institution under the first transaction, so far as not transferred by a previous further transaction.

(9) References in this section to a person shall be read, in relation to times after the death of the person concerned, as references to his personal representatives.

…

73 Alternative property finance: land sold to financial institution and re-sold to person

(1) This section applies where arrangements are entered into between a person and a financial institution under which—
 (a) the institution—
  (i) purchases a major interest in land ("the first transaction"), and
  (ii) sells that interest to the person ("the second transaction"), and
 (b) the person grants the institution a legal mortgage over that interest.

(2) The first transaction is exempt from charge if the vendor is—
 (a) the person concerned, or
 (b) another financial institution by whom the interest was acquired under other arrangements of the kind mentioned in section 71A(1) … entered into between it and the person.

(3) The second transaction is exempt from charge if the financial institution complies with the provisions of this Part relating to the first transaction (including the payment of any tax chargeable on a chargeable consideration that is not less than the market value of the interest and, in the case of the grant of a lease at a rent, the rent.).

(4) This section does not apply if—
 (a) the person enters into the arrangements as trustee and any beneficiary of the trust is not a person, or
 (b) the person enters into the arrangements as partner and any of the other partners is not a person.

(5) In this section—
 …
 (b) "legal mortgage"—
  (i) in relation to land in England …, means a legal mortgage as defined in section 205(1)(xvi) of the Law of Property Act 1925 (c. 20);
  …
  (iii) in relation to land in Northern Ireland, means a mortgage by conveyance of a legal estate or by demise or sub-demise or a charge by way of legal mortgage.

(6) References in this section to a person shall be read, in relation to times after the death of the person concerned, as references to his personal representatives.

English courts will not accept a choice of law clause in a commercial financing contract which seeks to apply only Islamic law or the *Shari'a* to such a contract. English courts have confirmed this position with respect to the Contracts (Applicable Law) Act 1990, which incorporated the Rome Convention into English law, holding that the Convention provides for only a territorial choice of law, not personal or religious law. The Rome Convention was replaced by the Rome Regulation (EC) No. 593/2008 (Rome I), which survives Brexit mostly intact. It can be presumed that the courts will hold the same position with respect to finance contracts which purport to conform to the *Shari'a*.[1]

Shamil Bank of Bahrain EC v Beximco Pharmaceuticals Ltd and others
[2004] EWCA Civ 19, [2004] 1 W.L.R. 1784, Court of Appeal

The first and second defendants were two Bangladeshi pharmaceutical companies, which were bound by various financing agreements with the claimant bank which were guaranteed by the third to fifth defendants. The claimant bank was incorporated under the laws of Bahrain. Although the principles of Islamic law were not incorporated into the commercial law of Bahrain, the bank held itself out as applying Islamic principles in the course of its business. The financing agreements sought to circumvent the prohibition under Islamic law against the charging of interest upon a loan by using a *Morabaha* agreement, recognised in Islamic law, as the sale contract. The agreements each contained a governing law clause which stated that "[s]ubject to the principles of the Glorious *Shari'a*, this agreement shall be governed by and construed in accordance with the laws of England." When the first and second defendants defaulted on their payments, the claimant bank applied for summary judgment against them and against the guarantors. The defendants claimed that, on the true construction of the governing law clauses, the agreements were enforceable only in so far as they were valid in accordance with both the principles of the *Shari'a* and English law, and that the agreements did not in fact comply with *Shari'a* law in that they were actually disguised loans with interest. After the first instance judge gave judgment for the bank, the defendants appealed on the ground, *inter alia*, that the judge had failed to consider whether the clauses were apt to incorporate the principles of *Shari'a* law into the agreements. The Court of Appeal found for the claimant, with Potter LJ giving the reasoned judgment with which Laws and Arden LJJ agreed. The following extracts from the

1 The issue is now governed by the Law Applicable to Contractual Obligations and Non-Contractual Obligations (Amendment etc.) (EU Exit) Regulations 2019, SI 2019/834.

judgment include the Court of Appeal's summary of the opinions of the experts on both sides on the question of what Islamic law required for a finance contract to be valid. In the event, the point was not decisive for the Court of Appeal, which found that the *Shari'a* was imprecise and instead applied English law as the governing law.

> 29. The rival expert evidence as to the validity of te agreements under Islamic law was as follows. The bank's expert, Dr Lau, the former director of the Centre of Islamic and Middle Eastern Law [SOAS, University of London], stated that the precise scope and content of Islamic law in general, and Islamic banking in particular, are marked by a degree of controversy within the Islamic world, best exemplified by the fact that the actual practice of Islamic banking differs widely within the Islamic world. Even within particular jurisdictions such as Pakistan, which are committed and constitutionally obliged to introduce Islamic financial systems, the issue is subject to ongoing debate and a high degree of uncertainty. In the absence of any agreement on the boundaries of "Islamic banking" or, indeed, on what ought to be the precise ingredients of a Morabaha agreement, it is in practice up to individual banks to determine the issue. In the absence of any legal prescription as to what does and what does not constitute Islamic banking or finance, most Islamic banks, including those in Bahrain, seek the advice of Islamic scholars who examine and approve particular agreements and forms of agreement, the role of the Religious Supervisory Committee being to formulate the bank's interpretation of the *Shari'a*.
>
> 30. Strictly interpreted "the Glorious *Shari'a'a*" refers to the divine law as contained in the Qur'an and Sunnah. However, most of the classical Islamic law on financial transactions is not contained as "rules" or "law" in the Qur'an and Sunnah but is based on the often divergent views held by established schools of law formed in a period roughly between 700 and 850 CE. The particular form and content of Morabaha agreements varies. If a bank's religious supervisory board is satisfied that the bank's activities are in accordance with *Shari'a* law, that concludes the matter, there being no provision in Bahrain law, or Islamic law generally, for an appeal by a customer of the bank against the board's rulings and certifications. Finally, even if the relevant agreements amounted to agreements to pay *Riba* [interest], the principal sums advanced could be validly claimed.
>
> 31. Dr Lau's conclusion was that the concern of the defendants that the sums advanced were not used to purchase the goods and/or equipment, the subject of the 1995 and 1996 Morabaha agreements, but rather as part of the general

working capital of the first and second defendants was of no relevance to the question whether or not the Morabaha agreements complied with Islamic law. He stated:

> In my opinion for the Morabaha agreements to be in accordance with Islamic law all that is required is that they are certified as such by Shamil Bank's Religious Supervisory Board and the principal amounts are disbursed in accordance with the terms of the 1995 and 1996 Morabaha agreements.

32. The position of the defendant's expert, Mr Khan, formerly Khan J, chairman of the *Shari'a* Appellate Bench of the Supreme Court of Pakistan, shortly stated was as follows. He acknowledged that "wherever a question of interpretation of the principles contained in the Qur'an and Sunnah is involved, the application of the rules of *Shari'a*'a has and will continue to give rise to disputes between different jurists". He also did not contradict the assertion of Dr Lau that most of the classical Islamic law on financial transactions was not to be found in the Qur'an and Sunnah. However, he made clear (as Dr Lau did not dispute) that the injunction against the payment of *Riba* is contained in both those holy books and that it is uncontroversial that under Islamic law interest charged on loans by banks is *Riba* and prohibited. Equally, any agreement in which, in substance, interest is being charged upon a loan is unlawful, void and unenforceable.

33. Mr Khan acknowledged that the *Shari'a* recognises two modes of financing as permissible, namely Morabaha and Ijarah agreements, but asserted that, for such transactions to be valid, the requirements prescribed and provided for in the agreement must be fulfilled, failing which the transaction as a whole will be void according to the principles and rules of *Shari'a*. On the basis of the (uncontradicted) assertion of the defendants that the advances were never applied or intended to be applied in the purchase or lease of any property, the relevant agreements were void. The ESUAS [the Morabaha agreements] were similarly void and unenforceable on the basis of a number of arguments advanced, the principal one of which was that, irrespective of their form as purported Ijarah leases of assets, the ESUAS simply constituted a rescheduling or roll-over of the 1995 and 1996 Morabaha agreements, the bank charging interest or an additional amount over and above the sums due in consideration of the giving of time. This too was *Riba* and accordingly prohibited and void.

34. Finally, so far as the position of the bank's religious supervisory board was concerned, Mr Khan stated that certification by the board that the operations of the bank were according to the *Shari'a* would not be a decision binding on any court dealing with the dispute under the law of *Shari'a*. The dispute would

fall to be resolved by the court in the light of its own view of the position under *Shari'a* law. In any event there was no evidence that the board had had knowledge of, nor was it required to approve, the particular transaction in this case, its function being one of overall supervision and approval of the methods and procedures adopted by the bank in the course of its business.

…

52. The general reference to principles of *Shari'a* in this case affords no reference to, or identification of, those aspects of *Shari'a* law which are intended to be incorporated into the contract, let alone the terms in which they are framed. It is plainly insufficient for the defendants to contend that the basic rules of the *Shari'a* applicable in this case are not controversial. Such "basic rules" are neither referred to nor identified. Thus the reference to the "principles of … *Shari'a*" stands unqualified as a reference to the body of *Shari'a* law generally. As such, they are inevitably repugnant to the choice of English law as the law of the contract and render the clause self-contradictory and therefore meaningless.

53. In these circumstances, having rightly conceded that English law is the governing law of the contract, Mr Hacker [counsel for the defendants] is left with little room for manoeuvre, save to assert that the court should accept his submission on the basis that otherwise the proviso to the governing law clause would be mere surplusage.

54. I do not agree. It seems to me that there is an appropriate alternative construction, namely that favoured by the [High Court] judge, i.e., that the words are intended simply to reflect the Islamic religious principles according to which the bank holds itself out as doing business rather than a system of law intended to "trump" the application of English law as the law to be applied in ascertaining the liability of the parties under the terms of the agreement. English law is a law commonly adopted internationally as the governing law for banking and commercial contracts, having a well known and well developed jurisprudence in that respect which is not open to doubt or disputation on the basis of religious or philosophical principle. I share the [High Court] judge's view that, having chosen English law as the governing law, it would be both unusual and improbable for the parties to intend that the English court should proceed to determine and apply the *Shari'a* in relation to the legality or enforceability of the obligations clearly set out in the contract. Reference to authority does not assist the defendants in this respect. In *Glencore International AG v Metro Trading International Inc* [2001] 1 Lloyd's Rep 283 the judge was concerned with, and heard evidence in relation to, the meaning and scope of the word "ghasb" (misappropriation) as a term used

but undefined in article 1326 of the Fujairah Civil Code which was the governing law in the case before him. As such he was obliged to interpret and apply the term in the dispute before him, with the assistance of rival experts in the law of Fujairah. The decision has no relevance to this case. As to the decision in *Al-Bassam v Al-Bassam* [2002] EWHC 2281 (Ch) the court was concerned with *Shari'a* law as being the law which the parties agreed was the law of succession applied in Saudi Arabia as the country of the deceased's domicile at the date of his death. Again, it has no relevance to this case, other than demonstrating that, where it is clear that a particular system of law governs a dispute before the English court, the court is obliged to apply it, with the assistance of expert evidence. Neither case was concerned with the construction of a disputed choice of law clause.

55. Finally, so far as the "principles of … *Shari'a*" are concerned, it was the evidence of both experts that there are indeed areas of considerable controversy and difficulty arising not only from the need to translate into propositions of modern law texts which centuries ago were set out as religious and moral codes, but because of the existence of a variety of schools of thought with which the court may have to concern itself in any given case before reaching a conclusion upon the principle or rule in dispute. The fact that there may be general consensus upon the proscription of *Riba* and the essentials of a valid Morabaha agreement does no more than indicate that, if the *Shari'a* law proviso were sufficient to incorporate the principles of *Shari'a* law into the parties' agreements, the defendants would have been likely to succeed. However, since I would hold that the proviso is plainly inadequate for that purpose, the validity of the contract and the defendant's obligations thereunder fall to be decided according to English law. It is conceded in this appeal that, if that is so, the first and second defendants are liable to the bank.

CHAPTER 13

Islamic Dress

As with many other topics covered in this book, anti-discrimination law and human rights law are both relevant in cases of disputes arising from restrictions applied to Islamic clothing. This chapter therefore follows the division between the two branches of law although they might both be invoked simultaneously in the cases.

1 Islamic Dress under Anti-discrimination Law

Azmi v Kirklees
[2007] IRLR 434, Employment Appeal Tribunal

One of the leading cases which was litigated and decided under the then applicable anti-discrimination law, it concerns the claim made by a Muslim woman who had acquired an employment position in a school as a bilingual support worker and subsequently asked to be allowed to wear the face veil, a request that was refused by the school management as well as the local authority. The case was decided under the Employment Equality (Religion or Belief) Regulations 2003, the United Kingdom's domestic legislation giving effect to European Union Council Directive 2000/78/EC in the sphere of religion and belief. The legislation has since been superseded by the Equality Act 2006 and the Directive's implementation is now given effect to by the current Equality Act 2010 which uses substantially the same wording as used in the Directive and the implementing Regulations of 2003. The case therefore remains relevant for future cases which may be decided under the Equality Act 2010, which remains in force despite Brexit. As can be seen, the claimant (appellant) did not succeed in her claim for either direct or indirect discrimination.

> 8. The Appellant is a devout Muslim. Since the age of 15 she has worn a long dress (the jabbah) and has also usually worn a veil which covers all of her head and face, save for her eyes, when in the presence of adult males. At her interview, the Claimant had worn a black tunic and headscarf; her face was not covered. At no time during the interview did she indicate that her religious beliefs required her to wear a veil or placed any limitation on her working. She attended the training day on 1 September 2005 in advance of term starting. On that occa-

sion she dressed in a similar manner without her face being covered. At the hearing, the Claimant was asked the reason for her apparent change in practice and she explained that her husband had suggested to her that she should go unveiled.

9. During the first week of term, the Appellant telephoned Mrs Maher to ask if she could wear the veil when teaching with male teachers, or whether arrangements could be made so she would not have to work with male teachers at all. Mrs Maher referred the matter to the headmaster and she discussed it with him on 9 September. They concluded that it was not possible to isolate the Appellant from male staff, since all the classes had some male teachers and, in addition, the Claimant was required to liaise from time to time with other male members of staff. Mr Smith spoke to the Claimant on that Friday to inform her that it was not possible to re-arrange her duties because of the substantial timetable changes that would be required. The Appellant then asked if she could consider the matter over the weekend.

10. On Monday 12 September, the Appellant spoke to Mr Smith and informed him that she was willing to work with male teachers but, to accord with her religious beliefs, she would have to wear a veil at all times when in the presence of male colleagues. This would include when she was speaking to and communicating with the children. Mr Smith had not encountered this issue before, since the other female Muslim staff wore the traditional headscarf but not a veil. He sought advice from the education department of the Respondent. They had no existing guidelines, though a similar situation at another Kirklees primary school had just been referred to them. The Respondents began holding meetings and conducting enquiries concerning the impact on staff wishing to wear a veil when carrying out educational duties at the Respondent's schools. There already existed a pack of material, provided to new teachers and assistants, in which there is reference to children learning a second language and which compares it to the way in which they acquire their first language. In particular it states:

> Gesture and body language including facial expression reinforce the spoken word.

11. The Respondent's education service prepared and produced advice to head teachers on the wearing of the veil during October 2005. It confirmed the Respondent's commitment to valuing cultural and religious diversity. It also referred to their responsibility to ensure that all members of staff were able to undertake their duties effectively. It stated:

> We believe the following principles are appropriate to our circumstances. Obscuring the face and mouth reduces the non-verbal signals required be-

> tween adult and pupil, both in the classroom and other communal parts of the School. A pupil needs to see the adult's full face in order to receive optimum communication. Schools are professional settings where communication is vital, both between adults and pupils and between adults. It follows that for teachers or support workers wearing a veil in the workplace will prevent full and effective communication being maintained. In our view the desire to express religious identity does not overcome the primary requirement for optimal communication between adults and children.

> 12. Mr Smith had agreed that, pending receipt of advice, the Appellant could wear the veil even when teaching the children. He decided to undertake an observation of her work. This took place on 21 September when she was supporting a male class teacher, Mr Lee, in a literacy session. He concluded that it was readily apparent that the children she was working with were seeking visual clues from her which they could not obtain because they could not see her facial expressions. He also thought that her diction was not as clear as it would have been if she were not wearing a veil. There were occasions when the Claimant had to speak at the same time as the teacher which meant that she had to be able to speak quietly but clearly to her group of children.

> 13. Mr Smith discussed his findings with the Appellant and indicated that his professional assessment was that she would be able to carry out her role more effectively if she were not wearing the veil when working directly with the children. The Appellant maintained that her religious belief required her to be veiled when in the presence of adult males. Mr Smith told her that she should not wear the veil when working directly with children in a classroom.

The appellant subsequently took time off work for stress.

> 28. She returned to work on 20 February 2006. Mr Smith discussed with her the instruction not to wear the veil when she was in class communicating with the children. The Appellant said she was unwilling to comply with this instruction. Following further discussions, Mr Smith arranged for her to be placed in year 3 on a temporary basis since one of the other BSWs in that year was off sick. This meant that for most of the time the Appellant would be able to work with female class teachers and would not need to be veiled when communicating with pupils. Mr Smith asked her to consider being unveiled at all times in the classroom, although he confirmed that she could continue to wear her veil in communal areas of the school, the library and the shared area. But the Claimant was not prepared to agree to this proposal.

29. Following further discussions with the Respondent's education department it was agreed that there would be a meeting with the Claimant prior to taking further action. This meeting was held on 23 February. As for the wearing of the veil, the Appellant indicated that she had been happy in the past few days in year 3 but it was pointed out that the basic management instruction remained that in the classroom she should not be veiled. The Appellant said that when working with males she would be veiled and she would not remove her veil. She was then suspended. This was confirmed by letter of the same date. Two reasons were given, first, she had not obeyed the instruction issued by Mr Smith not to be veiled whilst communication with the children, second, a failure to keep in contact with the school and submit sick notes during her recent absence.

…

1.1 *Direct Discrimination*

The following extract provides the reasoning of the Employment Appeal Tribunal in *Azmi v Kirklees* on the issue of direct discrimination under the Employment Equality (Religion or Belief) Regulations 2003.

…

51. The ET decided that this was not a case of direct discrimination. Its main reason for doing so was set out in paragraph 9.13. The Claimant had failed to show that she had suffered less favourable treatment than a comparator in similar circumstances. The Tribunal also found that there was no evidence of any prejudice or motivation which would cause the Tribunal to conclude that discrimination on the ground of her religion must exist.

52. There was a dispute before the ET as to the characteristics of the comparator. The Appellant argued that the comparator should be another Muslim woman who covered her head but not her face. The ET rejected that contention. It concluded that the comparator should be a person, not of the Muslim religion, who covered her face for whatever reason. On that basis the Tribunal concluded, having regard to the documents which were before it concerning the Respondent's teaching methodology for children reading English as a second language, that any such comparator would also have been suspended since that person's face and mouth would be obscured, which would be a barrier to effective learning by those children in circumstances where the Respondent's policy was that the education of children was paramount.

…

56. The ET, having chosen, in our judgment, the correct comparator, concluded, on the evidence before it, that such a person would have been issued an instruction and, if she had refused to comply with it, would have been suspended. Accordingly, it concluded that the claim for direct discrimination failed. In our judgment it was entitled so to conclude and did not err in law in so doing.

…

1.2 *Indirect Discrimination*

The following extract provides the reasoning of the court in *Azmi v Kirklees* on the issue of indirect discrimination under the Employment Equality (Religion or Belief) Regulations 2003.

…

63. … the ET had to consider whether the PCP [provision, criterion or practice] put persons of the Appellant's belief at a particular disadvantage when compared with others. It was not in dispute that it did and that the reason for that was that the Appellant believed that she was required by her religion to wear the veil, whereas persons of another religion or no religion would not have such a requirement. Accordingly, the ET found that there was a potential case of indirect discrimination and proceeded to consider whether the Respondent was able to show that the adoption of the PCP in this particular case was a proportionate means of achieving a legitimate aim.

…

65. The argument on this aspect of the case was focussed on whether the ET had erred in law in concluding that the means chosen were proportionate. The ET addressed this at paragraphs 18 to 25 of its decision. It referred back to the history of the matter, in particular the fact that the requirement was not imposed by the school immediately, but the Appellant was permitted to wear the veil, when she considered it appropriate, at all times up to 16 November 2006.

66. Second, the ET took into account the fact that, by confining the instruction that she must remove her veil to those occasions when she was teaching the children, and concluded that the means adopted were proportionate. The Claimant had the freedom to wear the veil at all other times, in particular when she was moving to different parts of the school. Any earlier confusion there may have been about this had been sufficiently clarified by Mr Smith in his relevant letter.

67. Third, the ET took account of the fact that, before issuing the instruction there had been observations of the Claimant teaching and assisting the children. Mr Smith had observed her and was concerned about how effective her communication was. There was detailed observation by Mrs Maher on 7 November when she took detailed notes which were produced to the Tribunal. In paragraph 22 of the decision the ET said as follows:

> Although Mrs Maher did suggest that the Claimant should take other action such as raising her voice, etc, this does not mean that there would necessarily have been communication with the children which was as good and effective as if she was not wearing the veil.

In addition to the paragraph to which we have referred, the ET reminded itself of the consideration which had been given by the Respondent to alternative ways for accommodating the Appellant's wish to wear her veil when in the classroom with a male teacher, including suggestions that she use a screen; or that she remain with her back to the teacher; or that she remove the target group from the classroom; or that she use more hand and body gestures; or that the timetable be changed so that she only taught with female teachers.

…

74. In respect of each of these possible alternatives, including actions such as raising her voice, the ET in paragraph 25 concluded that it was satisfied that the Respondent had shown that the imposition of the PCP was a proportionate means of achieving their legitimate aim. They did so … having conducted the kind of stringent investigation of the alternative means of achieving the aim by not imposing this requirement upon the Appellant, and having concluded that the Respondent had discharged the statutory burden upon it. In those circumstances, in our judgment, the ET did not err in law in its decision on whether the indirect discrimination that they found was justified within the terms of the statute. Accordingly, the appeal on indirect discrimination fails.

2 Islamic Dress under Article 9 of the ECHR

R (Begum) v. Headteacher and Governors of Denbigh High School
[2006] UKHL 15 (per Lord Bingham), House of Lords

In the *Begum* case, of a Muslim pupil whose school disallowed her claim to be allowed to wear a *jilbab*, a full-length gown that covered her neck, the House of Lords was asked to consider the question whether there was a violation of ECHR, Article 9 (freedom of religion).

2.1 *Interference*

In *Begum*, the House of Lords first considered the question whether there was an interference with Article 9(1), given the factual background of the case. Lord Bingham, from whose judgment the extracts below are reproduced, was in the majority on the question whether an interference with the freedom of religion in Article 9 had occurred at all, that majority deciding that no interference was present.

> 2. It is important to stress at the outset that this case concerns a particular pupil and a particular school in a particular place at a particular time. It must be resolved on facts which are now, for purposes of the appeal, agreed. The House is not, and could not be, invited to rule whether Islamic dress, or any feature of Islamic dress, should or should not be permitted in the schools of this country. That would be a most inappropriate question for the House in its judicial capacity, and it is not one which I shall seek to address.
>
> ...
>
> 10. On 3 September 2002, the first day of the autumn term, the respondent (then aged nearly 14) went to the school with her brother and another young man. They asked to speak to the head teacher, who was not available, and they spoke to the assistant head teacher, Mr Moore. They insisted that the respondent be allowed to attend the school wearing the long garment she had on that day, which was a long coatlike garment known as a jilbab. They talked of human rights and legal proceedings. Mr Moore felt that their approach was unreasonable and he felt threatened. He decided that the respondent should wear the correct school uniform and told her to go home, change and return wearing school uniform. His previous experience in such situations, with one exception, was that pupils always complied. He did not believe he was excluding the respondent, which he had no authority to do, but did not allow her to enter the school dressed as she was, this being (it was said) the only garment which met her religious requirements because it concealed, to a greater extent than the shalwar kameeze, the contours of the female body, and was said to be appropriate for maturing girls. The respondent then left with her brother and the other young man. The young men said they were not prepared to compromise over this issue.
>
> ...
>
> 15. The respondent's solicitor obtained opinions from three sources (two of them Imams previously consulted by the appellants) to the effect that the jilbab was the appropriate dress for mature Muslim women. This advice was passed on to the appellants, who did not accept it but repeatedly urged the respondent to

return to school. The chairman of the governors reviewed the matter and supported the action of the head teacher. The appellants reiterated that the respondent had not been excluded, that she had a place at the school but that she must wear one of the school's approved uniforms. The EWS met the respondent in September 2003 and offered her their help in getting a place at another school if that was what she wanted. In the same month there was forwarded to the school a statement made by the Muslim Council of Britain on the "Dress code for women in Islam": there was no recommended style; modesty must be observed at all times; trousers with long tops or shirts for school wear were "absolutely fine".

...

23. The Strasbourg institutions [i.e. the Commission and Court of Human Rights] have not been at all ready to find an interference with the right to manifest religious belief in practice or observance where a person has voluntarily accepted an employment or role which does not accommodate that practice or observance and there are other means open to the person to practise or observe his or her religion without undue hardship or inconvenience.

...

24. ... Even if it be accepted that the Strasbourg institutions have erred on the side of strictness in rejecting complaints of interference, there remains a coherent and remarkably consistent body of authority which our domestic courts must take into account and which shows that interference is not easily established.

25. In the present case the respondent's family chose for her a school outside their own catchment area. It was a school which went to unusual lengths to inform parents of its uniform policy. The shalwar kameeze, and not the jilbab, was worn by the respondent's elder sister throughout her time at the school, and by the respondent for her first two years, without objection. It was of course open to the respondent, as she grew older, to modify her beliefs, but she did so against a background of free and informed consent by her and her family. It is also clear that there were three schools in the area at which the wearing of the jilbab was permitted. The respondent's application for admission to one of these was unsuccessful because the school was full, and it was asserted in argument that the other two were more distant. There is, however, no evidence to show that there was any real difficulty in her attending one or other of these schools, as she has in fact done and could no doubt have done sooner had she chosen. On the facts here, and endeavouring to apply the Strasbourg jurisprudence in a reasonable way, I am of opinion that in this case (unlike Williamson, above, para 41, where a different conclusion was reached) there was no interference with the respondent's

> right to manifest her belief in practice or observance. I appreciate, however, that my noble and learned friends Lord Nicholls and Lady Hale of Richmond incline to a different opinion. It follows that this is a debatable question, which gives the issue of justification under article 9(2) particular significance.

2.2 *Justification for Interference with Article 9 Rights*

Especially given the difference of opinion among the judges on the interference point, in the same case of *Begum* Lord Bingham dealt with the question whether, assuming that there had been an interference, which the majority considered had not happened, such an interference might be justified:

> 26. To be justified under article 9(2) a limitation or interference must be (a) prescribed by law and (b) necessary in a democratic society for a permissible purpose, that is, it must be directed to a legitimate purpose and must be proportionate in scope and effect. It was faintly argued for the respondent that the school's uniform policy was not prescribed by law, but both the judge (para 78) and the Court of Appeal (paras 61, 83 and 90) held otherwise, and rightly so. The school authorities had statutory authority to lay down rules on uniform, and those rules were very clearly communicated to those affected by them. It was not suggested that the rules were not made for the legitimate purpose of protecting the rights and freedoms of others. So the issue is whether the rules and the school's insistence on them were in all the circumstances proportionate. This raises an important procedural question on the court's approach to proportionality and, depending on the answer to that, a question of substance.
>
> ...
>
> 33. The respondent criticised the school for permitting the headscarf while refusing to permit the jilbab, for refusing permission to wear the jilbab when some other schools permitted it and for adhering to their own view of what Islamic dress required. None of these criticisms can in my opinion be sustained. The headscarf was permitted in 1993, following detailed consideration of the uniform policy, in response to requests by several girls. There was no evidence that this was opposed. But there was no pressure at any time, save by the respondent, to wear the jilbab, and that has been opposed. Different schools have different uniform policies, no doubt influenced by the composition of their pupil bodies and a range of other matters. Each school has to decide what uniform, if any, will best serve its wider educational purposes. The school did not reject the respondent's request out of hand: it took advice, and was told that its existing policy conformed with the requirements of mainstream Muslim opinion.

34. On the agreed facts, the school was in my opinion fully justified in acting as it did. It had taken immense pains to devise a uniform policy which respected Muslim beliefs but did so in an inclusive, unthreatening and uncompetitive way. The rules laid down were as far from being mindless as uniform rules could ever be. The school had enjoyed a period of harmony and success to which the uniform policy was thought to contribute. On further enquiry it still appeared that the rules were acceptable to mainstream Muslim opinion. It was feared that acceding to the respondent's request would or might have significant adverse repercussions. It would in my opinion be irresponsible of any court, lacking the experience, background and detailed knowledge of the head teacher, staff and governors, to overrule their judgment on a matter as sensitive as this. The power of decision has been given to them for the compelling reason that they are best placed to exercise it, and I see no reason to disturb their decision. After the conclusion of argument the House was referred to the recent decision of the Supreme Court of Canada in *Multani v Commission scolaire Marguerite-Bourgeoys* [2006] SCC 6. That was a case decided, on quite different facts, under the Canadian Charter of Rights and Freedoms. It does not cause me to alter the conclusion I have expressed.

CHAPTER 14

Criminal Law

The general picture of Muslims revealed in the crime figures in Britain is striking. On average for the years 2015 to 2023 Muslims formed 16.16 per cent of the total prison population in England and Wales. In absolute numbers the population of Muslims in prison rose from 12,543 in 2015 to 15,271 in 2023, in some years constituting up to three times their proportion in the general population. Muslims made up 17.52 per cent of the total prison population in 2021, 17.40 per cent in 2022 and 17.86 per cent in 2023. Estimating a Muslim population of 7 per cent in England and Wales, a parliamentary briefing noted that in March 2024 there were 15,909 Muslims in prison in England and Wales, constituting 18 per cent of the prison population, an increase of 10.4 per cent since 2002.[1] The same briefing observed an over representation of Muslims in Scottish prisons, although older figures were used than those for England and Wales.

Muslims are over-represented in some sorts of criminal behaviour. For example, in recent years there have been successive revelations of Muslims being involved in Group Localised Child Sexual Exploitation (GLCSE), and they are probably over-represented in this activity, in what has been popularly termed "grooming gangs."[2] A greater proportion of Muslims is monitored for involvement in terrorism-related activity. A parliamentary briefing paper noted that, as of 31 March 2022, 158 or 68 per cent of terrorist and extremist prisoners in custody in Great Britain were Muslim.[3] The UK government has estimated that some 850 fighters had travelled to Syria to join ISIS, which amounts to one of the highest figures from any Western country.[4] In addition, some specific offences have been created in recent years, such as those relating to forced

1 Sturge, G. (2024), *UK prison population statistics*. House of Commons Library. The 2002–2014 period also saw a rise in the Muslim prison population in proportional terms and at a rate greater than the increase in Muslims in the general population. See Shaw, D. (2015), "Why the surge in Muslim prisoners?," *BBC News*, 11 March 2015. Available at: https://www.bbc.co.uk/news/uk-31794599.

2 Bhatti-Sinclair, K. and Sutcliffe, C.M.S. (2023), "Group localised child sexual exploitation offenders: Who and why?". Unpublished paper. At https://papers.ssrn.com/sol3/papers.cfm?abstract_id=3248665

3 Allen, G., Burton, M., and Pratt, A. (2022), *Terrorism in Great Britain: The statistics*: House of Commons Library, pp. 26–27.

4 "Tally of Britons joining ISIS and similar groups abroad grown to 850," theguardian.com, 14.08.2016 ⟨https://www.theguardian.com/world/2016/aug/11/britons-joining-isis-grown-to-850-100-killed-syria-khadiza-sultana⟩.

marriage or female genital mutilation, where it is thought that Muslims have a significant representation among the perpetrators.

Although Islamophobia has often been flagged in public, institutional and academic discourse as making Muslims more vulnerable to discrimination and hate crimes, it is unclear how prevalent it is. Among the factors responsible for this lack of clarity are that the very conception of Islamophobia is vague and rather expansive, and since claims of Islamophobia are self-reported, they are subject to quirkiness and liable to be unreliable. Nevertheless, alongside the recognition of religion in the civil anti-discrimination law, a number of religion-linked offences have been introduced in recent decades at the behest of Muslim campaigners, and include public order offences connected with religion and religiously aggravated offences.[5] Islamophobia as a notion meaning anti-Muslim hate also finds some elaboration in the judiciary's Equal Treatment Bench Book (see ch. 1, section 4). Despite the inherent methodological problems, the Bench Book tends to treat claims of Islamophobia and its prevalence uncritically. In February 2025, the British government announced that it would recognise Islamophobia, although it is assumed that this will not involve legislative change, but will rather be reflected in guidance issued to the police and prosecuting authorities.

1 Public Order Offences

The Racial and Religious Hatred Act 2006 provides for additional penalties in the criminal law applying to hate-related offences. The 2006 Act, which applies only to England and Wales, amends the Public Order Act 1986 by creating new offences of stirring up hatred against persons on religious grounds and amends section 24A of the Police and Criminal Evidence Act 1984 so that the powers of citizen's arrest do not apply here. Religious hatred is defined as hatred against a group of persons defined by reference to religious belief or the lack of it. For each offence the words, behaviour, written material, recordings or programmes must be threatening and intended to stir up religious hatred. The offences apply to the use of words or behaviour or the display of written material (section 29B), publishing or distributing written material (section 29C), the public performance of a play (section 29D), distributing, showing or playing a recording (section 29E), broadcasting or including a programme in a programme service

5 Meer, N. (2010), *Citizenship, identity and the politics of multiculturalism: The rise of Muslim consciousness*. Basingstoke: Palgrave Macmillan, Nash, P. (2022), *British Islam and English law: A classical pluralist perspective*. Cambridge: Cambridge University Press, pp. 45–80.

(section 29F), and the possession of written materials or recordings with a view to their display, publication, distribution or inclusion in a programme service (section 29G). There is an overriding clause protecting the freedom of expression in section 29J, but it applies only to Part 3A of the Act and not to other parts of this or other legislation.

In *Norwood v DPP*, a British National Party member was convicted of displaying a poster in the window of his house for probably causing harassment, alarm or distress under the Public Order Act, section 5 (extracted below) in a religiously aggravated manner. The poster contained a photograph of the Twin Towers in flames, the words "Islam out of Britain—Protect the British People," and a symbol of a crescent and star in a no entry sign.[6] The defendant applied to the European Court of Human Rights, complaining that the criminal proceedings against him violated the ECHR, Article 10. The European Court declared the application inadmissible, relying on Article 17 (destruction of Convention rights) to do so.[7] A slightly differently worded provision, section 4A, concerning intentional harassment, alarm or distress was added to the Public Order Act by the Criminal Justice and Public Order Act 1994. This offence has the requirement of intentionality but is not qualified by the act having to be within the sight or hearing of the person affected as the section 5 offence does. On 3 February 2025, Martin Frost was charged with causing racially and religiously aggravated intentional harassment, alarm and distress and admitted to so doing. He was prosecuted for having burnt pages of the Qur'an apparently demonstrating solidarity with Salwan Momika, an Iraqi Christian refugee who was shot dead the previous week after burning Qur'ans in Sweden during public demonstrations in 2023. These cases demonstrate that the freedom of speech guarantee of section 29J is unavailable when a person is accused of having committed offences that were not introduced into the Public Order Act by the Racial and Religious Hatred Act 2006. It should also be noted that the Online Safety Act 2023, Schedule 7, paras. 4 and 5 (not extracted here) extends some of the offences in the Public Order Act to online activities.

Public Order Act 1986

4A Intentional harassment, alarm or distress.

(1) A person is guilty of an offence if, with intent to cause a person harassment, alarm or distress, he—

6 *Norwood v DPP* [2003] EWHC 1564 (Admin).

7 *Norwood v United Kingdom*, Application No. 23131/03, 16 November 2004, (2005) 40 E.H.R.R. SE11.

(a) uses threatening, abusive or insulting words or behaviour, or disorderly behaviour, or
(b) displays any writing, sign or other visible representation which is threatening, abusive or insulting,

thereby causing that or another person harassment, alarm or distress.

(2) An offence under this section may be committed in a public or a private place, except that no offence is committed where the words or behaviour are used, or the writing, sign or other visible representation is displayed, by a person inside a dwelling and the person who is harassed, alarmed or distressed is also inside that or another dwelling.

(3) It is a defence for the accused to prove—
(a) that he was inside a dwelling and had no reason to believe that the words or behaviour used, or the writing, sign or other visible representation displayed, would be heard or seen by a person outside that or any other dwelling, or
(b) that his conduct was reasonable.

(5) A person guilty of an offence under this section is liable on summary conviction to imprisonment for a term not exceeding 6 months or a fine not exceeding level 5 on the standard scale or both.

5 Harassment, alarm or distress.

(1) A person is guilty of an offence if he—
(a) uses threatening or abusive words or behaviour, or disorderly behaviour, or
(b) displays any writing, sign or other visible representation which is threatening or abusive,

within the hearing or sight of a person likely to be caused harassment, alarm or distress thereby.

(2) An offence under this section may be committed in a public or a private place, except that no offence is committed where the words or behaviour are used, or the writing, sign or other visible representation is displayed, by a person inside a dwelling and the other person is also inside that or another dwelling.

(3) It is a defence for the accused to prove—
(a) that he had no reason to believe that there was any person within hearing or sight who was likely to be caused harassment, alarm or distress, or
(b) that he was inside a dwelling and had no reason to believe that the words or behaviour used, or the writing, sign or other

visible representation displayed, would be heard or seen by a person outside that or any other dwelling, or

(c) that his conduct was reasonable.

…

(6) A person guilty of an offence under this section is liable on summary conviction to a fine not exceeding level 3 on the standard scale.

…

Part 3A

Meaning of "religious hatred" and "hatred on the grounds of sexual orientation"

29A Meaning of "religious hatred"

In this Part "religious hatred" means hatred against a group of persons defined by reference to religious belief or lack of religious belief.

29AB Meaning of "hatred on the grounds of sexual orientation"

In this Part "hatred on the grounds of sexual orientation" means hatred against a group of persons defined by reference to sexual orientation (whether towards persons of the same sex, the opposite sex or both).

29B Use of words or behaviour or display of written material

(1) A person who uses threatening words or behaviour, or displays any written material which is threatening, is guilty of an offence if he intends thereby to stir up religious hatred or hatred on the grounds of sexual orientation.

(2) An offence under this section may be committed in a public or a private place, except that no offence is committed where the words or behaviour are used, or the written material is displayed, by a person inside a dwelling and are not heard or seen except by other persons in that or another dwelling.

…

(4) In proceedings for an offence under this section it is a defence for the accused to prove that he was inside a dwelling and had no reason to believe that the words or behaviour used, or the written material displayed, would be heard or seen by a person outside that or any other dwelling.

(5) This section does not apply to words or behaviour used, or written material displayed, solely for the purpose of being included in a programme service.

29C Publishing or distributing written material

(1) A person who publishes or distributes written material which is threatening is guilty of an offence if he intends thereby to stir up religious hatred or hatred on the grounds of sexual orientation.

(2) References in this Part to the publication or distribution of written material are to its publication or distribution to the public or a section of the public.

29D Public performance of play

(1) If a public performance of a play is given which involves the use of threatening words or behaviour, any person who presents or directs the performance is guilty of an offence if he intends thereby to stir up religious hatred or hatred on the grounds of sexual orientation.

(2) This section does not apply to a performance given solely or primarily for one or more of the following purposes—

  (a) rehearsal,

  (b) making a recording of the performance, or

  (c) enabling the performance to be included in a programme service;

  but if it is proved that the performance was attended by persons other than those directly connected with the giving of the performance or the doing in relation to it of the things mentioned in paragraph (b) or (c), the performance shall, unless the contrary is shown, be taken not to have been given solely or primarily for the purpose mentioned above.

(3) For the purposes of this section—

  (a) a person shall not be treated as presenting a performance of a play by reason only of his taking part in it as a performer,

  (b) a person taking part as a performer in a performance directed by another shall be treated as a person who directed the performance if without reasonable excuse he performs otherwise than in accordance with that person's direction, and

  (c) a person shall be taken to have directed a performance of a play given under his direction notwithstanding that he was not present during the performance;

  and a person shall not be treated as aiding or abetting the commission of an offence under this section by reason only of his taking part in a performance as a performer.

(4) In this section "play" and "public performance" have the same meaning as in the Theatres Act 1968.

(5) The following provisions of the Theatres Act 1968 apply in relation to an offence under this section as they apply to an offence under section 2 of that Act—

section 9 (script as evidence of what was performed),
section 10 (power to make copies of script),
section 15 (powers of entry and inspection).

29E Distributing, showing or playing a recording

(1) A person who distributes, or shows or plays, a recording of visual images or sounds which are threatening is guilty of an offence if he intends thereby to stir up religious hatred or hatred on the grounds of sexual orientation.

(2) In this Part "recording" means any record from which visual images or sounds may, by any means, be reproduced; and references to the distribution, showing or playing of a recording are to its distribution, showing or playing to the public or a section of the public.

(3) This section does not apply to the showing or playing of a recording solely for the purpose of enabling the recording to be included in a programme service.

29F Broadcasting or including programme in programme service

(1) If a programme involving threatening visual images or sounds is included in a programme service, each of the persons mentioned in subsection (2) is guilty of an offence if he intends thereby to stir up religious hatred or hatred on the grounds of sexual orientation.

(2) The persons are—
(a) the person providing the programme service,
(b) any person by whom the programme is produced or directed, and
(c) any person by whom offending words or behaviour are used.

Inflammatory material

29G Possession of inflammatory material

(1) A person who has in his possession written material which is threatening, or a recording of visual images or sounds which are threatening, with a view to—
(a) in the case of written material, its being displayed, published, distributed, or included in a programme service whether by himself or another, or

(b) in the case of a recording, its being distributed, shown, played, or included in a programme service, whether by himself or another,

is guilty of an offence if he intends thereby to stir up religious hatred or hatred on the grounds of sexual orientation.

(2) For this purpose regard shall be had to such display, publication, distribution, showing, playing, or inclusion in a programme service as he has, or it may reasonably be inferred that he has, in view.

29H Powers of entry and search

(1) If a justice of the peace is satisfied by information on oath laid by a constable that there are reasonable grounds for suspecting that a person has possession of written material or a recording in contravention of section 29G, the justice may issue a warrant under his hand authorising any constable to enter and search the premises where it is suspected the material or recording is situated.

(2) …

(3) A constable entering or searching premises in pursuance of a warrant issued under this section may use reasonable force if necessary.

(4) In this section “premises” means any place and, in particular, includes—

(a) any vehicle, vessel, aircraft or hovercraft,

(b) any offshore installation as defined in section 12 of the Mineral Workings (Offshore Installations) Act 1971, and

(c) any tent or movable structure.

29I Power to order forfeiture

(1) A court by or before which a person is convicted of—

(a) an offence under section 29B relating to the display of written material, or

(b) an offence under section 29C, 29E or 29G,

shall order to be forfeited any written material or recording produced to the court and shown to its satisfaction to be written material or a recording to which the offence relates.

(2) An order made under this section shall not take effect—

(a) until the expiry of the ordinary time within which an appeal may be instituted or, where an appeal is duly instituted, until it is finally decided or abandoned;

(b) …

(3) For the purposes of subsection (2)(a)—
   (a) an application for a case stated or for leave to appeal shall be treated as the institution of an appeal, and
   (b) where a decision on appeal is subject to a further appeal, the appeal is not finally determined until the expiry of the ordinary time within which a further appeal may be instituted or, where a further appeal is duly instituted, until the further appeal is finally decided or abandoned.

(4) …

29J Protection of freedom of expression

Nothing in this Part shall be read or given effect in a way which prohibits or restricts discussion, criticism or expressions of antipathy, dislike, ridicule, insult or abuse of particular religions or the beliefs or practices of their adherents, or of any other belief system or the beliefs or practices of its adherents, or proselytising or urging adherents of a different religion or belief system to cease practising their religion or belief system.

29JA Protection of freedom of expression (sexual orientation)

(1) In this Part, for the avoidance of doubt, the discussion or criticism of sexual conduct or practices or the urging of persons to refrain from or modify such conduct or practices shall not be taken of itself to be threatening or intended to stir up hatred.

(2) In this Part, for the avoidance of doubt, any discussion or criticism of marriage which concerns the sex of the parties to marriage shall not be taken of itself to be threatening or intended to stir up hatred.

Supplementary provisions

29K Savings for reports of parliamentary or judicial proceedings

(1) Nothing in this Part applies to a fair and accurate report of proceedings in Parliament, in the Scottish Parliament or in the National Assembly for Wales.

(2) Nothing in this Part applies to a fair and accurate report of proceedings publicly heard before a court or tribunal exercising judicial authority where the report is published contemporaneously with the proceedings or, if it is not reasonably practicable or would be unlawful to publish a report of them contemporaneously, as soon as publication is reasonably practicable and lawful.

29L Procedure and punishment

(1) No proceedings for an offence under this Part may be instituted except by or with the consent of the Attorney General.

(2) For the purposes of the rules against charging more than one offence in the same count or information, each of sections 29B to 29G creates one offence.

(3) A person guilty of an offence under this Part is liable—

(a) on conviction on indictment to imprisonment for a term not exceeding seven years or a fine or both;

(b) on summary conviction to imprisonment for a term not exceeding 12 months or a fine not exceeding the statutory maximum or both.

(4) In subsection (3)(b) the reference to 12 months shall be read as a reference to 6 months in relation to an offence committed before 2 May 2022.

29M Offences by corporations

(1) Where a body corporate is guilty of an offence under this Part and it is shown that the offence was committed with the consent or connivance of a director, manager, secretary or other similar officer of the body, or a person purporting to act in any such capacity, he as well as the body corporate is guilty of the offence and liable to be proceeded against and punished accordingly.

(2) Where the affairs of a body corporate are managed by its members, subsection (1) applies in relation to the acts and defaults of a member in connection with his functions of management as it applies to a director.

29N Interpretation

In this Part—

"distribute", and related expressions, shall be construed in accordance with section 29C(2) (written material) and section 29E(2) (recordings);

"dwelling" means any structure or part of a structure occupied as a person's home or other living accommodation (whether the occupation is separate or shared with others) but does not include any part not so occupied, and for this purpose "structure" includes a tent, caravan, vehicle, vessel or other temporary or movable structure;

"hatred on the grounds of sexual orientation" has the meaning given by section 29AB;

"programme" means any item which is included in a programme service;
"programme service" has the same meaning as in the Broadcasting Act 1990;
"publish", and related expressions, in relation to written material, shall be construed in accordance with section 29C(2);
"religious hatred" has the meaning given by section 29A;
"recording" has the meaning given by section 29E(2), and "play" and "show", and related expressions, in relation to a recording, shall be construed in accordance with that provision;
"written material" includes any sign or other visible representation.

2 Religiously Aggravated Offences

The original version of the Crime and Disorder Act 1998, section 28, referred to the concept of racially aggravated offences. It was amended by the Anti-terrorism, Crime and Security Act 2001 to create the composite notion of "racially or religiously aggravated offences" in England and Wales. Only the racially aggravated offences apply in Scotland. These are not independent offences but allow the adding on of an extra term to a sentence upon conviction where there is hostility based on, or towards, the victim's membership or presumed membership of a racial or religious group. The listed offences are assaults (section 29), criminal damage (section 30), public order offences (section 31) and harassment (section 32). More recently, under the Sentencing Act 2020, section 66 (in force from 1 December 2020), the notion of religiously aggravated offences became applied to any offence. The Crown Prosecution Service of England and Wales has issued a document, "Racist and Religious Hate Crime—Prosecution Guidance" in which it confirms that "[h]ostility is not defined in the legislation. Consideration should be given to ordinary dictionary definitions, which include ill-will, ill-feeling, spite, prejudice, unfriendliness, antagonism, resentment, and dislike".[8] The offences in the Malicious Communications Act 1988, section 1, the Communications Act 2003, section 127, and Part 10 of the Online Safety Act 2023 (not extracted here) may be particularly relevant to consider in the light of the notions of religiously aggravated

8 Racist and Religious Hate Crime—Prosecution Guidance, https://www.cps.gov.uk/legal-guidance/racist-and-religious-hate-crime-prosecution-guidance, updated 3 March 2022, accessed on 12 February 2025.

offences given the extensive concerns and prosecutions that have arisen in the context of social media and email use.[9]

Crime and Disorder Act 1998
PART II
CRIMINAL LAW

Racially or religiously aggravated offnces: England and Wales
28 Meaning of “racially or religiously aggravated”.
(1) An offence is racially or religiously aggravated for the purposes of sections 29 to 32 below if—
  (a) at the time of committing the offence, or immediately before or after doing so, the offender demonstrates towards the victim of the offence hostility based on the victim’s membership (or presumed membership) of a racial or religious group; or
  (b) the offence is motivated (wholly or partly) by hostility towards members of a racial or religious group based on their membership of that group.
(2) In subsection (1)(a) above—
  “membership”, in relation to a racial or religious group, includes association with members of that group;
  “presumed” means presumed by the offender.
(3) It is immaterial for the purposes of paragraph (a) or (b) of subsection (1) above whether or not the offender’s hostility is also based, to any extent, on any other factor not mentioned in that paragraph.
(4) In this section “racial group” means a group of persons defined by reference to race, colour, nationality (including citizenship) or ethnic or national origins.
(5) In this section “religious group” means a group of persons defined by reference to religious belief or lack of religious belief.

Sentencing Act 2020

66 Hostility
(1) This section applies where a court is considering the seriousness of an offence which is aggravated by—

9 See also the legal guidance on Communications Offences produced by the Crown Prosecution Service, https://www.cps.gov.uk/legal-guidance/communications-offences, which provides an idea of the prosecution approach to such offences, accessed on 12 February 2025.

(a) racial hostility,
(b) religious hostility,
(c) hostility related to disability,
(d) hostility related to sexual orientation, or
(e) hostility related to transgender identity.

This is subject to subsection (3).

(2) The court—
(a) must treat the fact that the offence is aggravated by hostility of any of those types as an aggravating factor, and
(b) must state in open court that the offence is so aggravated.

(3) So far as it relates to racial and religious hostility, this section does not apply in relation to an offence under sections 29 to 32 of the Crime and Disorder Act 1998 (racially or religiously aggravated offences).

(4) For the purposes of this section, an offence is aggravated by hostility of one of the kinds mentioned in subsection (1) if—
(a) at the time of committing the offence, or immediately before or after doing so, the offender demonstrated towards the victim of the offence hostility based on—
(i) the victim's membership (or presumed membership) of a racial group,
(ii) the victim's membership (or presumed membership) of a religious group,
(iii) a disability (or presumed disability) of the victim,
(iv) the sexual orientation (or presumed sexual orientation) of the victim, or (as the case may be)
(v) the victim being (or being presumed to be) transgender, or
(b) the offence was motivated (wholly or partly) by—
(i) hostility towards members of a racial group based on their membership of that group,
(ii) hostility towards members of a religious group based on their membership of that group,
(iii) hostility towards persons who have a disability or a particular disability,
(iv) hostility towards persons who are of a particular sexual orientation, or (as the case may be)
(v) hostility towards persons who are transgender.

(5) For the purposes of paragraphs (a) and (b) of subsection (4), it is immaterial whether or not the offender's hostility is also based, to any extent, on any other factor not mentioned in that paragraph.

(6) In this section—
  (a) references to a racial group are to a group of persons defined by reference to race, colour, nationality (including citizenship) or ethnic or national origins;
  (b) references to a religious group are to a group of persons defined by reference to religious belief or lack of religious belief;
  (c) "membership" in relation to a racial or religious group, includes association with members of that group;
  (d) "disability" means any physical or mental impairment;
  (e) references to being transgender include references to being transsexual, or undergoing, proposing to undergo or having undergone a process or part of a process of gender reassignment;
  (f) "presumed" means presumed by the offender.

3 Terrorism Offences

British legislation on terrorism was overhauled by the Terrorism Act 2000. It was envisaged as a permanent piece of legislation, unlike earlier statutes that were meant to have temporary effect.[10] The 2000 Act, which has been amended several times, contains an entirely new definition of "terrorism" (section 1) and "terrorist" (section 40). There is a list of specified offences and more general provisions on "the commission, preparation or instigation of acts of terrorism" (section 40). It has powers for the Secretary of State to proscribe organisations (section 3), and most of those listed today are Islamic organisations. De-proscription of an organisation may be applied for, and a refusal appealed against. A range of offences follows in connection with such proscribed organisations or their aliases, including belonging or professing to belong, support or inviting support; arranging, managing or assisting in arranging or managing meetings connected to an organisations; or addressing a meeting with the purpose of encouraging support for the organisation; wearing a uniform or wearing, carrying or displaying an article, or publishing an image or any of these, in such a way or in such circumstances as to arouse reasonable suspicion that the individual is a member or supporter of a proscribed organisation; or inviting, receiving, providing, using, possessing, arranging to make available, insuring

10 See Syrett, K. (2015), "The United Kingdom," in Roach, K. (ed.), *Comparative counter-terrorism law*. Cambridge: Cambridge University Press, pp. 167–202.

or laundering money or other property for terrorist purposes. There are wide powers of arrest, search and seizure. In Part VI of the Terrorism Act 2000, a number of specific offences are set out: engagement in weapons training (including training in biological and chemical weapons and radioactive materials), directing a terrorist organisation, possession of items and materials for terrorist purposes, and the collection or possession of information for terrorist purposes (including eliciting, publishing or communicating information about members of the armed forces, intelligence services or police). Further offences are added by Part I of the Terrorism Act 2006. These include: the publication of statements which directly or indirectly encourage or induce the commission, preparation or instigation of acts of terrorism (including in order to glorify the preparation or commission of such acts), disseminating terrorist publications, preparing acts of terrorism, attending a place used for terrorist training, making and possessing radioactive devices and materials in connection with an act of terrorism, using radioactive materials and damaging nuclear facilities in connection with an act of terrorism, and terrorist threats relating to radioactive devices and materials and nuclear facilities. The Anti-Terrorism, Crime and Security Act 2001, sections 113–114, meanwhile added specific offences of threats and hoaxes.

Terrorism Act 2000
Part I

Introductory
1 Terrorism: interpretation.
(1) In this Act "terrorism" means the use or threat of action where—
  (a) the action falls within subsection (2),
  (b) the use or threat is designed to influence the government or an international governmental organisation or to intimidate the public or a section of the public, and
  (c) the use or threat is made for the purpose of advancing a political, religious, racial or ideological cause.
(2) Action falls within this subsection if it—
  (a) involves serious violence against a person,
  (b) involves serious damage to property,
  (c) endangers a person's life, other than that of the person committing the action,
  (d) creates a serious risk to the health or safety of the public or a section of the public, or
  (e) is designed seriously to interfere with or seriously to disrupt an electronic system.

(3) The use or threat of action falling within subsection (2) which involves the use of firearms or explosives is terrorism whether or not subsection (1)(b) is satisfied.
(4) In this section—
  (a) "action" includes action outside the United Kingdom,
  (b) a reference to any person or to property is a reference to any person, or to property, wherever situated,
  (c) a reference to the public includes a reference to the public of a country other than the United Kingdom, and
  (d) "the government" means the government of the United Kingdom, of a Part of the United Kingdom or of a country other than the United Kingdom.
(5) In this Act a reference to action taken for the purposes of terrorism includes a reference to action taken for the benefit of a proscribed organisation.

…

Part v

Counter-terrorist Powers
40 Terrorist: interpretation.
(1) In this Part "terrorist" means a person who—
  (a) has committed an offence under any of sections 11, 12, 15 to 18, 54 and 56 to 63, or
  (b) is or has been concerned in the commission, preparation or instigation of acts of terrorism.
(2) The reference in subsection (1)(b) to a person who has been concerned in the commission, preparation or instigation of acts of terrorism includes a reference to a person who has been, whether before or after the passing of this Act, concerned in the commission, preparation or instigation of acts of terrorism within the meaning given by section 1.

Regina v Michael Adebolajo (Also known as Mujaahid Abu Hamza), Michael Adebowale
[2014] EWCA Crim 2779, Court of Appeal

Prior to committing the murder of a soldier, Lee Rigby, in London, the two defendants had converted to Islam and became radicalised. In their defence, they claimed that they were not eligible for a murder conviction because they believed that they were fighting a war and, therefore, their killing of the soldier did not come within the definition of a killing committed "under the Queen's peace" as required by the common law definition of murder. Presumably, the reference to "war" here is one to "*jihad*". The Court of Appeal considered but dismissed this (and other) grounds of their appeal.

> Adebolajo is a British citizen. He was aged 29 at the time of the murder. He is married with four stepchildren and two children. He had three convictions in 2008: failing to surrender to custody, possession of an air weapon, and assault on a constable.
>
> 6. Adebowale is also a British citizen. At the time he was aged 22. He lived with his mother in Deptford, having left school at the age of 16. He had convictions in 2008 and 2009 for possession of cocaine. Although brought up as a Christian, he had converted to Islam when he was aged 17.
>
> 7. After converting to Islam both were radicalised. Each became an extremist. They decided between themselves, in order to advance their extremist cause as they saw it, to murder a soldier in public in broad daylight. They would do so in a way that would generate maximum media coverage. That included getting themselves killed by armed officers who would be bound to attend the scene in the aftermath of the murder. They saw themselves as martyrs who would each gain a place, as they saw it, in paradise. Each plainly had a political or ideological aim in planning the barbaric murder they intended to carry out.
>
> …
>
> 11. Adebolajo and Adebowale got out of the car, armed with knives. Over a period of two to three minutes they butchered Lee Rigby. Adebolajo concentrated on Lee Rigby's neck. He hacked it repeatedly. He first used a substantial cleaver-type knife. He then used another knife. All this was part of an attempt to decapitate him. Its purpose was to have the maximum horrific effect. Adebolajo failed in that process. Nonetheless, he caused horrendous injuries. Adebowale, in contrast, concentrated on Lee Rigby's torso. He stabbed him a number of times in the chest. This was done in a frenzied fashion with severe force. The judge rightly described what had taken place as a "bloodbath."
>
> 12. This was seen, as was intended, by members of the public, in furtherance of their aim to achieve their political and ideological cause and the terrorism

they espoused. Once they had finished their murderous assault, both carried and dragged Lee Rigby's body into the road and dumped it there. They brought the traffic to a halt.

13. Thirteen minutes then elapsed between that event and the arrival of the armed police. A number of members of the public came to the scene. Adebolajo and Adebowale, in pursuance of their ideological and political aim, and the terrorism which they espoused, gloried in what they had done. Each held a gun at one point or another and used it to warn off any male member of the public who looked as they he might intervene. Adebolajo handed out a prepared written statement seeking to justify their cause and their actions. In addition, carrying the bloodied cleaver in bloody hands and knowing he was being filmed, Adebolajo made a political statement. Images were broadcast around the world. The effect of the two statements was to seek to justify their joint actions as being retaliation for deaths in Muslim lands and to incite the removal of the Government in the United Kingdom.

…

15. The judge, who heard evidence from Adebolajo, was satisfied that he was the leader of the joint enterprise, but that Adebowale enthusiastically played his part. It was evident from the way in which the matter proceeded that, apart from what the two intended as part of their political cause, they inflicted upon the family of Lee Rigby indescribable suffering with which they must live for the rest of their lives. That is a matter we take much into account.

…

17. The first relates to the definition of murder. The Defence Statement sets out the following:

> At all times the [applicant Adebolajo] honestly believed he was fighting a war. He believed he was a soldier fighting that war. He only targeted a serving member of the British armed forces because they were engaged in fighting an unjust war on behalf of the State.
>
> …

20. The submission of [counsel for Adebolajo] Mr Gottlieb to Sweeney J was that it had been the law for centuries that the Crown had to prove that a murder was committed under the Sovereign's peace; that did not include killing in the course of a war. The Crown, it was submitted, had to prove that Adebolajo was under "The Queen's Peace" and not at war with the Queen. Whether or not there was a war or rebellion at the time that Lee Rigby was killed was irrelevant. Adebolajo

fell to be dealt with upon the facts as he (Adebolajo) honestly, though mistakenly, believed them to be, namely he was at war with the Queen.

21. It was not surprising it was submitted that this element of the offence of murder in relation to the Queen's peace did not normally feature in murder cases because prior to 1997 reliance by a defendant on a state of war would have been likely to involve an admission of treason. On the basis that this argument was available, Adebolajo was therefore entitled to put before the jury his defence that his killing of Lee Rigby was part of a war with the British Government, involving a people's struggle against forceful occupation and aggression; he had not been under the Queen's peace, but at war with the Queen.

22. In support of this argument Mr Gottlieb put before the judge a 28 page skeleton argument and a number of authorities, the list running to some 20 cases. After hearing argument, the judge ruled that, if an element of the offence of murder was that the killing had to be under the Queen's peace, it was a requirement that the victim or deceased be under the Queen's peace and not the killer, as was advanced by Mr Gottlieb. Accordingly, any belief of either appellant, however genuine, as to the existence of a state of war between him and Her Majesty the Queen justifying the carrying out of the killing was entirely irrelevant. The sole issue was whether it was proved that Lee Rigby himself was under the Queen's peace. The judge directed the jury accordingly.

…

33. The law is now clear. An offender can generally be tried for murder wherever committed if he is a British subject, or, if not a British subject, the murder was committed within England and Wales. The reference to "the Queen's peace", as originally dealt with in the cases to which we have referred, went essentially to jurisdiction. Although the Queen's Peace may play some part still in the elements that have to be proved for murder as regards the status of the victim (and it is not necessary to examine or define the ambit of that), it can only go to the status of the victim; it has nothing whatsoever to do with the status of the killer. The argument was completely hopeless. We have set out at some length why it was hopeless; it should never have been advanced. We dismiss this ground of appeal as entirely misconceived.

Begg v British Broadcasting Corporation

[2016] EWHC 2688 (QB)

This defamation clam was brought by Shakeel Begg, the Chief Imam at Lewisham Islamic Centre, who claimed damages against the Defendant ("the BBC") for libel in respect of an hour-long broadcast of the Sunday Politics current affairs television programme on BBC1 in November 2013. Although it is not a criminal law or specifically a terrorism case, its importance lies in the court's approach to the issue of *jihad*, extremism and terrorism in Islam, which it addresses at some length. The programme was hosted by the well-known journalist and broadcaster, Andrew Neil, and watched by over 838,000 people, and subsequently viewed on the BBC's app, iPlayer, and YouTube. The programme opened with a roving reporter posing the question, "[a]re mosques doing enough to counter extremism?" The broadcast then switched to the studio where Mr Neil interviewed an invited studio guest from the Muslim Council of Britain, particularly on the subject of the treatment of women under Islam. Among the points made by Mr Neil was a specific claim: "[t]he East London Mosque, which you personally and the MCB are closely associated with, it's also the venue for a number of extremist speakers and speakers who espouse extremist positions. This year Shakeel Begg, he spoke there and hailed jihad as 'the greatest of deeds'." The defendant, the BBC, accepted that the claimant did not preach *jihad* as "the greatest of deeds" at the East London Mosque, but asserted that he did so elsewhere; and it also accepted that the claimant did not so preach in 2013, but that he had done so in previous years. The defendant claimed that neither of those errors was of significance, and that the substance of its charges against the claimant remained true. The claimant denied being an extremist speaker and denied that any of his previous speeches and utterances, on their true interpretation, demonstrated that he espoused extremist views. The claimant also put forward a positive case that he had always been against extremism and relied on his inter-faith and community work in support of this. The judge found on the facts that the BBC had succeeded in its defence of justification; that the words complained of were substantially true in their meanings: (1) that the claimant was an extremist Islamic speaker who espoused extremist Islamic positions; and (2) that the claimant had recently promoted and encouraged religious violence by telling Muslims that violence in support of Islam would constitute a man's greatest deed. The extracts below show the way in which the court approached the issue of *jihad*, extremism and terrorism in Islam. Although these findings would come under findings of fact rather than law, and therefore they would not technically bind a future court, they might nevertheless be interesting to examine as an example of a court's construction of the issues of Islamic law, including by considering elements of the experts' evidence.[11]

11 In *Abdulrazaq v Hassan* [2019] EWHC 2930 (QB) the judge took judicial notice of "the

> 78. I heard evidence from the Claimant's expert, Robert Gleave, Professor of Arabic Studies at Exeter University, and the BBC's expert, Dr Matthew Wilkinson, Research Fellow at the Centre of Islamic Studies at the School of Oriental & African Studies (SOAS). They were both instructed to prepare reports by reference to the Claimant's speeches: (a) explaining the various different meanings of the word *"jihad"* in the contexts used by the Claimant; (b) translating and explaining the various Arabic words and *hadith* (sayings and actions of the Prophet Muhammad) used in the passages quoted by the Claimant; and (c) explaining the roles and significance of some of the historical figures cited by the Claimant in his speeches.
>
> The judge nevertheless considered that there was an asymmetry in their reports in some respects; that their instructions and perspectives and methodologies differed but that hefound them useful in certain respects.
>
> …
>
> 83. The experts, Professor Gleave and Dr Wilkinson, have provided me with a deeper understanding of the structure, terminology and fundamental concepts, *mores* and *tropes* of Islam and the perspectives particular to a Muslim audience when considering Muslim theology and ideology. Their expert evidence is of assistance, in particular, as to the meaning of Arabic words, the interpretation to be given to various *hadiths*, what particular historical Islamic figures would be seen to stand for by a Muslim audience, and the range of meanings which the word *jihad* may bear in particular contexts.
>
> 84. I have also had regard to the various views which the experts have expressed on aspects of the Claimant's various speeches. I have, however, assessed the ordinary English, syntax and import of the speeches for myself. Insofar as what the Claimant said, and its meaning, are clear as a matter of plain English, that is a matter for the Court rather than expert evidence. In my judgment, ultimately, the main thrust of the Claimant's messages in each case has been quite clear and would have been quite clear to a Muslim audience.

The judge then summarised some of the early history of Islam and the context of the Qur'anic revelations.

---

uncontroversial fact that within the Arab world many states regard the Muslim Brotherhood as a terrorist organisation. Whether it is proscribed in the United Kingdom does not seem to me to be relevant." The court did not decide whether the association of the claimant with terrorism because of his alleged Muslim Brotherhood links was defamatory and suggested the parties resolve the matter by alternative dispute resolution.

...

Islam is a religion of peace

94. It is common ground that Islam is a religion of peace. The *Qur'an* is a book of peace.

95. The words *Islam, Muslim* and *Salaam* all share the same Arabic triconsonantal root, *s-l-m*, which denotes *"peace"*. *Islam* means "submission to the will of God/Allah," i.e. at peace with God. *Muslim* means a person who has submitted to God/Allah, i.e. at peace with God. *Salaam* is the Arabic word for peace.

96. The fundamental philosophy and world-view of Islam is "unity-in-diversity." God is one God who created Heaven and Earth and the entire universe, including every human being. God, as the Source and Creator of life on Earth, is the unifying feature that underlies the whole of existence and binds humankind. Adam and Eve are cited by the *Qur'an* as the father and mother of the whole of humanity. Noah, Moses, Abraham, Jesus and Muhammad are referred to and cited as Prophets chosen by God. A large part of the *Qur'an* is directed at humankind in general, without any distinction being made between believer or non-believer. We are all brothers and sisters and creatures of God by dint of being from the tribe of Adam (*Banu*). Within this essential unity, the *Qur'an* recognises natural diversity and plurality:

> *O mankind! Lo! We have created you male and female, and have made you nations and tribes that you may know one another. The noblest of you, in the sight of Allah, is the best in conduct. Allah is Knower, Aware.* (*Qur'an*, 49:13)

97. Islam includes unconditional respect for humanity regardless of faith, since all human beings are God's creatures:

> [*L*]*et him who believes in Allah and the Last Day be generous to his neighbour, and let him who believes in Allah and the Last Day be generous to his guest* (narrated by the Companion, Abu Hurairah).

Extremism in religion is forbidden in Islam

98. *Islam* forbids anything extreme. This includes extremism in religion. The *Qur'an* commands:

> *Oh People of the Book, do not go to excess in your religion.* (*Qur'an*, 4: 171 and 5: 77).

99. Prophet Muhammad said:

"Distance yourselves from being extreme in religion" and, *"Beware of going to extremes in religion, for those before you were only destroyed through excessiveness".*

100. The great 14th Century Damascene scholar, ibn Taymiyya, said that extremism in religion means deviating from a "Middle Path" between two extremities.

The meaning of "Jihad"

101. The word *iihad* or *jihād* (جهاد) is an Arabic participle which means literally *"struggling", "exerting oneself"* or *"striving".* It is the nominal participle from the triconsonantal Arabic root *j h d.* In modern parlance, the word *jihad* has, unfortunately, become synonymous with "holy war"; but *jihad* has more complex, varied and subtle meanings in classical Islam which must be viewed and understood in their proper historical context.

102. Scholars distinguish between the linguistic (*lughawi*) and religious meaning of *jihad.* The religious use of the term *jihad* in Islam is shorthand for *jihad fiy sabilillah* which means *"striving in the cause* (literally, path) *of God"* (in *Qur'anic* and contemporary usage).

103. There was broad agreement between the experts as regards the origin, tradition and meaning of *jihad* in Islam. *Jihad* is an ancient, multi-faceted tradition of "striving or struggling" in the cause of God, to obey God and His Law and to establish and preserve Islam. It was common ground that the prevalent message of the *Qur'an* is one of peace and tolerance, but it allows reasonable self-defence (like the Common Law).

104. The word *jihad* appears in 41 verses in the *Qur'an* (in 11 Meccan verses and 30 Median verses). None refers explicitly to an armed struggle. There are 21 references in the context of "striving" generally because of religious beliefs and 12 references in the context of "armed combat" in defence of Islam (*qital*). It is significant that all the verses of the *Qur'an* which refer to the conduct of armed combat (*qital*) came after the Prophet Muhammad and his Companions fled from persecution from Mecca to Medina (*hijra*) in 622 CE as explained above.

Categorisation of Jihad in Islam

105. Classical categorisation of *jihad* in Islam by jurists such as the Maliki5 jurist, Ibn Rushd (Averroes), involved four main categories: (i) *jihad* of the heart

(*jihad bil qalb/nafs*) concerned with combating the evil insinuations of the ego and the devil; (ii) *jihad* by the tongue (*jihad bil lisan*) is concerned with speaking the truth and spreading the word of Islam; (iii) *jihad* by the hand (*jihad bil yad*) concerned with doing what is right and combating injustice; (iv) *jihad* by the sword (*jihad bis saif*) which refers to armed combat (*qital*) in the way of God, or holy war (*qital fi sabilillah*), the final resort if other types of *jihad* fail and the integrity of the Islamic religion and safety of the Muslim community is threatened.

106. The first category, *jihad* of the heart (*jihad bil qalb/nafs*), is classically referred to as the "Greater Struggle" (*al-jihad al-akbar*) as it concerns the daily business of training the ego to obey God's injunctions. The fourth category, *jihad* by the sword (*jihad bis saif*), is commonly referred to as the "Lesser Struggle" (*jihad al-asghar*).

Qital

107. The *Qur'anic* word for armed defensive combat is in fact "*qital*" not *jihad*. It was only during the later formalisation of the doctrines of Islam and the doctrinal formulations of *jihad* as "striving in the path of God" that *qital* was included officially as one of the many forms of *jihad fiy sabilillah* (striving in the path of God). Regrettably, the wider concept of *jihad* has now become confused with the narrow concept of *qital* (a concept which is highly regulated by Islamic law—see further below). In modern times, *qital* has come to monopolise the popular meaning of the word *jihad* both in the Muslim-majority world and in Western minds. This means, unfortunately, that whenever most people use the word *jihad*, they are almost always referring (incorrectly) to *qital*, i.e. armed combat.

108. The *Qur'an* and the *Sunna* lay down strict codes for the ethics of both declaring and conducting *qital* (*la ta 'tadu*):

(1) The established Islamic doctrinal conditions laid down by the *Qur'an* and the *Sunna* for the declaration of armed combat (*qital*) include, *e.g.*, (i) exhaustion of all peaceful avenues, (ii) self-defence against a known armed aggressor (which could never include civilian populations), and (iii) declaration of war by the recognised 'leader' of a Muslim political entity.

(2) The stipulations in the *Qur'an* and the *Sunna* for the ethics of conducting *qital* include, *e.g.*, (i) proportionate force, (ii) only combatants may be fought, not civilians, (iii) crops and civic infrastructure may not be damaged, (iv) looting, plunder and property violation is prohibited, (v) the use

of human shields is forbidden, and (vi) prisoners of war must be humanely treated (see in particular *Qur'an*, 2:190–194).

109. The general and historical context of *Qur'an* 2:190–194 was a concern raised by Muhammad's followers as to whether they were permitted to retaliate and defend themselves when attacked by their persecutors within the sacred precincts in Mecca when on pilgrimage. The *Qur'an* provides:

> *Fight in God's cause against them that fight you but do not overstep the limits. God does not love those that overstep the limits.* (*Qur'an*, 2:190191)

110. Propagation of the false notion that *jihad* in effect means naked *qital*, shorn of its proper historical context and limitations, has been used by extremists to radicalise elements in contemporary society. This distorted notion of *jihad* continues to be used, illegitimately, as a powerful tool of violent Islamist radicalisation, especially in respect of young Muslim men, for whom fighting a "war" "in the cause of God" has a natural historical and emotional appeal.

111. Islamist extremists have routinely diluted, or entirely ignored, these conditions and regulations for (*qital*) in order to seek to justify terrorist attacks against defenceless civilians (notably "9/11" and "7/7").

Is qital only defensive?

112. The experts disagreed on the nature of armed *jihad* (*qital*) in Islam. Professor Gleave stated that the majority of *Sunni* and *Shia'* jurists were of the view that the *Qur'an* licences both legitimate offensive and defensive *jihads*. Dr Wilkinson stated that the *Qur'anic* warrant for armed *jihad* is always as armed *defence* of Islam and Muslim life from prior aggression and that this is the overwhelmingly majority scholarly view in both *Sunni* and *Shia'* Islam. They agreed that what constitutes "defence" and "offence" in the context of armed *jihad* is sometimes contested in Muslim circles.

113. It is not necessary finally to determine this theological issue for the purposes of this judgment, but in so far as it is relevant to do so, it is clear in my view, that the *Qur'an* permits only defensive *jihad* (*al-jihad a-difa'i*).

Salafism

114. *Salafism* is the movement within Islam which argues that Muslim practice should return to that of the 7th Century, the time of Islam's earliest "pious ancest-

ors" (*salaf salih*). *Salafism* in Islam, therefore, generally refers to Islam as practised by the earliest Muslim communities. *Salafi* Islam, is sub-divided into myriad sub-groups. There is a wide spectrum of *Salafist* views. In practice, *Salafism* often tends to scriptural literalism shorn of the necessary contextual reasoning (*asbab an-nuzul*). As Dr Wilkinson explains, *Salafists* are inclined to ignore the contextual understandings of Islam as developed by the four Canonical Schools of Islamic Law and sometimes "cherry-pick" verses of the *Qur'an* and sayings of the Prophet Muhammad to form religious-legal judgments without the necessary contextual reasoning (*asbab annuzul*). Most extreme and violent Islamist extremists would claim to be *Salafi* Muslims, but they take this process of scriptural literalism and contextual ignorance to an extreme extent, i.e. scriptural determinism.

115. Professor Gleave accepts that the majority of *Salafis* do not call for military offensive *jihad*, but simply call for devout Muslims to spread the message of Islam through a process called *da'wah* (call), that is, presenting to non-Muslims and calling on them to recognise the truth of Islam. *Jihadi Salafism* is an "offshoot" of mainstream *Salafism* which "supplements" the religious obligation of *da'wah* (call) with military action, which they refer to simply as "*jihad*".

What is extreme Islam?

116. I turn to consider what is properly to be considered "*extreme*" in the context of Islam and Islamic doctrinal positions. It is necessary to do so in order to determine that the BBC's plea of justification for the WCO is made out, *viz. "The Claimant is an extremist Islamic speaker who espouses extremist Islamic positions"*. The various speeches and posts relied upon by the BBC were given by the Claimant on Islamic issues in his capacity as an Imam and directed to predominantly Muslim audiences. The analysis of what is "*extreme*" and what are "*extremist Islamic positions*" is, therefore, necessarily to be judged initially through the prism of Islam.

117. What is "extreme" is, by definition, something which is not "moderate". Thus, "*extremist*" Islamic positions can be seen in contra-distinction to "moderate" or "mainstream" Islamic positions. Dr Wilkinson usefully defines moderate Islam as essentially those ideas, doctrines and worldviews consensually agreed by *Sunni* and *Shia'* Islamic Law Muslim scholars, mainstream *Salafi* scholars and Muslims, generally to constitute the essential doctrines, teachings and spirit of Islam, according to *Qur'an* and *Sunna*, applied in such a way as to be suitable for the context of contemporary Britain. I agree with this as a general working definition.

Extremist Islamic positions

118. In my view, the following constitute "*extremist*" Islamic positions (or *indicia* thereof).

119. First, a "Manichean" view of the world. A total, eternal "Manichean" worldview is a central tenet of violent Islamic extremism. It divides the world strictly into "Us" versus "Them": those who are blessed or saved (i.e. the "*right kind*" of Muslim) on the one hand and those who are to be damned for eternity (i.e. the "*wrong kind*" of Muslim and everyone else) on the other. For violent Islamic extremists, the "*wrong kind*" of Muslim includes moderate *Sunni* Muslims, all *Shia* Muslims, and many others who are "*mete for the sword*" and can be killed, and anyone who associates or "*collaborates*" with them. Violent Islamic extremists divide the world strictly into the Abode of Islam (*Dar al-Islam*), the Abode of Unbelief (*Dar al-Kufr*) and the Abode of War (*Dar al-Harb*). The ultimate agenda of violent Islamic extremists is the overthrow of all democratic states, including Muslim democratic states, and the creation of a global *Caliphate* or Islamic State and the imposition of a primitive, literalist interpretation of *Shari'a* Law by force (as exemplified by e.g. "ISIS"). The clearest exposition of this "Manichean" philosophy is to be found in Sayyid Qutb's "*Milestones*" who called for a war against *jahiliyyah* (unbelief) (see further below).

120. Second, the reduction of *jihad* (striving in God's cause) to *qital* (armed combat) ("the Lesser Jihad"). An interpretation of *jihad* that simply equiperates *jihad* with *qital* and ignores the numerous peaceable meanings of *jihad* (and "the Greater Jihad") would *a priori* be extreme. Such an interpretation would give *jihad* an exclusively violent meaning which it does not have.

121. Third, the ignoring or flouting of the conditions for the declaration of armed *jihad* (*qital*), i.e. the established Islamic doctrinal conditions for the declaration of armed combat (*qital*) set out above. Thus, terrorist insurgency, "leaderless" *jihadist* attacks by groups or individuals against civilians, or the waging of aggressive war against another country or people, cannot properly constitute lawful *qital* under Islamic doctrine. Accordingly, encouragement of such actions would, therefore, be classified as "*extremist*" Islamic positions.

122. Fourth, the ignoring or flouting of the strict regulations governing the conduct of armed *jihad*, i.e. the stipulations in the *Qur'an* and the *Sunna* for the ethics of conducting *qital* set out above. Thus, the use of excessive violence, attacks on civilians, indiscriminate "suicide" violence and the torture or the murder of

prisoners would constitute violation of these regulations of *jihad*, and, therefore, be classified as "*extremist*" Islamic positions.

123. Fifth, advocating armed fighting in defence of Islam (*qital*) as a universal *idividual* religious obligation (*fard al 'ayn*). *Qital* has been adjudicated from early to classical to modern times by the vast majority of Islamic scholars as being a *collective* religious obligation (*fard al-kifaya*) unless one is directly under attack. Thus, encouraging young Muslim men or women to believe that it was their individual religious duty to go off and 'fight in the name of Allah' would be an "*extremist*" Islamic position.

124. Sixth, any interpretation of *Shari'a* (i.e. religious law laid down by the *Qur'an* and the *Sunna*) that required breaking the "law of the land." Under *Shari'a*, Muslims are required to obey the law of the land, unless that law of the land explicitly required them to break the *Shari'a*.

125. Seventh, the classification of all non-Mslims as unbelievers (*kuffar*). Extremist Islamists cite irreconcilable differences between belief (*iman*) and unbelief (*kufr*) and classify as all non-Muslims as unbelievers (*kuffar*). In mainstream Islam, however, "People of the Book," i.e. Christians and Jews, are not classed as *kuffar*.

126. Eighth, the extreme *Salafist* Islamism doctrine that the precepts of the Muslim faith negate and supersede all other natural ties, such as those of family, kinship and nation. This is redolent of the extreme *Salafist* Islamist outlook which cites absolute, irreconcilable differences between belief (*iman*) and unbelief (*kufr*) (see Sayyid Qutb below).

127. Ninth, the citing with approval of the *fatwa* (legal opinions) of Islamic scholars who espouse extremist views (e.g. the *Salafi-Wahabi* scholar, Sheikh Abdul Aziz bin Baz), or referring with approbation to notorious violent, extremist, Islamic ideologues (e.g. Sayyid Qutb and Abdullah Azzam).

128. Tenth, any teaching which, expressly or implicitly, encourages Muslims to engage in, or support, terrorism or violence in the name of Allah.

Islam forbids terrorism

129. Islam forbids terrorism. Islamic notions of terrorism (*hiraba*) bear similarities to the UK statutory definition as regards unauthorised threats to the wellbeing

and property of individual citizens and to the State. The *Qur'an* and the *Sunna*, i.e. the primary sources of Islamic Law, provide that the crime of sowing sedition and perpetrating terror, to "*cause corruption in the land*" in peaceful territories is one of the most severe crimes in Islam (*Qur'an*, 5:33). "*Corruption*" is defined as armed rebellion against a legitimate ruler, "*those who take up weapons to spread fear*", highway robbery, kidnapping and other acts that would today be classed as terrorist activity. Muslims suffered terrorism in the first century of Islam at the hands of the Khwarij sect.

130. Terrorism in Islam (*hiraba* or *irhab*) was defined by the 11th Century Chief Judge of Muslim Lisbon, Ibn ʿAbd al-Barr, as follows:

> *Anyone who disturbs the free passage in the streets and renders them unsafe to travel, striving to spread corruption in the land by killing people or violating what God has made it unlawful to violate, is guilty of terrorism* [*hiraba*]*, be he a Muslim or a non-Muslim, free or slave, and whether he actually realises his goal of taking money and killing or not.*

131. Thus, the "9/11" and "7/7" bombers would have been guilty of terrorism (*hiraba*) under Islamic law.

4 Forced Marriage Offences

Under the civil provisions on forced marriage (ch. 15, section 2.1.2), the courts have a power to issue forced marriage protection orders (FMPOs), the breach of which can attract a maximum of five years' imprisonment. Since then, the Anti-social Behaviour, Crime and Policing Act 2014, section 121, introduced a self-standing offence of forced marriage which carries a maximum penalty of seven years' imprisonment. Like the civil provisions on forced marriage, the definition of marriage is wider than that of a marriage that would ordinarily be recognised in civil law because the words "whether or not legally binding" are included (section 121(4)). This indicates that legislators have included those *nikah* marriages which may not otherwise be recognised in the civil law as constituting valid marriages. The Marriage and Civil Partnership (Minimum Age) Act 2022 in turn inserted additional provisions into section 121 (subsections 3A–7A) relating to children who are specified to be those under the age of 18. In the case of those who lack capacity (subsection 2) and for children under 18 (subsection 3A), it is irrelevant that the conduct of the offender amounts to violence, threats or any other form of coercion (or deception in the case of children). These specific recent provisions on children do not apply in Scotland as they do in England and Wales. The Scottish provisions also differ in that, instead of a reference to those lacking capacity, they refer to those "incapable of consenting to marriage or civil partnership by reason of mental disorder" (section 122(2)). Schedule 6 of the Anti-social Behaviour, Crime and Policing Act 2014 makes provision for the anonymity of an alleged victim of a forced marriage which extends to publication of their identity in general and not merely that related to court proceedings.[12] The Court of Appeal has observed that an indirect effect of the existence of the criminal law provisions is that they can be used to construe a forced marriage as being void on grounds of public policy.[13]

Anti-social Behaviour, Crime and Policing Act 2014

121 Offence of forced marriage: England and Wales

(1) A person commits an offence under the law of England and Wales if he or she—
  (a) uses violence, threats or any other form of coercion for the purpose of causing another person to enter into a marriage, and
  (b) believes, or ought reasonably to believe, that the conduct may cause the other person to enter into the marriage without free and full consent.

(2) In relation to a victim who lacks capacity to consent to marriage, the offence under subsection (1) is capable of being committed by any conduct carried out for the purpose of causing the victim to enter into a marriage (whether or not the conduct amounts to violence, threats or any other form coercion).

(3) A person commits an offence under the law of England and Wales if he or she—
  (a) practises any form of deception with the intention of causing another person to leave the United Kingdom, and
  (b) intends the other person to be subjected to conduct outside the United Kingdom that is an offence under subsection (1) or would be an offence under that subsection if the victim were in England or Wales.

(3A) A person commits an offence under the law of England and Wales if he or she carries out any conduct for the purpose of causing a

12 Similar provisions apply to victims of sexual offences under the Sexual Offences (Amendment) Act 1992, which is relevant in cases of child sexual exploitation or grooming.

13 *Re SA* (*Declaration of Non-Recognition of Marriage*) [2023] EWCA Civ 1003, [2024] 2 All E.R. 875.

child to enter into a marriage before the child's eighteenth birthday (whether or not the conduct amounts to violence, threats, any other form of coercion or deception, and whether or not it is carried out in England and Wales).

(4) "Marriage" means any religious or civil ceremony of marriage (whether or not legally binding).

(5) "Lacks capacity" means lacks capacity within the meaning of the Mental Capacity Act 2005.

(5A) "Child" means a person under the age of 18 years.

(6) It is irrelevant whether the conduct mentioned in paragraph (a) of subsection (1) or subsection (3A) is directed at the victim of the offence under either of those subsections or another person.

(7) A person commits an offence under subsection (1) or (3) only if, at the time of the conduct or deception—
  (a) the person or the victim or both of them are in England or Wales,
  (b) neither the person nor the victim is in England or Wales but at least one of them is habitually resident in England and Wales, or
  (c) neither the person nor the victim is in the United Kingdom but at least one of them is a UK national.

(7A) A person commits an offence under subsection (3A) only if—
  (a) the conduct is for the purpose of causing the child to enter into a marriage in England or Wales,
  (b) at the time of the conduct, the person or child is habitually resident in England and Wales, or
  (c) at the time of the conduct, the child is a United Kingdom national who—
    (i) has been habitually resident in England and Wales, and
    (ii) is not habitually resident or domiciled in Scotland or Northern Ireland.

(8) "UK national" means an individual who is—
  (a) a British citizen, a British overseas territories citizen, a British National (Overseas) or a British Overseas citizen;
  (b) a person who under the British Nationality Act 1981 is a British subject; or
  (c) a British protected person within the meaning of that Act.

(9) A person guilty of an offence under this section is liable—
  (a) on summary conviction, to imprisonment for a term not exceeding the general limit in a magistrates' court or to a fine or both;

(b) on conviction on indictment, to imprisonment for a term not exceeding 7 years.

(10) In relation to an offence committed before May 2022, the reference to the general limit in a magistrates' court in subsection (9)(a) is to be read as a reference to six months.

5 Female Genital Mutilation Offences

The Female Genital Mutilation Act 2003 makes provision for civil measures and criminal sanctions to be applied when the offence is committed. Female genital mutilation (FGM) involves procedures which include the partial or total removal of the external female genital organs for cultural or other non-therapeutic reasons. It is stated to be medically unnecessary, extremely painful and has serious health consequences at the time when the mutilation is carried out, as well as later on in life.

FGM has been a specific criminal offence in the UK since the passage of the Prohibition of Female Circumcision Act 1985. The Female Genital Mutilation Act 2003 repeals and re-enacts the provisions of the 1985 Act and gives them extra-territorial effect after the recommendation of an All Party Parliamentary Group on Population, Development and Reproductive Health which reported in 2000. The 2003 Act also increases the maximum penalty, on conviction on indictment, for FGM from five to 14 years' imprisonment. The Act applies to England and Wales and Northern Ireland but does not extend to Scotland, where the relevant legislation is the Prohibition of Female Genital Mutilation (Scotland) Act 2005.

The 2003 Act, section 1, makes it an offence for a person to perform an FGM operation on a girl, although an exception is provided for a surgical operation on a girl (including a woman) which is necessary for her physical or mental health, or during labour or birth. The acts in question are excising, infibulating or otherwise mutilating the whole or any part of a girl's labia majora, labia minora or clitoris. In assessing a girl's mental health no account is to be taken of any belief that the operation is needed as a matter of custom or ritual. Consequently, an FGM operation could not be argued to be lawful on the ground that a girl's mental health would suffer if she did not conform with the prevailing custom of her community.

Sections 2 and 3 respectively cover assisting ("aids, abets, counsels or procures") a girl to carry out an FGM operation or doing so overseas in relation to a national or habitual resident of the United Kingdom. Offences under sections 1, 2 and 3 attract a maximum sentence of 14 years' imprisonment when the conviction is on indictment but a maximum of six months and/or a statutory maximum fine after a summary conviction. Section 3A, introduced by the Serious Crime Act 2015, makes it an offence to fail to protect a girl from the risk of genital mutilation. The section 3A offence attracts a maximum sentence of seven years' imprisonment when the conviction is on indictment, but a maximum of six months and/or a statutory maximum fine after a summary conviction. Any of the prohibited acts done outside the UK by a UK national or habitual resident are also criminal offences (section 4). As with Forced Marriage Protection Orders (FMPOs), the victims are granted anonymity (section 4A and Schedule 1).

Under section 5, a healthcare professional, a teacher, or a social care worker in Wales must report it to the police if they discover that an act of female genital mutilation appears to have been carried out on a girl who is aged under 18.

In a manner similar to that for FMPOs, under the 2003 Act, section 5A and Schedule 2, courts are empowered to make FGM protection orders (FGMPOs). Breaching an FGMPO attracts a maximum sentence of five years' imprisonment when on indictment and a maximum of six months and/or a statutory maximum fine after a summary conviction. Since their introduction in July 2015 and up to the end of December 2023, a total of 614 FGMPO applications were made and 864 FGMPOs were made by family courts in England and Wales.[14]

While it is obvious that the practice of FGM is widespread and not restricted to Muslims, the cases in the courts reveal that Muslims who are connected to the UK are involved in the practice, which has also come to the attention of the courts. It has been observed during court proceedings that "the evidence is that FGM is part of the cultural norms of parts of the Somali community and that 98% of women in Somaliland have been subject to FGM."[15] Official figures which are compiled from attendances in England at National Health Service facilities and then entered into the FGM Enhanced Dataset show a significant number and proportion of cases connected to East Africa, North Africa and West Asia by the country of birth of the victim and where FGM was performed.[16] Evidence as to the practice of FGM can also come up indir-

14 Family Court Statistics Quarterly: October to December 2023, published in March 2024, https://www.gov.uk/government/statistics/family-court-statistics-quarterly-october-to-december-2023/family-court-statistics-quarterly-october-to-december-2023#forced-marriage-protection-orders-and-female-genital-mutilation-protection-orders.

15 *SA v AA* [2023] EWHC 2016 (Fam) at para. 5 and similarly at para. 98.

16 *Female Genital Mutilation (FGM) Enhanced Dataset April 2022 to March 2023, England, experimental statistics, Annual Report*, 10 August 2023, https://digital.nhs.uk/data-and-information/publications/statistical/female-genital-mutilation/april-2022-to-march-2023.

ectly through asylum claims,[17] in proceedings related to forced marriage[18] and in care proceedings,[19] and has even been identified in procedures that apply to victims of trafficking.[20] Naturally, claims of FGM can be manufactured to achieve other ends.[21]

Female Genital Mutilation Act 2003

1 Offence of female genital mutilation

(1) A person is guilty of an offence if he excises, infibulates or otherwise mutilates the whole or any part of a girl's labia majora, labia minora or clitoris.

(2) But no offence is committed by an approved person who performs—

   (a) a surgical operation on a girl which is necessary for her physical or mental health, or

   (b) a surgical operation on a girl who is in any stage of labour, or has just given birth, for purposes connected with the labour or birth.

---

17 *Secretary of State for the Home Department v Suffolk County Council and others* [2020] EWCA Civ 731, [2020] 3 W.L.R. 742, where proceedings in the family court for an FGM order concerning a Shia Muslim girl against her return to Bahrain appeared to contradict the Immigration and Asylum Chamber of the First-tier Tribunal's finding on asylum on FGM grounds.

18 *SA v AA* [2023] EWHC 2016 (Fam) where the proceedings did not take place under the forced marriage legislation, but there was a claim by the mother of three children that their father, from whom she was separated, would cause the children to undergo FGM and forced marriages.

19 *Leeds City Council v M, F, B, G* (*B and G by their children's guardian Victoria Wilson*) [2015] EWFC 3 concerning care proceedings with respect to the two children of a Muslim family of which, according to the local authority and expert witnesses, the girl child had undergone FGM, a claim which the judge did not accept.

20 *Regina* (*MN*) *v Secretary of State for the Home Department* (*AIRE Centre and another intervening*) [2020] EWCA Civ 1746, [2021] 1WLR 1956 where the victim was from Nigeria but the judgment does not state whether she was a Muslim.

21 In *Nottingham County Council v OA, MN* [2022] EWFC 102, in rejecting the application for an FGMPO for an infant child of an Egyptian Muslim mother, the judge observed at para. 25, "[t]he irresistible feeling that I was left with, and which remains with me, and which I find, is that the mother had been advised to use the system and complain, first, of domestic abuse, and then of the risks of FGM for the purposes of advancing her settlement application." For a case of travel to Egypt with a child to see the converted wife's Egyptian husband and his relatives, leading the local authority to apply for an FGMPO, see *In re X* (*Female Genital Mutilation Protection Order*) (*No. 2*) [2019] EWHC 1990 (Fam), [2019] 4 W.L.R. 114.

(3) The following are approved persons—
 (a) in relation to an operation falling within subsection (2)(a), a registered medical practitioner,
 (b) in relation to an operation falling within subsection (2)(b), a registered medical practitioner, a registered midwife or a person undergoing a course of training with a view to becoming such a practitioner or midwife.

(4) There is also no offence committed by a person who—
 (a) performs a surgical operation falling within subsection (2)(a) or (b) outside the United Kingdom, and
 (b) in relation to such an operation exercises functions corresponding to those of an approved person.

(5) For the purpose of determining whether an operation is necessary for the mental health of a girl it is immaterial whether she or any other person believes that the operation is required as a matter of custom or ritual.

6 Conscientious Objection

Khan v Royal Air Force Summary Appeal Court
[2004] EWHC (Admin) 2230, [2004] H.R.L.R. 40

Conscientious objection can typically arise in situations of being liable to act against one's own conscience, for example, in circumstances of military service or conflict. The question has arisen whether there is a right of refusal of compulsory military service on grounds of conscience or religion. The matter was litigated in the context of a reservist who was called up for service in the Royal Air Force. He had not been particularly religiously observant during his earlier period of service but became more so once he was discharged and effectively became a reservist before being called up for service for the Iraq war albeit in a non-combatant medical role. He left the service without permission and was convicted of being absent without leave under the Air Force Act 1955, section 38. He appealed against his conviction to the RAF summary appeal court which dismissed his appeal, ruling that his conscientious objection, although accepted as genuine, was no defence. He then appealed to the Divisional Court.

> 19. Another question which arises in this context is as to the exact content of the appellant's conscientious objection or belief as manifested. The facts found by the summary appeal court put this matter in these terms: "because to do so

> was against his religion: he did not want to fight against members of his own religion" (what the appellant told F/S Penfold on February 25, 2003, findings of fact, para.11); "It was against his religion. He did not want to be sent off to kill his brothers" (what the appellant told Cpl Macdonald on February 26, 2003, findings of fact, para.13); "they should understand that I'm a Muslim and this war thing I can't do it because of my religious beliefs" (what the appellant said in interview on March 5, 2003, findings of fact, para.17); and "a war against Iraq would not be right. He did not believe that his religion allowed it" (evidence before the summary appeal court, findings of fact, para.27); and "a genuine and deep belief that the impending invasion of Iraq was wrong and that to be in any way a participant in it would be contrary to his religion" (the summary appeal court's own conclusion, findings of fact, para.30). Mr Blake [the appellant's counsel] glossed these findings in his submissions in a number of ways. He began by saying the appellant's objection was to fighting Muslims; he ended by saying that his objection was to participating in any way, even as a medical non-combatant, in armed services preparing for war (in Iraq).
>
> 20. Mr Blake's skeleton also raised an issue under Art. 14 of the Convention, coupled with Art. 9, in terms of discrimination between the appellant as a Muslim and members of other religions, in that no Muslim cleric equivalent to a Christian chaplain was available on base to assist Muslims with religious problems about service in the war in Iraq: in circumstances where such a war would be likely to pose particular dilemmas for Muslim former servicemen. …

The Court held that whether the imposition of sanctions on conscientious objectors to compulsory military service might infringe the ECHR, Article 9(1), was a point which had been left open by the European Court of Human Rights, and in the present case Article 9 did not provide a defence to the appellant being charged with being absent without leave. The appellant would not manifest his belief until he expresses it in some way to his service. In some circumstances, the mere act of absence or desertion could be such an expression. Although the appellant was given repeated opportunities to voice any concerns, he did not manifest his belief until he informed his service of it in a formal way. Therefore, he had not manifested his belief. Until the recalled reservist had formally applied for discharge as a conscientious objector there was no material interference with the manifestation of a belief, and there had been no interference in the present case. While the regulations for reserve forces did not expressly make provision for conscientious objection they did cater for compassionate reasons. The appellant's right to invoke a claim to conscientious objection, whether at the time of his call-out or at any time thereafter, was therefore prescribed by law. Assuming that Article 9(1) was engaged, any interference was justified. The RAF was entitled to maintain a system of reservist recall and to discipline those accepted back into the service who go absent without leave and do so prior to raising any question of conscientious objection.

CHAPTER 15

Family Law

The law on family relations can be divided into situations where foreign law is considered in British courts and tribunals and matters that are regarded as coming under the scope of the substantive rules that govern purely internal situations. This chapter follows this division and, in so doing, focuses on marriage and divorce as the key areas under each division.

1 Private International Law

Private international law, or conflicts of law, is the mechanism by which legal systems grant recognition to claims with a "foreign" element. Private international law should reduce in importance the more established and settled a population becomes and its foreignness recedes, but because the British Muslim population is very active transnationally, one can expect private international law to remain significant. As with the experience of other European countries, especially in the domain of family relations, questions of Muslim law arise frequently in British legal systems.[1]

Given the dominance of the South Asian Muslim population in Britain, issues concerning Muslims and the laws in South Asian countries come up more often than for other groups of Muslims. Additional factors contribute to making the relative visibility of South Asian Muslims more pronounced in private international law contexts, such as the fact that Muslims from Turkey, Northern Cyprus or the Balkans are not governed by an official Islamic law;[2] and the ambiguity resulting from instability in countries such as Afghanistan,

1 Giunchi, E. (ed.) (2014), *Muslim family law in Western courts*. Abingdon: Routledge, Mehdi, R., Menski, W., and Nielsen, J.S. (eds.) (2012), *Interpreting divorce laws in Islam*. Copenhagen: DJØF Pub, Mehdi, R., and Nielsen, J.S. (eds.) (2011), *Embedding mahr (Islamic dower) in the European legal system*. 1st edn. Copenhagen: DJØF, Shah, P., Foblets, M.-C., and Rohe, M. (eds.) (2014), *Family, religion and law: Cultural encounters in Europe*. Farnham: Ashgate. For the most focused discussion on Britain see Pearl, D. and Menski, W. (1998), *Muslim family law*. London: Sweet & Maxwell.

2 That is, except for Muslims from Western Thrace in Greece who are governed in personal law matters by Islamic law. See Tsitselikis, K. (2016), *Annotated legal documents on Islam in Europe: Greece*. Leiden: Brill. However, this group is hardly visible in Britain.

Eritrea, Iraq, Somalia, and Syria, all of which have featured in the top ten asylum countries in recent years.[3] Uncertainties are likely to creep in as to what law is relevant because of a more general tension between applicable legislation, doctrinal claims related to Islamic law and the prevailing customs of any particular group, as well as inter-jurisdictional shopping.

Certain features of British legal systems make them quite distinct from their continental European civil law counterparts. The latter prioritise nationality or citizenship to determine relevant connecting factors to other jurisdictions and "apply" foreign law in their courts so long as it is not contrary to considerations of *ordre public*. British legal systems, meanwhile, prioritise domicile as a connecting factor, although residence and citizenship or nationality do still play a minor role. The slippery and malleable concept of domicile still determines capacity to enter into certain legal relations such as polygamous marriage.[4] Where domicile is ascertained, the further question might be what particular rule should apply to test the validity of relationships, particularly marriage. Should the dual domicile test apply, i.e., is validity to be judged according to the capacity granted by the domicile of both parties to a marriage, or should the intended matrimonial home test be applied, i.e. the jurisdiction in which a couple intends to set up its home?[5] As in other countries, immigration law often adds to the complications, implicitly affirming the intended matrimonial home theory because of the need to show monogamy or a certain minimum age at marriage when applying for spouse visas (although not for other purposes such as visitor visas).

The approach of *applying* the relevant foreign law is not common in British courts unless, for example, where commercial contracts specify an applicable law while giving jurisdiction to the British (usually English) courts and in the case of immovable property where the law of situs governs.[6] More usually,

3 Refugee Council, August 2022.

4 See Torremans et al. (2017), *Cheshire, North & Fawcett: Private international law*. 15th edn. Oxford: Oxford University Press, pp. 148–172 for a summary of the concept of domicile and the problems with it. See also Büchler, A. (2016), *Islamic law in Europe? Legal pluralism and its limits in European family laws*. Farnham: Routledge, pp. 27–56, a discussion which includes residence as a connecting factor in Switzerland.

5 For the variants of domicile, see Shah, P, (2003), "Attitudes to Polygamy in English Law," *International and Comparative Law Quarterly*, pp. 369–400. The fact that there is judicial support for either test makes things less certain. See also Torremans, P. et al. (2017), *Cheshire, North & Fawcett: Private international law*. 15th edn. Oxford: Oxford University Press, pp. 913–918.

6 E.g., see *Shamil Bank of Bahrain EC v Beximco Pharmaceuticals Ltd* (No. 1) [2004] 1 WLR 1784, discussed at ch. 12, section 2 above. On succession see also Torremans, P. et al., ibid., pp. 1338–1364.

however, the law of the forum (i.e., English or Scottish law) is applied to decide the substantive claim. In other words, foreign law is not "applied" in the sense in which it is in civil law countries but is merely noted as a "fact" which helps to assess the validity of legal relationships concluded in other jurisdictions.[7] This key difference between some civil and common law countries means that, in the former set of countries, foreign law has a stronger position as part of the official law. In the case of Muslims who are connected to places where Islamic law prevails, this means that Islamic law has a notionally stronger official position in those civil law countries.

Although treaties increasingly feature in Europe as part of the applicable rule complex, this is far less so in Britain, which relies on the common law approach and reforming legislation. However, treaty law may be relevant when the UK is also a party to a multilateral convention (e.g. the Hague Convention on Protection of Children and Co-operation in respect of Intercountry Adoption 1993, to which both the UK and India have been parties since 2003); takes part in an arrangement as part of the EU legal system (e.g. the Brussels Convention on jurisdiction and the enforcement of judgements in civil and commercial matters); or is a party to some other arrangement with Commonwealth countries (e.g. on the enforcement of judgments with Pakistan and India, which seems increasingly relevant in practice today).[8]

While they are within the domain of judicial practice, considerations of public order are increasingly used by legislatures to hem in judicial decision-making, and judges are thereby obliged to conform to what are effectively legislated assessments of what public order requires. For example, from the 1970s, British judges were already constrained by legislation demanding that only divorces obtained abroad through "judicial or other proceedings" may be recognised by English courts, effectively preventing them from recognising non-state forms of divorcing, which affect the Muslim *talaq* in particular.[9]

7 For questions of foreign law as being of "fact" and the role of the courts and expert witnesses with regard to foreign law see Torremans, P. et al., ibid., pp. 105–113.

8 Under the Foreign Judgments (Reciprocal Enforcement) Act 1933.

9 Pearl, D. and Menski, W. (1998), *Muslim family law*. London: Sweet & Maxwell, pp. 87–97. The formulation "judicial and other proceedings" was derived from the Hague Convention on the Recognition of Divorces and Legal Separations 1970, Article 1. Similar reforms have occurred more recently in Belgium too. See Rohe, M. (2014), "Family and the Law in Europe: Bringing together secular legal orders and religious norms and needs," in Shah, P.S., Foblets, M.-C., and Rohe, M. (eds.), *Family, religion and law: Cultural encounters in Europe*, pp. 49–78 at pp. 63–64, Janssens, Y. (2016), *Annotated legal documents on Islam in Europe: Belgium*. Leiden; Boston: Brill, pp. 159–160.

1.1 *Marriage*

The general rule on the recognition of the form of marriage conducted abroad is that the *lex loci celebrationis* applies. In other words, if a marriage is conducted in the accepted form in the place celebrated then it should be recognised in British legal systems. The Court of Appeal has spelt out the basic rule in *Akhtar*.

Secretary of State for Work and Pensions v Nasim Akhtar
[2021] EWCA Civ 1353, [2022] 1 W.L.R. 421, Court of Appeal

> …
>
> *Validity of marriage*
>
> 60. Under English rules of private international law: (a) the general rule is that the formal validity (i e the formalities) of a marriage is governed by the law of the country where the marriage was celebrated, Dicey at para 17R-001; and (b) the general rule is that capacity to marry (or essential validity) is governed by the law of each party's antenuptial domicile, Dicey at para 17R-057. Bigamy is "a matter of capacity", Dicey at para 17-082.[10]
>
> 61. If a marriage is valid in respect of both form and capacity it will be recognised as valid under English law and, as a result, the parties will be recognised as having the status of husband or wife.

This leads to some inconsistencies in how marriages performed abroad and those celebrated in British legal systems are treated. For example, in the larger South Asian countries, the registration of marriage is optional, as it is in Iran and Morocco, and such "unregistered marriages" ought to be recognised in British legal systems.[11] However, if the couple undergoes a *nikah* on British

10 The references are to Lord Collins of Mapesbury et al. (eds) (2012), *Dicey, Morris and Collins on the conflict of laws*. London: Sweet & Maxwell.

11 See Pearl, D. and Menski, W. (1998), *Muslim family law*. London: Sweet & Maxwell, pp. 151–153 for the legality of Muslim marriages that are not registered in India, Pakistan and Bangladesh despite the legislative provisions providing for (but not requiring) registration in the latter two countries. See Alim, N. and Yassari, N. (2016), "Between procedure and substance: A review of law making in Egypt," in Yassari, N. (ed.), *Changing God's law: The dynamics of Middle Eastern family law*. Milton Park, Abingdon: Routledge, pp. 113–130, at p. 117 on Pakistan, Morocco, and Iran, and who also points out that in Egypt, when registration is not done, withholding recognition of a Muslim marriage for divorce purposes does not follow.

territory, that will not lead to recognition in English law except when there is long cohabitation and recognition by others of a couple as husband and wife.[12] In Scotland, it may lead to the recognition of a couple as cohabitees but not as being married. The Family Law (Scotland) Act 2006 provided legal recognition to cohabitees (sections 26–29) but simultaneously removed the effect of "the rule of law by which marriage may be constituted by cohabitation with habit and repute" (section 3(1)).

There used to be the problem of recognition of an actually monogamous marriage being deemed "potentially polygamous" when conducted in a jurisdiction and under a law that allowed polygamy. This was solved by the Private International Law (Miscellaneous Provisions) Act 1995, section 5(1), which allows such actually monogamous marriages to be recognised.[13] Meanwhile, actually polygamous marriages conducted abroad are now accorded recognition in most legal situations except for some matters of social security.[14] British legal systems do not, however, recognise polygamous marriages when conducted within their jurisdictions.

The form of marriage is merely one aspect of the conditions for recognition of marriages conducted abroad. The other is the issue of capacity which is determined by whether one's domicile is in the British legal systems or elsewhere.[15] The basic position is that domicile in, say, England prevents a person from having the capacity to contract a marriage which the English legal system internally prohibits, such as a polygamous or child marriage. The Private International Law (Miscellaneous Provisions) Act 1995 does not disturb the prohibition on the recognition of actually polygamous marriages entered into by English domiciliaries when abroad. A *nikah* performed in British jurisdictions will not, however, attract criminal liability when it leads to a *de facto* polygamous marriage.[16]

---

12 For an English case that was used to uphold the validity in English law of an unregistered Muslim marriage see *Al-Mudaris v Al-Mudaris* [2001] 2 FLR 6.

13 See Torremans, P. et al. (2017), *Cheshire, North & Fawcett: Private international law*. 15th edn. Oxford: Oxford University Press, pp. 940–941.

14 See ibid., pp. 943–944. In *Bibi v Chief Adjudication Officer* 1 FLR 375 the first wife of a polygamous marriage was not entitled to a widowed parent's allowance. In *Secretary of State for Work and Pensions v Nasim Akhtar* [2021] EWCA Civ 1353 the court rejected the claim that the term "spouse" should be extended to grant a bereavement and a widow's parent allowance to a surviving widow who had entered into an actually polygamous marriage.

15 This is a simplification of a potentially more complicated set of rules on domicile which can be applied to ascertaining whether a marriage can be recognised. See ch. 15, section 1 above.

16 Torremans, P. et al. (2017), *Cheshire, North & Fawcett: Private international law*. 15th edn. Oxford: Oxford University Press, pp. 941–942.

Private International Law (Miscellaneous Provisions) Act 1995

5. Validity in English law of potentially polygamous marriages

(1) A marriage entered into outside England and Wales between parties neither of whom is already married is not void under the law of England and Wales on the ground that it is entered into under a law which permits polygamy and that either party is domiciled in England and Wales.

(2) This section does not affect the determination of the validity of a marriage by reference to the law of another country to the extent that it falls to be so determined in accordance with the rules of private international law.

The following are the provisions of the Matrimonial Causes Act 1973, sections 11 and 47, as amended by the Private International Law (Miscellaneous Provisions) Act 1995. The amended section 11(d) ensures that a potentially polygamous (actually monogamous) marriage by a person domiciled in England and Wales is no longer void. The amended version of section 47 ensures that a court may nevertheless grant a remedy under matrimonial law when the marriage is actually polygamous.

Matrimonial Causes Act 1973

11. Grounds on which a marriage is void.

A marriage which takes place after the commencement of this Act shall be void on the following grounds only, that is to say—

(a) that it is not a valid marriage under the provisions of the Marriage Acts 1949 to 1986 (that is to say where—
   (i) the parties are within the prohibited degrees of relationship;
   (ii) either party is under the age of; or
   (iii) the parties have intermarried in disregard of certain requirements as to the formation of marriage);

(b) that at the time of the marriage either party was already lawfully married or a civil partner;

(…)

(d) in the case of a polygamous marriage entered into outside England and Wales, that either party was at the time domiciled in England and Wales.

For the purposes of paragraph (d) of this subsection a marriage is not polygamous if at its inception neither party has any spouse additional to the other.

47. Matrimonial relief and declarations of validity in respect of polygamous marriages.

(1) A court in England and Wales shall not be precluded from granting matrimonial relief or making a declaration concerning the validity of a marriage by reason only that either party to the marriage is, or has during the subsistence of the marriage been, married to more than one person.

Since capacity to enter into marriage is determined by the domicile of a person, the validity of polygamous marriages and child marriages would be affected by whether a connection can be made to domicile in one of the British jurisdictions.

A Local Authority v X & Anor (Children)
[2013] EWHC 3274 (Fam)

In this case, a local authority applied for care proceedings concerning a mother, who was herself a child, and also her baby. The mother had been forced into a marriage at the age of 14 with a man in Pakistan. Collateral to those care proceedings the local authority also asked for permission to invoke the inherent jurisdiction of the High Court and a declaration of non-recognition of the marriage of the young mother. Some of the relevant facts appear in the text of the judgment below. Although the judge expected the mother, instead of the local authority, to apply for nullity, he was clearly of the view that because she was an English domiciliary and therefore lacked capacity in English law to contract a marriage in Pakistan at the age of 14, the marriage must be void.

> 4. I will refer to the mother as "X," which is not the initial letter of any of her names. She is the youngest of a number of children of Muslim parents who immigrated to England from Pakistan.
>
> 5. There is evidence that her father travelled to live in England about forty years ago. His wife travelled to live in England around the time of their marriage. They have both lived here as their home ever since, although they make return holiday visits to Pakistan. Over thirty years ago the father became a citizen of the United Kingdom. "X" herself was born in 1997.
>
> 6. Late in 2011, her father, accompanied by one of her adult brothers, took "X" to Pakistan. There she underwent a ceremony of marriage to a man living in

Pakistan which I will assume has formal legal validity under the law of the place where it was contracted. On the date of the marriage "X" was aged fourteen.

7. The domicile of origin of "X" is necessarily the domicile of her father on the date of her birth in 1997. On the facts that I have very briefly summarised it appears, on a balance of probability, that he was domiciled in England and Wales on that date and, accordingly, that her domicile of origin is England and Wales. There is nothing at all to suggest that the father's domicile changed between the date of her birth in 1997 and the date of the marriage in late 2011, so as to change her own domicile by dependency. Accordingly, it appears, on a balance of probability, that her domicile on the date of the marriage remained England and Wales.

8. Under the law of England and Wales the minimum age of both parties to a valid marriage is governed by the Marriage Act 1949 if either party is domiciled in England and Wales on the date of marriage. Section 2 of the Marriage Act 1949 provides as follows:

> A marriage solemnised between persons either of whom is under the age of sixteen shall be void.

Section 11 of the Matrimonial Causes Act 1973 provides, so far as is material, that:

> A marriage celebrated after 31 July 1971 shall be void on the following grounds only, that is to say—
>
> (a) that it is not a valid marriage under the provisions of the Marriage Acts 1949 to 1986 (that is to say, where—
>
> (i) …;
>
> (ii) either party is under the age of sixteen; …)

9. On the date of the marriage "X" was under the age of sixteen. In fact, she was still only fourteen. It follows, therefore, as a matter of mixed fact and law, that the marriage in question is, so far as concerns the law of England and Wales, void. Further, the case of *Pugh v Pugh* [1951] P 482 clearly establishes that the statutory provisions as to minimum age are extraterritorial in effect. If either party was domiciled here on the date of the marriage (as she was) and one of them was under the age of 16 (as she was), it makes no difference that both parties may have been of sufficient minimum age and had capacity under the law of the domicile of the other party or under the law of the place where the marriage was contracted.

10. "X" has given an account of the circumstances surrounding that marriage which are, frankly, harrowing to read. I have not heard any oral evidence, nor has the father or relevant brother of "X" had any opportunity to file any evidence in

answer to the statement of "X" herself; but on her account in that statement this was a grave example of a marriage which was forced under considerable duress, involving at one stage the production of a gun and physical violence upon "X."

11. The marriage was consummated about two weeks later after further threats to "X" if she did not permit her husband, who was aged about twenty four, to have sexual intercourse with her. As a result, while still aged fourteen, she became pregnant with the baby to whom I have referred.

12. "X" returned to England and the baby was born in the autumn of 2012 and is now aged just over one. The local authority commenced care proceedings in relation to both "X" and her baby. These are still ongoing and it is not necessary to make any reference in this judgment to the continuing issues in those proceedings.

13. The local authority advance two essential reasons for seeking the declaation to which I have referred to the effect that that marriage is not recognised as a valid marriage in England and Wales.

14. The first reason is that they consider that it would be advantageous to "X" to have the legal status of that marriage in England and Wales clarified by such a declaration. In that, they are supported by "X" herself and by "X"'s guardian in the care proceedings and by the baby's guardian in the care proceedings.

15. The second reason is to clarify, for the purpose of the proceedings in relation to the baby, the legal status of the baby's father. The father is not named on the baby's birth certificate. At the moment, the local authority does not know the identity, and still less the whereabouts, of the man with whom "X" went through the ceremony of marriage, who is, indeed, the genetic father of the baby. Under English law, if he was validly married to "X" at the time of, or at any time between, the conception or birth of the baby, then he has parental responsibility for the baby. (See sections 2 (1) and (3) of the Children Act 1989, read with section 1 of the Family Law Reform Act 1987.) If he was not validly married to her at any time during that period, then (not being himself domiciled here) he does not. That, of course, has some consequential effects upon his status within the care proceedings in relation to the baby and also within the application that the local authority has issued for a placement order in relation to the baby.

16. So far as that second reason or purpose is concerned, I hold by this judgment, as a mixed finding of fact and law for the purpose of the care and placement

proceedings, (but not making any declaration to this effect), that the marriage between "X" and the father of the baby is, on a balance of probability, void. Under English law, the father was not validly married to the mother on the date of the baby's conception or birth. Section 1(3)(a) of the Family Law Reform Act 1987, read together with section 1(1) of the Legitimacy Act 1976, provides that a child shall nevertheless be treated as legitimate (with the consequence that the father does have parental responsibility) if at the time of the child's conception either of the parties reasonably believed that the marriage was valid. However section 1(1) of the Legitimacy Act 1976 is subject to subsection (2). Subsection (2) provides that subsection (1) only applies where the father of the child (viz. of the baby in this case) was domiciled in England and Wales at the time of the birth which, patently, the father of this baby was not. I therefore hold that the father does not have parental responsibility for the baby.

1.2 *Divorce*

The legislation limiting the recognition of overseas divorces, with specified exceptions, to those obtained by "judicial or other proceedings" dates back to the early 1970s, and there has been significant case law concerning its interpretation.[17] More recently, the Family Law Act 1986 consolidated and rationalised some of the provisions that primarily govern under what circumstances an overseas divorce is to be recognised for British legal systems ("the law of the part of the United Kingdom"). The earlier case law on when a divorce has been obtained through "judicial or other proceedings" still matters, especially since it is concerned with the laws of particular countries where those divorces were obtained and has clarified whether divorces obtained in specific ways in those countries either qualify as "proceedings" divorces (in which case Family Law Act 1986, section 46(1) applies) or do not (in which case section 46(2) applies). It can be noted that the concepts of habitual residence, domicile and nationality are used as *alternatives* for "proceedings" divorces (section 46(1)), while domicile and habitual residence are applied as *cumulative* conditions in the case of non-proceedings divorces (section 46(2)). While domicile can be imputed from the birth, life and actions of a person, habitual residence and nationality may be easier to ascertain factually. In "proceedings" cases under section 46(1) the fact of dual nationality, as is often the case with British Pakistanis, may allow the other criteria to be by-passed and therefore facilitate the choice of divorce by Islamic law as applied in Pakistan.[18]

17 Pearl, D. and Menski, W. (1998), *Muslim family law*. London: Sweet & Maxwell, pp. 87–97.

18 The holding of dual nationality obviously leaves holders vulnerable to being deprived of

While the legislation of the 1970s referred to divorces and legal separations, the 1986 Act adds references to "annulment." It is unclear at this stage whether this addition would affect the approach towards Muslim overseas divorces. The Muslim Family Laws Ordinance 1961 (MFLO), which applies in both Pakistan and (as amended) in Bangladesh, does not refer to annulment although it does refer to divorce (when a man pronounces a *talaq*) and to both "divorce" and "dissolution" (in the case of a *talaq* delegated to a wife). The term "dissolution" does not appear in the relevant sections of the 1986 Act, however (although it does appear in other parts of the Act). Meanwhile, the legislation of undivided colonial India, the Dissolution of Muslim Marriages Act, 1939, which all of the current states of India, Pakistan and Bangladesh inherit, refers to "dissolution" without mention of divorce. It can probably be assumed that "dissolution" in the South Asian enactments can be interpreted as "divorce" for the purpose of the British legislation, and it does not appear that the inconsistent terminology has led to the point being raised in litigation.

One of the main factors that dominates the case law in this area is whether a divorce has followed the procedure set out in the MFLO 1961 of Pakistan. If it has, effectively by the husband providing notice to the chairman of the relevant official body that he has pronounced a *talaq*, then the British courts and tribunals appear to recognise the divorce. If this procedure is not followed, a "bare *talaq*" is recognised only in the limited circumstances spelled out in the Family Law Act 1986, section 46(2), although the same "bare *talaq*" is bound to be recognised within Pakistan and Bangladesh, as well as in India where there is no parallel to the MFLO.[19] It may be that section 46(2) has avoided mention of nationality as a connecting factor for a "bare talaq" to be recognised because of the knowledge that many British Pakistanis hold dual nationality. A similar process applicable in Saudi Arabia that involves giving notice to a court has also

British citizenship on grounds related to criminality. See, e.g., *R3 v Secretary of State for the Home Department* [2023] EWCA Civ 169 for a case of deprivation of British citizenship of a British-Pakistani dual national on grounds of it being conducive to the public good because he had travelled to Syria to join a group aligned with Al-Qaeda.

19 See the extensive discussion of the relevant British case law in Pearl, D. and Menski, W. (1998), *Muslim family law*. London: Sweet & Maxwell, pp. 382–393. On the common assumption that a bare *talaq* is valid in India as well as Pakistan and Bangladesh, see the discussion of the relevant case law in ibid., pp. 297–383. Some experts on the effect of the MFLO of Pakistan maintain that it changed the law with respect to divorce which no longer allows a bare *talaq* to be recognised. See, e.g. the expert evidence of Ian Edge in *K v K* [2007] EWHC 2945 (Fam). This view goes against the Pakistani case law, however. For the view that court rulings in Pakistan are contradictory see Sardar Ali, S. (2016), "Family law reform in postcolonial Pakistan," in Yassari, N. (ed.), *Changing God's law: The dynamics of Middle Eastern family law*. Milton Park, Abingdon: Routledge, pp. 34–67 at p. 54.

been recognised as amounting to "proceedings," as has the procedure applicable in Lebanon.[20] In the British case law, there is a prevailing assumption that the MFLO does not apply to "Azad Kashmir", i.e. that part of Kashmir under Pakistani occupation.[21]

Even where the "proceedings" rule in section 46(1) is applied in British legal systems, some problems can arise. The Pakistani and Bangladeshi procedures do not clearly envisage the involvement of a wife when a *talaq* with notice has been given, even though they contemplate a sort of arbitration council to be set up to reconcile the parties, while those of other countries such as Saudi Arabia do not envisage the wife's involvement at all. The Family Law Act 1986, section 51(3)(a), allows the validity of an overseas "proceedings" divorce to be rejected if the divorce was obtained without giving notice to, or to allow participation in the proceedings by, the other party. This is a discretion courts enjoy and they have generally been satisfied if the wife knows of the *talaq*, even when that knowledge arose some time after it was pronounced and she was denied any effective involvement in the process.[22] There is also the provision in section 51(3)(c) allowing rejection on grounds of public policy.

Family Law Act 1986

45 Recognition in the United Kingdom of overseas divorces, annulments and legal separations.

(1) Subject to sections 51 and 52 of this Act, the validity of a divorce, annulment or legal separation obtained in a country outside the British Islands (in this Part referred to as an overseas divorce, annulment or legal separation) shall be recognised in the United Kingdom if, and only if, it is entitled to recognition—
  (a) by virtue of sections 46 to 49 of this Act, or
  (b) by virtue of any enactment other than this Part.

46 Grounds for recognition.

(1) The validity of an overseas divorce, annulment or legal separation obtained by means of proceedings shall be recognised if—

20 *H v S* Case No. FD11D01981, High Court of Justice Family Division, 2011 WL 6329609 (Saudi Arabia); *El Fadl v El Fadl* [2000] 1 FLR 175 (Lebanon).

21 *Chaudhary v Chaudhary* [1985] 2 WLR 350 at 356; *NC (bare talaq, Indian Muslims, recognition)* [2009] UKAIT 16; *H v S (Recognition of Overseas Divorce)*, 2011 WL 6329609 (2011), para. 19.

22 *H v S* Case No. FD11D01981, High Court of Justice Family Division, 2011 WL 6329609.

(a) the divorce, annulment or legal separation is effective under the law of the country in which it was obtained; and
(b) at the relevant date either party to the marriage—
(i) was habitually resident in the country in which the divorce, annulment or legal separation was obtained; or
(ii) was domiciled in that country; or
(iii) was a national of that country.

(2) The validity of an overseas divorce, annulment or legal separation obtained otherwise than by means of proceedings shall be recognised if—
(a) the divorce, annulment or legal separation is effective under the law of the country in which it was obtained;
(b) at the relevant date—
(i) each party to the marriage was domiciled in that country; or
(ii) either party to the marriage was domiciled in that country and the other party was domiciled in a country under whose law the divorce, annulment or legal separation is recognised as valid; and
(c) neither party to the marriage was habitually resident in the United Kingdom throughout the period of one year immediately preceding that date.

(3) In this section "the relevant date" means—
(a) in the case of an overseas divorce, annulment or legal separation obtained by means of proceedings, the date of the commencement of the proceedings;
(b) in the case of an overseas divorce, annulment or legal separation obtained otherwise than by means of proceedings, the date on which it was obtained.

(4) Where in the case of an overseas annulment, the relevant date fell after the death of either party to the marriage, any reference in subsection (1) or (2) above to that date shall be construed in relation to that party as a reference to the date of death.

(5) For the purpose of this section, a party to a marriage shall be treated as domiciled in a country if he was domiciled in that country either according to the law of that country in family matters or according to the law of the part of the United Kingdom in which the question of recognition arises.

…

51 Refusal of recognition.

...

(3) Subject to section 52 of this Act, recognition by virtue of section 45 of this Act of the validity of an overseas divorce, annulment or legal separation may be refused if—
  (a) in the case of a divorce, annulment or legal separation obtained by means of proceedings, it was obtained—
    (i) without such steps having been taken for giving notice of the proceedings to a party to the marriage as, having regard to the nature of the proceedings and all the circumstances, should reasonably have been taken; or
    (ii) without a party to the marriage having been given (for any reason other than lack of notice) such opportunity to take part in the proceedings as, having regard to those matters, he should reasonably have been given; or
  (b) in the case of a divorce, annulment or legal separation obtained otherwise than by means of proceedings—
    (i) there is no official document certifying that the divorce, annulment or legal separation is effective under the law of the country in which it was obtained; or
    (ii) where either party to the marriage was domiciled in another country at the relevant date, there is no official document certifying that the divorce, annulment or legal separation is recognised as valid under the law of that other country; or
  (c) in either case, recognition of the divorce, annulment or legal separation would be manifestly contrary to public policy.

...

54 Interpretation of Part II.

(1) In this Part—

“annulment” includes any nullity of marriage order or decree or declarator of nullity of marriage, however expressed;

“part of the United Kingdom” means England and Wales, Scotland or Northern Ireland;

“proceedings” means judicial or other proceedings.

(2) In this Part “country” includes a colony or other dependent territory of the United Kingdom but for the purposes of this Part a person shall be treated as a national of such a territory only if it has a law of citizenship or nationality separate from that of the United Kingdom and he is a citizen or national of that territory under that law.

K v K
[2007] EWHC 2945 (Fam)

The husband and wife married in Pakistan in 1966 and started living together thereafter in the UK. The husband gave notice of divorce to the chairman of the union council in Pakistan in 1987. Although the wife, who still lived in the UK, disputed whether she had been given notice of these proceedings, the judge found on the facts that at some point she had come to know of the divorce which was granted and effective in Pakistan. The wife petitioned for divorce in the English court and the husband sought a declaration that the couple were already divorced by virtue of the Pakistani divorce. The Family Law Act 1986, section 51(3), was raised in the proceedings, it being argued that neither notice nor an opportunity to take part in the proceedings was given to the wife.

> 14. By s.51 (3) the validity of an overseas divorce may be refused in the following circumstances. The first ground is if the divorce was obtained "without such steps having been taken for giving notice of the proceedings to a party to the marriage as, having regard to the nature of the proceedings and all the circumstances, should reasonably have been taken."
>
> 15. The second ground is if the divorce was obtained "without a party to the marriage having been given (for any reason other than lack of notice) such opportunity to take part in proceedings as, having regard to those matters, he should reasonably have been given."
>
> 16. For the purpose of interpretation of these sections I have been referred to the decision of Hughes J as he then was in El Fadl v El Fadl (2000) 1 FLR 175. The case involved the validity of a talaq pronounced in Lebanon of which the wife was not given notice.
>
> 17. It was held that the consent or objection of the wife to the divorce was irrelevant. It was not necessary for her to have notice of the pronounced in order to give effect to the talaq, which had been recorded in the Sharia court in accordance with Lebanese law. That registration was sufficient for the talaq properly to be described as proceedings within s.46. Furthermore, it was not a proper exercise of discretion to refuse a divorce which was valid by the personal law of both parties at the relevant time, as had been known to them for many years.
>
> …

78. I turn to the law. The first question is whether the announcement of the talaq and giving notice to the union council amounts to "proceedings" within s.46 (1) of the Family Law Act 1986. The mere pronouncement of divorce before witnesses has been held not to be enough, *Chaudhary v Chaudhary (1985) Fam 19*. In that case Balcombe J as he then was said—

> … 'proceedings' requires some form of State machinery to be involved in the divorce process: not necessarily machinery established by the state, since existing religious machinery recognised by the state is sufficient … The act or acts of one or both of the parties to the marriage, without more, cannot amount to proceedings; there must be the intervention of some other body, a person with a specific function to fulfil such as the Union Council in the case of the talaq considered in.

79. There is the express provision of the MFLO 1961. Under s. 7 it is provided—

> "Talaq" "(1) Any man who wishes to divorce his lie wife shall, as soon as may be after the announcement of talaq in any form whatsoever, give the Chairman notice in writing of his having done so, and shall supply a copy thereof to the wife."
>
> "Chairman" is defined as the Chairman of the Union Council.

80. Lord Scarman in *Quazi v Quazi* (1980) AC 744 said at p. 824 that the following were capable of qualifying as proceedings

> … any act or acts, officially recognised as leading to divorce in the country where the divorce was obtained, and which itself is recognised by the law of the country as an effective divorce.

81. I am satisfied that that is the position in Pakistan where notice has been given after talaq to the relevant chairman of the Union Council as I find occurred in 1987. Accordingly I find that what happened here amounts to proceedings for the purpose of S.46 (1).

82. The final question is how I should exercise my discretion in the light of the facts as I have found them to be. The decision of Hughes J in *El Fadl* is not binding on me but it is of persuasive authority. If I may respectfully say so, I accept his analysis and propose to follow it.

83. Though the wife was not given notice of the divorce nor the opportunity to take part, I rely on the following passage from the judgment of Hughes J.

> … I am satisfied that however much a unilateral divorce without notice may offend English sensibilities, comity between nations and belief systems

> requires at least this much, that one country should accept the conscientiously held but very different standards of another, where they are applied to those who are domiciled in it (p. 190) ...
>
> I am satisfied that where, as here, the talaq is the prevailing form of divorce in the country of both parties, where it had been validly executed there, so that the marriage is at the end in the country, where it was contracted, and to which both parties belonged and where there is no evidence of forum shopping, not only does public policy not call for non-recognition, in the end it summonses recognition.

84. Here the difference is that the wife had been away from Pakistan for 25 years when the divorce took place. She is likely to be domiciled here. However she was born, brought up, and married in Pakistan to someone of the same background. They both have family there. The husband returned when their marriage came to an end. It is not an uncommon situation.

85. There are a great many people living in the UK from Pakistan and many move freely between both countries. Where there are as here close links to each country, it is important that marriages and divorces recognised by the country where they take place should be recognised in the other country unless there are good reasons for not doing so.

86. I see no good reasons here. That the wife has been away from Pakistan for a long period and is no longer domiciled there are factors. Also she was not given notice of the divorce nor the opportunity to participate. That is a feature of a talaq divorce. But neither party wishes the marriage to continue. The husband has expressly accepted that the wife has a valid financial claim under Part III of the Matrimonial and Family Proceedings Act 1984.

87. In the exercise of my discretion, I do not consider the matters to which I have referred should deter me from exercising my discretion to recognise the divorce obtained by the husband in Pakistan in 1987 which was valid from 1 April 1988. ...

2 Marriage and Divorce

2.1 *Marriage*

The Matrimonial Causes Act establishes the grounds under which a marriage may be void or voidable and therefore also the capacity to marry which, as seen (ch. 15, section 1.1), also affects the ability of British domiciliaries to marry abroad. Section 11(d), concerned with polygamous marriages, is reproduced above. Meanwhile, the Immigration Rules on the admission of polygamous spouses at paragraph 278 prohibit the admission of a person if the marriage is polygamous and another person has already been in the United Kingdom or been granted a certificate of entitlement to the right of abode or entry clearance as a spouse of the sponsor. This makes the Immigration Rules line up with the prohibition on the ability to marry polygamously within the jurisdiction.

Other circumstances contained in the Matrimonial Causes Act, section 11, that may potentially lead to a void marriage are marrying below the minimum age and marriage within prohibited degrees. With effect from 27 February 2023, the minimum age at which a person may marry within England and Wales is 18. Previously, the age at which a person could marry within the jurisdiction was 16. Since December 2004, the Immigration Rules at paragraph 277 require a person admitted as a spouse or partner to be aged 18 or over. The later change to the Matrimonial Causes Act means that the rules of admission as a spouse for immigration purposes and the permitted age for marriage now line up with each other. A change to the Immigration Rules in 2008 to require those admitted to the UK to be 21, which was justified by the government as a means by which to deter forced marriages, was struck down by the Supreme Court as being incompatible with the UK's human rights obligations.[23] The Immigration Rules therefore reverted to 18 as the age for admission as a spouse. It should be made clear that the Immigration Rules refer to age at the application for admission and not the age at marriage, which may well have been earlier.

To ascertain who falls within the prohibited degrees of marriage, one has to turn to the Marriage Act 1949 (as amended), section 1, and Schedule 1. As far as Muslims are concerned it is possible that some marriages between Muslims do fall within the prohibited degrees and could therefore be void.

Matrimonial Causes Act 1973

11 Grounds on which a marriage is void.
A marriage celebrated after 31st July 1971 other than a marriage to which section 12A applies, shall be void on the following grounds only, that is to say—
(a) that it is not a valid marriage under the provisions of the Marriage Acts 1949 to 1986 (that is to say where—

23 *R (on the application of Quila and another)* (FC) *(Respondents) v Secretary of State for the Home Department* (Appellant) [2011] UKSC 45.

(i) the parties are within the prohibited degrees of relationship;
(ii) either party is under the age of eighteen; or
(iii) the parties have intermarried in disregard of certain requirements as to the formation of marriage);

Immigration Rules part 8: family members

277. Nothing in these Rules shall be construed as permitting a person to be granted entry clearance, leave to enter, leave to remain or variation of leave as a spouse or civil partner of another if either the applicant or the sponsor will be aged under 18 on the date of arrival in the United Kingdom or (as the case may be) on the date on which the leave to remain or variation of leave would be granted. In these rules the term "sponsor" includes "partner" as defined in GEN 1.2 of Appendix FM.

278. Nothing in these Rules shall be construed as allowing a person to be granted entry clearance, leave to enter, leave to remain or variation of leave as the spouse and civil partner of a man or woman (the sponsor) if:
(i) his or her marriage or civil partnership to the sponsor is polygamous; and
(ii) there is another person living who is the husband or wife of the sponsor and who:
  (a) is, or at any time since his or her marriage or civil partnership to the sponsor has been, in the United Kingdom; or
  (b) has been granted a certificate of entitlement in respect of the right of abode mentioned in Section 2(1)(a) of the Immigration Act 1988 or an entry clearance to enter the United Kingdom as the husband or wife of the sponsor.

  For the purpose of this paragraph a marriage or civil partnership may be polygamous although at its inception neither party had any other spouse or civil partner.

Marriage Act 1949

PART I

RESTRICTIONS ON MARRIAGE

1 Marriages within prohibited degrees.
(1) A marriage solemnized between a person and any person mentioned in the list in Part 1 of Schedule 1, shall be void.

(2) Subject to subsection (3) of this section, a marriage solemnized between a person and any person mentioned in the list in Part 2 of Schedule 1, shall be void.

(3) Any such marriage as is mentioned in subsection (2) of this section shall not be void by reason only of affinity if both the parties to the marriage have attained the age of twenty-one at the time of the marriage and the younger party has not at any time before attaining the age of eighteen been a child of the family in relation to the other party.

…

SCHEDULE 1

PART 1

PROHIBITED DEGREES: KINDRED

1(1) The list referred to in section 1(1) is—

Adoptive child
Adoptive parent
Child
Former adoptive child
Former adoptive parent
Grandparent
Grandchild
Parent
Parent's sibling
Sibling
Sibling's child

(2) In the list "sibling" means a brother, sister, half-brother or half-sister.

PART 2

DEGREES OF AFFINITY REFERRED TO IN SECTION 1(2) AND (3)

2 The list referred to in section 1(2) is as follows—

Child of former civil partner
Child of former spouse
Former civil partner of grandparent
Former civil partner of parent
Former spouse of grandparent
Former spouse of parent
Grandchild of former civil partner
Grandchild of former spouse

2.1.1 Unregistered Marriages

A succession of cases has emerged in the British courts and tribunals in the past four decades in which the requirements of a valid marriage ceremony as stipulated in the Marriage Act 1949 have not been followed. A majority of those cases concerns Muslims. The Marriage Act 1949, section 26, makes provision for Anglican, Jewish and Quaker marriage ceremonies to be recognised as leading to a valid marriage. In effect, the Marriage Act expects members of those religious groups not specifically mentioned to undergo a secular registration ceremony. The Marriage Act provides for registration of marriage in a registered building, in a marriage superintendent registrar's premises or in approved premises, often a community hall, hotel, stately home or museum, among others.[24] In these contexts, an authorised person or a marriage registrar must conduct the relevant formalities, and an imam could be recognised as an authorised person or a registrar and could register a marriage alongside a *nikah* in a registered building or approved premises respectively. Although there have been claims that few Muslim mosques are registered buildings, a look at the official list of places of worship registered for marriage reveals a fairly large number of mosques.[25] It may be, however, that few Muslims would choose to undergo a marriage ceremony in a mosque.

Although Muslims support marriage in principle, they nevertheless stand out as having a high non-registration rate. They tend to conduct marriages through a *nikah* without going through the Marriage Act formalities.[26] The reasons for non-registration provided in the research include the lack of importance thought to attach to civil registration and importance being attached to the *nikah* while knowing or not knowing of its lack of validity in English law; the fact that Islam does not make registration mandatory; lack of time and convenience to arrange the registration, although much time, attention and expense do go into planning the Islamic marriage ceremony; unwillingness to allow English law to interfere in marital property arrangements, as well as polygamy and

24 For a list of such approved premises see *Civil marriages and partnerships: approved premises list* https://www.gov.uk/government/publications/civil-marriages-and-partnerships-approved-premises-list.

25 For such an observation made by the Court of Appeal citing studies see *Akhter v Khan (Attorney General and others intervening)* [2020] EWCA Civ 122, at para. 13. Also see Grillo, R.D. (2015), *Muslim families, politics and the law: A legal industry in multicultural Britain*. Farnham: Ashgate, pp. 43–44 including possible reasons why a low rate of registrations persists. See, however, *Places of worship registered for marriage*, https://www.gov.uk/government/publications/places-of-worship-registered-for-marriage.

26 See ibid., p. 41, citing other studies, which points out that "the great majority of Muslim couples married in the UK have not registered their marriages".

child marriages, which would result in any formal marriages being voided and attracting criminal penalties.[27] A combination of parliamentarians and official bodies as well as Muslim activists have conducted various campaigns to increase the rate of official registrations, but these do not appear to have gained traction among Muslims and have attracted criticisms by some Muslim bodies.[28]

In the cases emerging in recent decades, most often, the courts have held that unregistered *nikah*-only marriages are "non-marriages," which has attracted some criticism. In the case of *Akhter v Khan* (extracted below), the Court of Appeal conceded that instead of "non-marriage" the term "non-qualifying ceremony" ought to be used. Claims are made, however, that the marriages in question ought to be recognised either as valid because of the presumption of marriage or as void under the Matrimonial Causes Act 1973, section 11(a)(iii) ("the parties have intermarried in disregard of certain requirements as to the formation of marriage"). Although declaring a marriage void sounds like a non-recognition of marriage, it would actually mean that the remedies incidental to marriage breakdown or inheritance are available. As the leading case, *Akhter v Khan,* indicates however the senior judges have tried to hold the ground against such claims, the Court of Appeal reversing a High Court decision to hold an unregistered marriage void.

Marriage Act 1949

49 Void marriages.
If any persons knowingly and wilfully intermarry under the provisions of this Part of this Act—

27 See, ibid., pp. 42, 50–56; Akhtar, R. (2015), "Unregistered Muslim marriages: An emerging culture of celebrating rites and conceding rights," in Miles, J., Mody, P., and Probert, R. (eds.), *Marriage rites and rights*. Oxford: Hart, pp. 167–192, Uddin, I. (2020), "Reformulation of Islamic matrimonial law: British Muslims, contemporary understandings and normative practices," *Journal of Muslim Minority Affairs*, 40(1), pp. 6–25. One survey conducted for a Channel 4 documentary, *The Truth about Muslim Marriage*, found that 66 % of Muslim women who went through a *nikah*-only wedding knew that it did not have validity in English law. See Shah, P. (2017), "Does Channel 4's Documentary Provide the Truth about Muslim Marriage?," *Areo Magazine*, 7 December 2017, for a critical discussion of the survey results. Hyde, C. (2021), *Child sexual exploitation thematic child safeguarding practice review.* Bradford: Bradford Partnership, records two cases of under-age victims of child sexual exploitation, one as having been married in a nikah ceremony to her adult abuser and one who talked of doing so and travelling to Afghanistan. In such cases, in addition to charges for other crimes, forced marriage penalties may also be applicable (see ch. 14, section 4).

28 Grillo, R.D. (2015), *Muslim families, politics and the law: A legal industry in multicultural Britain.* Farnham: Ashgate, pp. 41–47.

(a) without having given due notice of marriage to the superintendent registrar;
(b) without a marriage schedule having been duly issued by the superintendent registrar of the registration district in which the marriage was solemnized;
...
(d) on the authority of a marriage schedule which is] void by virtue of subsection (2) of section thirty-three of this Act;
(e) in any place other than the church, chapel, registered building, office or other place specified in the notices of marriage and (if so specified) in the marriage schedule;
(ee) in the case of a marriage purporting to be in pursuance of section 26(1)(bb) of this Act, on any premises that at the time the marriage is solemnized are not approved premises;
(f) in the case of a marriage in a registered building (not being a marriage in the presence of an authorised person), in the absence of a registrar of the registration district in which the registered building is situated;
(g) in the case of a marriage in the office of a superintendent registrar, in the absence of the superintendent registrar or of a registrar of the registration district of that superintendent registrar;
(gg) in the case of a marriage on approved premises, in the absence of the superintendent registrar of the registration district in which the premises are situated or in the absence of a registrar of that district; or
(h) in the case of a marriage to which section 45A of this Act applies, in the absence of any superintendent registrar or registrar whose presence at that marriage is required by that section;

the marriage shall be void.

Akhter v Khan (Attorney General and others intervening)
[2020] EWCA Civ 122, [2020] 2 WLR 1183, Court of Appeal

In this case, the wife petitioned for a divorce after some 18 years of marriage. The *nikah* had been conducted in the United Kingdom by an imam in the presence of members of the parties' families and community. The husband did not undertake the intended civil ceremony, however. The parties lived as a married couple and had four children. The husband defended the divorce petition on the basis that the parties had not entered into a valid marriage because the *nikah* had not complied with the formalities of the Marriage Act 1949. The wife did not argue that the *nikah* had given rise to a valid marriage, but that, among other things, it had created a void marriage, within section 11(a)(iii) of the Matrimonial Causes Act 1973, and therefore a decree of nullity was available to her. The judge in the lower court granted a decree of nullity, holding that the parties had entered into a void marriage rather than a wholly invalid one.

This case is prominent not only because it is one of the few occasions on which the Court of Appeal has dealt with the status of an unregistered *nikah*-only marriage, but also because the wife claimed and the lower court accepted that not to recognise the marriage as void would amount to a breach of ECHR, s 8 (the right to private and family life) and 12 (the right to marry), alongside the best interests principle in the Convention on the Rights of the Child.[29] A key question in the case therefore became whether the court should hold the marriage void or merely a non-qualifying marriage.

> 43. In summary, therefore, s. 49 [of the Marriage Act] only applies when the parties "knowingly and wilfully intermarry *under* the provisions of this Part of this Act". Likewise, section 25 of the 1949 Act only applies when the parties "knowingly and wilfully intermarry *according* to the rites of the Church of England".
>
> 44. We deal with non-marriages below but, as Mr Nagpal [counsel for the Attorney General] submitted, these provisions support the conclusion that there is a threshold which must be crossed before a ceremony or other acts will be within the scope of the 1949 Act at all. The words "according" and "under" must have some meaning. In our view, they support the conclusion that to "intermarry *according to* the rites of the Church of England" requires a marriage that can, at least, be said to be according to these rites. Similarly, the words "intermarry *under* the provisions of this Part of this Act" must mean more than simply the performance of a ceremony of marriage in England. It must be a marriage which can be defined or described as a marriage being contracted *under* Part II of the 1949 Act.
>
> 45. As is pointed out in the article referred to above, *The Legal Treatment of Islamic Marriage Ceremonies*, at p. 390, when dealing with the intention of the parties, "it is only where the parties 'intermarry under the provisions of [the] Act' that the court is directed to consider whether they did so knowingly and

29 The case was subsequently referred to as supporting the non-extension of the term "spouse" to a *nikah*-only marriage for the purpose of a widowed parent's allowance by the Upper Tribunal in *AR v Secretary of State for Work and Pensions* [2020] UKUT 165 (AAC), where human rights arguments were also submitted.

wilfully".[30] In the view of the authors, with which we agree, "it would be wrong in principle for those who know that they are flouting the law to have more rights than those who do not". In our view, this also supports the conclusion that there is a threshold which has to be crossed before it can be said that the parties have intermarried under the provisions of Part II of the 1949 Act.

…

50. Mr Hale [counsel for the first intervener, who was a petitioner in separate nullity proceedings] submitted that the 1949 Act does not preclude the court from finding a marriage void in circumstances other than those set out in that Act. We do not agree with this submission at least in respect of the circumstances of this case and certainly in respect of the court's power to grant a decree of nullity. As appears to have been agreed below, s. 11 of the 1973 Act prescribes *when* the court will have jurisdiction to grant a decree of nullity. Williams J recorded, at [51], Mr Le Grice QC's acknowledgment that "there is no residual inherent power in the High Court to grant a decree of nullity save under statute". Further, as set out above, s. 11(a)(iii) is clearly referring to non-compliance with those formalities which the 1949 Act expressly stipulates will make a marriage void. As set out in *A v A*, at [50]–[51] (Dr Lushington in *Catterall v Sweetman (1845) 1 Rob Eccl 304* and Lord Penzance in *Greaves v Greaves (1872) LR 2 P & D 423*), it has long been established that the statutory provisions delineate when non-compliance with one of the required formalities will make a marriage void.

51. We would also refer to s. 58(5)(a) of the Family Law Act 1986 which prohibits a court from making a declaration "that a marriage was at its inception void". In our view, the combined effect of these provisions is clear, namely that whether the court can grant a decree of nullity because a marriage is void is to be determined by the provisions of s. 11 and, through s. 11(a)(iii), by the provisions of the 1949 Act.

…

63. We would, therefore, have concluded that, to prevent the regulatory system being fundamentally undermined and in a manner which would be contrary to the need for certainty in the interests of the parties and in the public interest, we would have decided that there are some ceremonies of marriage which do not create even void marriages. In summary, in some cases the extent of non-

30 The article in question is Probert, R. and Saleem, S. (2018), 'The legal treatment of Islamic marriage ceremonies', *Oxford Journal of Law and Religion*, 7(3), pp. 376–400.

compliance with the formal requirements stipulated under the 1949 Act means that the manner in which the marriage has been "solemnized" (to use the word from the 1949 Act, including s. 29), is such that the parties have not intermarried *under* the provisions of Part II or, when relevant, *according* to the rites of the Church of England.

64. As referred to above, however, we agree with observations that have been made about the unsatisfactory nature of the expression "non-marriage". We consider that the focus should be on the ceremony and would propose that they should be called a "non-qualifying ceremony" to signify that they are outside the scope of both the 1949 and the 1973 Acts.

Issue (i):

65. We conclude on issue (i) that, it is clear, for the reasons given above, that there can be ceremonies which do not create a marriage, or even a void marriage, within the scope of the 1949 and the 1973 Acts and which do not, therefore, entitle the parties to a decree of nullity.

…

81. It being "irrefutable" that there is no absolute right to be divorced under [ECHR] Article 12, the question is whether Article 12 applies to nullity. In our judgment it does not. Logic alone would dictate this to be the case but, in any event, casting back to the ECtHR's words in *Johnston* [*Johnston and Others v Ireland* [1986] ECHR 17, (1986) 9 EHRR 203], if Article 12 cannot cover "the dissolution of a marriage", it cannot cover a situation where a marriage is declared null and void ab initio.

…

103. In addition, the question of whether a marriage is void must, in our view, depend on the facts as they were at the date of the alleged marriage. A marriage either is or is not void and either is or is not within the scope of the 1949 Act at the date of its alleged solemnisation. The determination of whether a marriage is void or not cannot, in our view, be wholly (or in part) dependent on future events, such as the intention to undertake another ceremony or whether there are children. We return to this below but, putting it more broadly, it cannot be the case that the legal effect of a ceremony of marriage can depend on whether the parties have children either at the date of the ceremony or subsequently. There is no basis, under Article 8 or by virtue of the impact of Article 3 of the United Nations Convention on the Rights of the Child 1990 ("UNCRC"), by which the legal

effect of the same ceremony could be converted including from a non-marriage to a void marriage.

...

106. In our judgment therefore:

i) Whilst the Petitioner's Article 8 right to respect to family life is undoubtedly engaged, the failure of the state to recognise the *Nikah* as a legal marriage is not in breach of those rights;

ii) The right or otherwise to the grant of a decree of nullity does not in itself engage Article 8.

The fact that at the time of the *Nikah* ceremony both parties knew that in order to contract a legal marriage they had to go through a civil ceremony, and intended to do so, does not undermine either of those conclusions or permit reliance on Article 8 as a means to allow a flexible interpretation of s. 11 of the 1973 Act.

...

Issue (i):

121. Returning to issue (i), we conclude, for the reasons given above, that the judge's approach is not supported by either the ECHR or the UNCRC. We are also of the view that they do not support any departure from the current legal approach as also summarised above. Accordingly, we repeat, there can be ceremonies which do not create a marriage, even a void marriage, within the scope of the 1949 and the 1973 Acts and which do not, therefore, entitle the parties to a decree of nullity.

2.1.2 Forced Marriage

Legislation now applies to forced marriages in British jurisdictions, with a mixture of civil and criminal provisions. Separate legislation with slightly different provisions applies in England, Wales and Northern Ireland on the one hand, and in Scotland on the other.[31] Under the Family Law Act 1996, as amended by the Forced Marriage (Civil Protection) Act 2007, courts can grant forced marriage protection orders (FMPOs) when petitioned to do so by the person "to be protected" i.e., the one being forced into a marriage or by a relevant third party. Amendments by the Anti-social Behaviour, Crime and Policing Act 2014

31 For the background to the English, etc. legislation, see Grillo, R.D. (2015), *Muslim families, politics and the law: A legal industry in multicultural Britain*. Farnham: Ashgate, pp. 59–91.

introduced a new section 63CA of the Family Law Act 1996, which made the breaching of an FMPO a criminal offence, with a possible maximum sentence of five years with a fine. This is in addition to the free-standing offence of forced marriage which attracts a maximum of seven years' imprisonment (see ch. 14, section 4).

Under the Family Law Act 1996, section 63S, a "marriage" means "any religious or civil ceremony of marriage (whether or not legally binding)." This makes the forced marriage legislation wider in scope by including unregistered marriages where only a *nikah* has been performed. This approach can be contrasted with the condition of recognising marriages in other contexts where legislation has not been interpreted to extend to unregistered marriages solemnised with a *nikah* only (see the case of *Akhter v Khan*, at ch. 15, section 2.1.1 above). In practice, the wording contained in FMPOs may be wider than that relating strictly to marriage, and this appears to be allowed under the Family Law Act 1996, section 63B. For example, in the case of *The Chief Constable of West Yorkshire Police v FP, MP, PP* the FMPO referred to the subject of the order undergoing "any ceremony (or purported ceremony) of marriage, civil partnership, betrothal or engagement."[32] FMPOs can also include travel bans and orders to retain passports and other travel documents of any of the relevant parties,[33] and it appears to be a practice that extends to passports of non-British nationals.[34]

The Scottish legislation, the Forced Marriage etc. (Protection and Jurisdiction) (Scotland) Act 2011, has slightly different provisions. That Act made it a criminal offence to breach an FMPO earlier than in England, Wales and Northern Ireland. The Scottish legislation, section 4(3), envisages the Sheriffs' courts acting in criminal proceedings as being among the courts that can make the FMPOs, whereas the Family Law Act 1996 envisages only the family court and the High Court being able to do so.

Although numbers have fluctuated, family court statistics in England and Wales indicate that there has been an overall long-term upward trend from the

32 *The Chief Constable of West Yorkshire Police v FP, MP, PP* [2024] EWFC 130.

33 *In re K (Secretary of State for Justice and another intervening)* [2020] EWCA Civ 190; [2020] 2 W.L.R. 1279 where the court set out general rules on travel and passport orders and where it also addressed the question of an indefinite passport confiscation as a potential violation of ECHR, Articles 3 and 8.

34 Although it has not been specifically stated, this seems to have happened in *London Borough of Enfield v M, F, K & L (By their Children's Guardian, Jasmin Wedderburn)*, Case No: ZW20C00468, Family Court Sitting at Barnet, 2022 WL 00350398. *M (Children: Care Proceedings: Passport Order)* [2017] EWCA Civ 69 is a care proceedings case, where the father's Libyan as well as British passports were withheld.

introduction of FMPOs in November 2008 until the end of 2019, with a less pronounced increase thereafter. In 2023, 287 applications were made for FMPOs, up by 7 per cent compared to 2022; and 414 orders were made in 2023, up by 20 per cent on the previous year. An increase in the number of orders does not necessarily represent an increase in the prevalence of forced marriage. It can be put down to greater awareness, including the fact that in 2020 health education became compulsory across all state-funded schools in England, including Relationships Education in primary schools and Relationships and Sex Education (RSE) in secondary schools (see ch. 7, section 7). The number of orders also outweighs the number of applications because of reasons such as one application covering more than one person and extensions to existing FMPOs.[35] The Government's Forced Marriage Unit, which is a joint unit of the Foreign and Home Offices, found that of the cases it was approached about in 2023, 67 (24 per cent) involved victims whose mental capacity to consent to marriage was in doubt, and the case law testifies to the frequent intervention and requests for FMPOs made by local authorities in cases of this kind.[36] Concerns have been expressed by the Forced Marriage Unit about gay Muslims, especially males, being forced into marriages.[37]

It can be noted that the Scottish legislation on forced marriage contains a different, more expansive formulation of what constitutes "force" as compared to the legislation that applies in England, Wales and Northern Ireland (i.e. the Family Law Act 1996, section 63A(6), below). The Scottish legislation, in section 1(6) specifies that "force" includes to "(a) coerce by physical, verbal or psychological means, threatening conduct, harassment or other means, (b) knowingly [to] take advantage of a person's incapacity to consent to marriage or to understand the nature of the marriage."

It is conceivable that the circumstances which enable a voidable marriage to be declared void extend to the circumstances which would make a marriage into a forced marriage. Although the terminology used to define a forced mar-

35 Family Court Statistics Quarterly: October to December 2023, published in March 2024, https://www.gov.uk/government/statistics/family-court-statistics-quarterly-october-to-december-2023/family-court-statistics-quarterly-october-to-december-2023#forced-marriage-protection-orders-and-female-genital-mutilation-protection-orders.

36 Forced Marriage Unit statistics 2023, 9 May 2024, https://www.gov.uk/government/statistics/forced-marriage-unit-statistics-2023/forced-marriage-unit-statistics-2023#sexual-orientation-of-victims.

37 'More men being forced into marriage', 1 July 2010, https://www.gov.uk/government/news/more-men-being-forced-into-marriage, accessed on 12 February 2025; Casey, L. (2016), *The Casey Review: A review into opportunity and integration*. London: Her Majesty's Stationery Office, pp. 111–112.

riage is different from that which is used to define a voidable marriage in the Matrimonial Causes Act, section 12(1), they would overlap in practice. Therefore, the psychological and other threats that could constitute a forced marriage would conceivably be the kind of circumstances that could constitute a lack of consent in consequence of duress in section 12(1). Also, local authorities often tend to intervene in situations where the lack of consent is due to the unsoundness of mind mentioned in section 12(1). The Court of Appeal has confirmed that there is no restriction on the power of a court to declare a marriage void whether it is technically a voidable marriage under section 12(1) rather than a marriage that is void at the outset.[38]

In a series of cases, usually ones in which the authorities have intervened to challenge the marriage with a person living in Bangladesh or Pakistan, the courts have been prone to avoid the implication that the marriage is voidable, because to hold that would mean that the marriage was valid until the time when it was declared voidable. Although in *A Local Authority v X & Anor (Children)* (discussed at ch. 15, section 1.1) the court expected the victim of a forced marriage, who was underage at the time she was married, to initiate nullity proceedings, it nevertheless found that the marriage was void without making a declaration to that effect.[39]

More generally, the higher courts have preferred to rely on their inherent power to refuse to recognise a forced marriage as valid. In the leading case, which other courts have since followed, the Court of Appeal held that English law would find it repugnant to public policy to recognise a marriage in which the English-domiciled spouse had autism and severe impairment of intellectual functioning such that he did not have the intellectual capacity to marry.[40] Since the decision depended on the inherent jurisdiction of the court,

38 *Westminster City Council v C and others* [2008] EWCA Civ 198, [2009] 2 WLR, followed by *Re SA (Declaration of Non-Recognition of Marriage)* [2023] EWCA Civ 1003, [2024] 2 All E.R. 875.

39 *A Local Authority v X & Anor (Children)* [2013] EWHC 3274 (Fam).

40 *Westminster City Council v C and others* [2008] EWCA Civ 198, [2009] 2 WLR. That case was applied in *Re SA (Declaration of Non-Recognition of Marriage)* [2023] EWCA Civ 1003, [2024] 2 All E.R. 875 in the nearly identical circumstances of a marriage conducted in Bangladesh of a significantly intellectually impaired person with her cousin. For a further rich discussion of the inherent jurisdiction of the court and the cases in which it had been used previously see *A Local Authority v Ma, Na, Sa (by her children's guardian LJ)* [2005] EWHC 2942 (Fam). The case concerned whether to extend the exercise of inherent powers to prevent a marriage from being arranged by the parents of a profoundly deaf vulnerable Pakistani Muslim woman now that she was over 18 years of age. A similar case would today presumably be dealt with by an FMPO under the Forced Marriage (Civil Protection) Act 2007.

a marriage solemnised in British jurisdictions could similarly be subject to non-recognition and therefore not depend on one of the parties to it bringing an action for nullity of the marriage under section 12(1)(c). The Court of Appeal has taken the view that non-recognition of a marriage on public policy grounds could be justified because of the civil law provisions which allow courts to make an FMPO and the offence of forced marriage which carries a maximum term of imprisonment of seven years.[41]

Matrimonial Causes Act 1973

12 Grounds on which a marriage is voidable.

(1) A marriage celebrated after 31st July 1971, other than a marriage to which section 12A applies, shall be voidable on the following grounds only, that is to say—

...

(c) that either party to the marriage did not validly consent to it, whether in consequence of duress, mistake, unsoundness of mind or otherwise;

Family Law Act 1996

63A Forced marriage protection orders

(1) The court may make an order for the purposes of protecting—

(a) a person from being forced into a marriage or from any attempt to be forced into a marriage; or

(b) a person who has been forced into a marriage.

(2) In deciding whether to exercise its powers under this section and, if so, in what manner, the court must have regard to all the circumstances including the need to secure the health, safety and well-being of the person to be protected.

(3) In ascertaining that person's well-being, the court must, in particular, have such regard to the person's wishes and feelings (so far as they are reasonably ascertainable) as the court considers appropriate in the light of the person's age and understanding.

(4) For the purposes of this Part a person ("A") is forced into a marriage if another person ("B") forces A to enter into a marriage (whether with B or another person) without A's free and full consent.

41 *Re SA (Declaration of Non-Recognition of Marriage)* [2023] EWCA Civ 1003, [2024] 2 All E.R. 875.

(5) For the purposes of subsection (4) it does not matter whether the conduct of B which forces A to enter into a marriage is directed against A, B or another person.

(6) In this Part—
"force" includes coerce by threats or other psychological means (and related expressions are to be read accordingly); and
"forced marriage protection order" means an order under this section.

63B Contents of orders

(1) A forced marriage protection order may contain—
  (a) such prohibitions, restrictions or requirements; and
  (b) such other terms;
as the court considers appropriate for the purposes of the order.

(2) The terms of such orders may, in particular, relate to—
  (a) conduct outside England and Wales as well as (or instead of) conduct within England and Wales;
  (b) respondents who are, or may become, involved in other respects as well as (or instead of) respondents who force or attempt to force, or may force or attempt to force, a person to enter into a marriage;
  (c) other persons who are, or may become, involved in other respects as well as respondents of any kind.

(3) For the purposes of subsection (2) examples of involvement in other respects are—
  (a) aiding, abetting, counselling, procuring, encouraging or assisting another person to force, or to attempt to force, a person to enter into a marriage; or
  (b) conspiring to force, or to attempt to force, a person to enter into a marriage.

63C Applications and other occasions for making orders

(1) The court may make a forced marriage protection order—
  (a) on an application being made to it; or
  (b) without an application being made to it but in the circumstances mentioned in subsection (6).

(2) An application may be made by—
  (a) the person who is to be protected by the order; or
  (b) a relevant third party.

(3) An application may be made by any other person with the leave of the court.

(4) In deciding whether to grant leave, the court must have regard to all the circumstances including—
   (a) the applicant's connection with the person to be protected;
   (b) the applicant's knowledge of the circumstances of the person to be protected; and
   (c) the wishes and feelings of the person to be protected so far as they are reasonably ascertainable and so far as the court considers it appropriate, in the light of the person's age and understanding, to have regard to them.

(5) An application under this section may be made in other family proceedings or without any other family proceedings being instituted.

(6) The circumstances in which the court may make an order without an application being made are where—
   (a) any other family proceedings are before the court ("the current proceedings");
   (b) the court considers that a forced marriage protection order should be made to protect a person (whether or not a party to the current proceedings); and
   (c) a person who would be a respondent to any such proceedings for a forced marriage protection order is a party to the current proceedings.

(7) In this section—
"family proceedings" has the samc meaning as in Part 4 (see section 63(1) and (2)) but also includes—
   (a) proceedings under the inherent jurisdiction of the High Court in relation to adults;
   (b) proceedings in which the court has made an emergency protection order under section 44 of the Children Act 1989 (c. 41) which includes an exclusion requirement (as defined in section 44A(3) of that Act); and
   (c) proceedings in which the court has made an order under section 50 of the Act of 1989 (recovery of abducted children etc.); and

"relevant third party" means a person specified, or falling within a description of persons specified, by order of the Lord Chancellor.

(8) An order of the Lord Chancellor under subsection (7) may, in particular, specify the Secretary of State.

63CA Offence of breaching order

(1) A person who without reasonable excuse does anything that the person is prohibited from doing by a forced marriage protection order is guilty of an offence.

(2) In the case of a forced marriage protection order made by virtue of section 63D(1), a person can be guilty of an offence under this section only in respect of conduct engaged in at a time when the person was aware of the existence of the order.

(3) Where a person is convicted of an offence under this section in respect of any conduct, that conduct is not punishable as a contempt of court.

(4) A person cannot be convicted of an offence under this section in respect of any conduct which has been punished as a contempt of court.

(5) A person guilty of an offence under this section is liable—
   (a) on conviction on indictment, to imprisonment for a term not exceeding five years, or a fine, or both;
   (b) on summary conviction, to imprisonment for a term not exceeding the general limit in a magistrates' court, or a fine, or both.

(6) A reference in any enactment to proceedings under this Part, or to an order under this Part, does not include a reference to proceedings for an offence under this section or to an order made in proceedings for such an offence.

(7) "Enactment" includes an enactment contained in subordinate legislation within the meaning of the Interpretation Act 1978.

…

63S Interpretation of Part 4A

In this Part—

…

"marriage" means any religious or civil ceremony of marriage (whether or not legally binding); and

2.2 *Divorce*

The Divorce Reform Act 1969 was a reforming piece of legislation that sought to get away from the prior blame-based law on divorce, which set spouses against one another even when there were no real quarrels between them. The 1969 Act, whose relevant provisions were included in the Matrimonial Causes Act 1973, section 1, obliged the petitioner to show that "the marriage has broken down irretrievably." They could do this by satisfying the court that one of five facts were present: adultery; unreasonable behaviour; desertion; separation for two years with consent, or five years without the need for consent. The court also had a duty to inquire into the facts as alleged by the parties. Although the one formal ground and five facts were expressed in the legislation, the important dimension was procedural. The procedure has meant that in practice divorce was consensual since the overwhelming majority of petitions (more than 98 per cent) were not contested, making the specific assertion of one of the facts a formality. Uncontested divorces would not get a formal hearing in court but the decrees nisi and absolute were pronounced in court, thus ending the matter. This contrasted with the claim that, unlike other systems of divorcing, including the Islamic one, British legal systems required a court to be involved in the process.[42] Recent changes with the Divorce, Dissolution and Separation Act 2020 (in force from 6 April 2022) recognise the consensual nature of divorce. The Matrimonial Causes Act, section 1, is amended by the 2020 Act to require a mere statement of irretrievable breakdown, which the court must accept as conclusive evidence. The change of language compared to that of the earlier legislation is quite significant, although it may recognise the procedural realities which were already in play prior to it.

Matrimonial Causes Act 1973
(as amended by the Divorce, Dissolution and Separation Act 2020)

1 Divorce on breakdown of marriage

(1) Subject to section 3, either or both parties to a marriage may apply to the court for an order (a "divorce order") which dissolves the marriage on the ground that the marriage has broken down irretrievably.

(2) An application under subsection (1) must be accompanied by a statement by the applicant or applicants that the marriage has broken down irretrievably.

(3) The court dealing with an application under subsection (1) must—
   (a) take the statement to be conclusive evidence that the marriage has broken down irretrievably, and
   (b) make a divorce order.

(4) A divorce order—
   (a) is, in the first instance, a conditional order, and
   (b) may not be made final before the end of the period of 6 weeks from the making of the conditional order.

42 Poulter, S. (1986), *English law and ethnic minority customs*. London: Butterworth, p. 98.

(5) The court may not make a conditional order unless—
  (a) in the case of an application that is to proceed as an application by one party to the marriage only, that party has confirmed to the court that they wish the application to continue, or
  (b) in the case of an application that is to proceed as an application by both parties to the marriage, those parties have confirmed to the court that they wish the application to continue;

and a party may not give confirmation for the purposes of this subsection before the end of the period of 20 weeks from the start of proceedings.

Divorce is obviously intimately connected to the issue of marriage in the context of both private international law and that part of the law that applies to purely internal situations. Many of the cases to do with marriage are initiated because a petition of divorce has been initiated by one party to a marriage and then contested by raising issues about the validity of marriage. Conversely, marriage-based claims in family or administrative contexts, such as social security or immigration, or even criminal law, can also rest on the existence of a prior divorce. Since the Domicile and Matrimonial Proceedings Act 1973, divorces in any part of the British islands have to be obtained by a court of civil jurisdiction. This condition is now contained in the Family Law Act 1986, section 44. This was a response to the judiciary taking steps to recognise Islamic divorces effected when a *talaq* had notified to the Pakistani High Commission, treating them as MFLO divorces.[43] In turn, this led to the phenomenon of Muslim men having recourse to the law of their countries of origin by either travelling there and divorcing overseas or trying to effect a transnational divorce. This has led to the rise of a case law concerning the private international law on proceedings and non-proceedings divorces which has been noted (ch. 15, section 1.2). One way in which transnational divorces have been used to circumvent the restriction on Islamic divorces being effected within the jurisdiction is by so-called divorces by post where the husband pronounces a *talaq* while in the UK and then notifies the relevant authority in Pakistan in order to comply with the MFLO rules on divorce. The intricate interplay of the law applying to purely domestic situations and private international law shows that they cannot be so easily compartmentalised, and provides yet another

43 *Qureshi v Qureshi* [1972] Fam. 173; [1971] W.L.R. 518 was particularly significant in provoking the parliamentary legislation of 1973.

good example of how a sphere of law has been impacted on by significant Muslim immigration.[44]

Family Law Act 1986

44 Recognition in United Kingdom of divorces, annulments and judicial separations granted in the British Islands.

(1) Subject to section 52(4) and (5)(a) of this Act, no divorce or annulment obtained in any part of the British Islands shall be regarded as effective in any part of the United Kingdom unless granted by a court of civil jurisdiction.

(2) Subject to section 51 of this Act, the validity of any divorce, annulment or judicial separation granted by a court of civil jurisdiction in any part of the British Islands shall be recognised throughout the United Kingdom.

***R. v Secretary of State for the Home Department Ex p. Fatima* (*Ghulam*)**
[1986] A.C. 527

A Pakistani man pronounced a *talaq* in England against his wife, who was resident in Pakistan. In compliance with the Pakistan MFLO 1961 he pronounced the *talaq* against his wife and made a statutory declaration that he had done so before a solicitor. Copies of that document were sent to the wife and to the chairman of the relevant union council in Pakistan. As no reconciliation was effected, the marriage was dissolved according to Pakistani law 90 days after the receipt by the chairman of the notice of the *talaq*. He then acted as sponsor to his Pakistani fiancee's application for leave to enter the United Kingdom. On arrival in the UK the applicant was refused leave to enter by an immigration officer on the ground that he was not satisfied that the intended marriage could take place within a reasonable time as her sponsor's divorce was not recognised in the UK. The applicant applied for judicial review of the decision of the immigration officer. The High Court refused the application on the ground that the sponsor's divorce could not be recognised as a valid decree under the provisions of sections 2 and 3(1) of the Recognition of Divorces and Legal Separations Act 1971, which contained an earlier expression of the "proceedings" requirement and, in turn, the Court of Appeal dismissed the applicant's appeal.

44 See Pearl, D. and Menski, W. (1998), *Muslim family law*. London: Sweet & Maxwell, pp. 87–95 for the details.

On appeal to the House of Lords, Lord Ackner gave the main speech with which their other Lordships agreed.

> Given that the pronouncement of the talaq was the institution of the proceedings, then such institution took place in the United Kingdom and not in Pakistan where the divorce was obtained. Accordingly its validity cannot be recognised since the requirements of section 3(1) set out above cannot be satisfied. This demonstrates that the wording of section 2 and section 3(1) when read together make it clear that the "proceedings" in section 2(a) must be a single set of proceedings which have to be instituted in the same country as that in which the relevant divorce was ultimately obtained.
>
> Mr. Kadri [counsel for the appellant] strongly urged that if the wording of sections 2 and 3 of the Recognition Act is only apt to cover "judicial or other proceedings" which take place exclusively abroad, then such a construction frustrates the purpose of the Act. He relied upon the observations of Lord Diplock in *Quazi v. Quazi*, at p. 804, that the purpose of the Act was to enable the United Kingdom to give effect in its domestic law to the Hague Convention on the Recognition of Divorces and Legal Separations (1970) (Cmnd. 6248). He described the mischief which the Convention was designed to cure as that of "limping marriages," that is to say "marriages that were recognised in some jurisdictions as having been validly dissolved, but in other jurisdictions as still subsisting." In considering the policy of the legislature I agree with the Court of Appeal and with Taylor J. that we should have in mind the provisions of the Domicile and Matrimonial Proceedings Act 1973 which made further provision concerning the recognition of divorces and legal separations and which provided by section 16(1) as follows:
>
> > No proceedings in the United Kingdom, the Channel Islands or the Isle of Man shall be regarded as validly dissolving a marriage F unless instituted in the courts of law of one of those countries.
>
> That provision was intended to reverse the decision in *Qureshi v. Qureshi* [1972] Fam. 173, where recognition was given to full talaq proceedings which took place wholly within the United Kingdom. It is thus clearly the policy of the legislature to deny recognition to divorces obtained by persons within the jurisdiction, and therefore subject to the laws of the United Kingdom, by any proceedings other than in a United Kingdom court. It would seem contrary to that policy to encourage the obtaining of divorces essentially by post by Pakistani nationals resident in this country by means of the talaq procedure.
>
> For the reasons set out above, which are in essence those expressed by the courts below, I agree that the immigration officer was entitled to take the view that he could not be satisfied that the proposed marriage would take place within a reasonable time.

Hussain v Parveen
[2022] EWCA Civ 1434

Although the *Fatima* case (above) has reinforced the idea that divorces must be obtained wholly within one jurisdiction or another and does not entertain divorces by post, the more recent case of *Hussain v Parveen* nevertheless upheld the validity of the second marriage of a Pakistani woman who had been divorced by her first husband by the same means, i.e., a *talaq* declared in England and then sent to the relevant union council in Pakistan as in the *Fatima* case above. Moylan L.J., with whom the other Lord Justices agreed, gave the judgement of the court.

> 85. In deciding what justice requires, the court should give weight, and probably significant weight, to the general policy objectives of seeking to uphold the validity of a marriage and of seeking to avoid creating a limping marriage.
>
> 86. I do not think it necessary for the purposes of the present case but, if I was to seek to narrow the approach down, I would be inclined broadly to adopt that proposed in Cheshire, at p. 54, because, by applying the choice of law rules applicable to the main question to the issues of both capacity and recognition, it seems to me more likely to achieve those policy objectives. This is because the issue raised by this appeal will only arise when a spouse has the capacity to marry by the law of their domicile but their previous divorce (or nullity) is not recognised under the FLA 1986.
>
> 87. I certainly consider that that approach should be applied in the present case. In my view, as set out in Dicey, at [2-049], "the principal question is whether the second marriage is invalid for bigamy". This "raises a question of capacity" which, in respect of the wife, is governed by the law of Pakistan. I also consider that the question of the validity of the wife's previous divorce should be determined by the law of Pakistan, under which it was effective to determine her first marriage. This would mean that the wife had capacity to marry the husband and that the marriage is not void under section 11(b) of the MCA 1973.
>
> …
>
> 89. Also in deciding what justice requires, I need to consider whether there are any public policy reasons why the marriage should not be recognised. I accept that there might be public policy reasons why the divorce recognition rules should take priority over the marriage capacity rules. Mr Murray relied on what Lord Ackner said in *In Re Fatima*, at p. 534 G, I repeat:

> It is thus clearly the policy of the legislature to deny recognition to divorces obtained by persons within the jurisdiction, and therefore subject to the laws of the United Kingdom, by any proceedings other than in a United Kingdom court. It would seem contrary to that policy to encourage the obtaining of divorces essentially by post by Pakistani nationals resident in this country by means of the talaq procedure.

In my view, the key words for the purposes of the present appeal are "divorces obtained by persons within the jurisdiction, and therefore subject to the laws of the United Kingdom". These would apply to the wife's previous husband. They do not apply to the wife and, in the circumstances of the present case, I do not consider that they should be applied to the wife. I see no reason why the wife should be subject to this policy consideration when, at all relevant times, she was domiciled in and lived in Pakistan. I see no reason why she should be expected to obtain legal advice in England and, if she was able to do so, to commence divorce proceedings in England. She was, in my view, entitled to rely on her first marriage having been determined by a divorce which was valid in Pakistan. The public policy objectives would be sufficiently achieved by denying recognition of the divorce to the wife's previous husband because of his connections with the UK.

90. In conclusion, therefore, the wife's marriage to the husband is valid as she had the capacity to marry because her previous divorce was effective under the law of Pakistan. The fact that that divorce is not entitled to recognition under the FLA 1986 does not mean that she did not have the capacity to marry.

3 Children

3.1 *Circumcision*

P (Circumcision: Child in Care), Re

[2021] EWHC 1616 (Fam), High Court of Justice Family Division

The decision to circumcise a boy because of the requirement of his Muslim identity can give rise to discussions in legal contexts. In this case, the issue became complicated because the prospective permanent carers of a Muslim child, who were not his parents or relatives, did not wish to see him circumcised at the age of 21 months, while his parents did wish that to happen. They had not shown a broader interest in his upbringing as a Muslim, and they did not have much contact with him, while being permitted to do so. The Local Authority and the Children's Guardian both contended that the decision about the child's circumcision should not be taken immediately but deferred until later in the boy's life.

> 1. The application before the Court concerns P. He is a boy aged 21 months. He is currently subject to an interim care order in favour of X Local Authority ("the Local Authority"); he has lived all his life with extended maternal family members (Mr and Mrs R), who (it is agreed by all parties) are likely soon to become his permanent carers under a Special Guardianship Order.
>
> 2. P's parents are Muslim: his father by birth and heritage, and his mother by conversion to Islam some years ago.
>
> 3. By application dated 25 November 2020 brought under the Court's inherent jurisdiction, P's mother ("the mother") seeks the court's authorisation for P to be circumcised, in accordance with the custom of the Muslim faith; she wishes this procedure to be undertaken forthwith, and in any event before P's second birthday. The application is supported by P's father. The Local Authority and the Children's Guardian both contend that the decision about P's circumcision should not be taken now, but should be deferred until later in P's life.
>
> …
>
> 7. Mr and Mrs R are not Muslim. It is nonetheless agreed that they will care for P throughout his life; they have been positively assessed as Special Guardians for P, and the parents agree that this order should now be made. Mr and Mrs R have agreed that they will respect P's Muslim heritage; they have acknowledged the parents' preference for P to follow a broadly (but not strictly) *halal* diet.
>
> …
>
> 13. Ms Shaikh argues on the mother's behalf that circumcision of P represents an important component of his identity and cultural and religious heritage; she accepts that male circumcision is recommended not obligatory in the Islamic faith (she suggests that "it is the usual practice").
>
> 14. Ms Shaikh argues that the combined and strongly held views of the parents should carry considerable weight with the court. She further points to the fact that the Local Authority had initially been willing to contemplate, even allow the parents to arrange, for P to be circumcised when he was a new-born infant, but it had not happened; in this respect, I must observe that the mother fails to acknowledge that neither she nor the father took the appropriate or necessary steps to arrange it. The mother is concerned that if P is not circumcised now,

he will not choose to be circumcised later in his life as he would be deterred by the likely pain and discomfort which the procedure would then cause him. The mother has requested that P follow a *halal* diet, and this is largely to be followed; however, it is noted that this request was only made after he had been with Mr and Mrs R for over a year.

...

16. Mr Lindsay submits that, like the mother, the father is concerned that if left until later in his life P would not choose to be circumcised as he would not be sufficiently motivated by his faith to do so.

...

18. In December 2020, both parents made a commitment to provide items for P which would aid his understanding of the Muslim faith and identity; they also agreed that they would attend regular contact with their son. They have (as I have already mentioned re: contact) done neither. I note that the Local Authority has in the circumstances provided P with three child friendly board books: "My First book about Allah," "My First Book about the Prophet Muhammad" and "My First Book about the Qur'an" (authored by Sara Khan and detailed to be teachings for toddlers and young children).

19. The Local Authority contends that the decision on circumcision should now be deferred. Ms McCallum accepts that when P was first born in the summer 2019, the Local Authority was indeed willing to contemplate P's circumcision in accordance with the tenets of the Muslim faith. They had placed the expectation on the parents to make plans for this, and to propose a suitable clinic; the parents did not do so. Only in October 2020 did the father first make any specific proposals for this procedure to be undertaken. Ms McCallum contends that if the parents wish to promote P's identity and cultural heritage, this could be achieved more meaningfully for P by them committing to seeing him in contact as planned, and providing cultural/religious books for P as agreed. She contends that circumcision for P must be seen in the wider context of his religious and cultural identity.

20. The Children's Guardian echoes the views of the Local Authority.

...

22. I have been referred to a number of authorities relevant to this issue, though all previous decisions referred to me have been taken in the context of private law. Counsel have surprisingly not been able to locate any High Court or Court of

Appeal authority in which the court has been required to consider circumcision of a child in interim care, as a contested issue, in public law proceedings.

23. Taking the statutory framework first, it is of course accepted that the parents both have parental responsibility for P, and will retain that parental responsibility even when the permanent arrangements for P are, as seems likely given the evidence filed and the consent of the parties, endorsed by the Court. The Local Authority currently has parental responsibility (senior parental responsibility) for P under section 33(3) Children Act 1989 ('CA 1989') though this will be ceded if/when Special Guardianship Orders are made in favour of Mr and Mrs R. No party argues that as a matter of statutory construction either the parents or the Local Authority have the decisive "say" in relation to the issue.

24. It is also nted that the Local Authority is required, for as long as it has an interim care order, not to take any step to change his religious upbringing. Section 33(6) of the CA 1989 provides that: "… [w]hile a care order is in force with respect to a child, the local authority designated by the order shall not—(a) cause the child to be brought up in any religious persuasion other than that in which he would have been brought up if the order had not been made; …"

…

27. From the legislation and authorities cited to me, the following important guiding principles can be collected:

General

i) While it can never be reasonable parenting to inflict any form of FGM on a child, the position is different with male circumcision; "Society and the law, including family law, are prepared to tolerate non-therapeutic male circumcision performed for religious or even for purely cultural or conventional reasons, while no longer being willing to tolerate FGM in any of its forms";

Welfare

ii) The welfare of the child, both in the immediate and long-term, is the paramount consideration in reaching a decision about circumcision for a male child (the law in its current form is in section 1(1) Children Act 1989); this is uncontroversial in the instant case, and has been the starting point of all previous decisions;

iii) The welfare checklist (section 1(3) CA 1989) is engaged;
iv) Religious upbringing of a child in care may be a matter of great importance; the significance of the issue will vary from case to case depending on the strength of the religious beliefs and observance of the child's parents; on any account, this factor will need to be incorporated within (and not in place of) the wider welfare review;
v) A local authority is under a duty to ensure that a child in their care is not brought up in any different religious persuasion from that followed by his parents prior to the care order. If the local authority breaches that duty, it will be exceeding the limitation imposed on its exercise of parental responsibility by section 33(6)(a) CA 1989;

Medical issues

vi) That the circumcision procedure is irreversible is a matter of significance when looking at the short and longer term implications for the child;
vii) The court must review the medical risks and benefits of such a procedure, particularly where it is proposed for a non-therapeutic purpose; Views of parents and others.
viii) The religious views and wishes of both parents carry significant weight (they may of course as between themselves have different views/wishes); the court should pay these views 'serious heed'. The court will be slow to conclude that a parent faithfully striving to follow the teachings of their religion is acting unreasonably;
ix) The court is not bound to give effect to the wishes of the parents about religious upbringing "when satisfied that the child's welfare requires otherwise, and in giving effect to them the court has power to do so in such a manner as it may consider to be best in the child's interests";
x) The views of the primary carers of the child (if not the parents) also carry significant weight; it is a strong thing to impose a medically unnecessary surgical intervention on a residential carer/parent who is opposed to it;
xi) The particular environment in which the child is going to be raised is an important factor; if the environment is one in which circumcision is not a part of family life, or in which it is not in conformity with the religion practised by his primary carer, this would be a relevant factor; I would add this:
xii) That where a disputed issue of non-therapeutic circumcision arises again in relation to a child in care, it is appropriate for the matter to be referred promptly to the court for resolution. In this instance, the mother has done so; it may be more appropriate for the Local Authority to take the initiative in such circumstances.

29. As a matter of law, no party holds the "trump card" before the court. Had there been no interim care order in place, these two parents acting in agreement, and exercising their shared parental responsibility, would have been able to provide consent for P's circumcision for either therapeutic or non-therapeutic reasons. But P is currently subject to an interim care order; the Local Authority currently has senior parental responsibility, and presently opposes the procedure. I am satisfied that section 33(3)(b)/(4) CA 1989 does not give the Local Authority absolute authority to oppose the procedure; I am equally satisfied that in opposing the procedure the authority is not offending against the statutory proscription on causing P "to be brought up in any religious persuasion other than that in which he would have been brought up if the order had not been made" (section 33(6))—P remains a Muslim boy being raised broadly in accordance with Muslim tenets.

30. The issue for determination requires me to exercise a pure welfare-based jurisdiction. The authorities referred to above are of some assistance in shaping that welfare judgement; the principles extracted from those authorities it seems to me apply as much in public law as in private law.

31. While not merely mechanically adhering to the CA 1989 statutory checklist, its structure provides useful checkpoints to my decision. No assessment of P's ascertainable wishes and feelings can be obtained on this issue, given his age. The social worker nonetheless made a reasonable point when observing that: "[w]hen [P] is older he may be very happy that he was circumcised—he may strongly align with the Muslim faith and traditions and may be happy that the procedure has been undertaken. However, there is also a possibility that [P] may not align himself with the Muslim faith or traditions as an older child and may view his circumcision in a negative way. The only way those involved with [P] would be able to garner his wishes and feelings on being circumcised is if the procedure took place when he is of an age where he can express his own wishes and feelings."

32. I am wholly satisfied that P should be brought up, as his parents wish, as a Muslim child albeit that he will be living in a non-Muslim household (these are current relevant "background" and "relevant characteristics"). It is important that P retains, and is allowed to develop an interest in, the profound and rich tenets of the Islamic faith. I recognise and accept that circumcision is an important and symbolic demonstration of his commitment to Islam, and that it is one of the five acts which are intended to fulfil the expectation of cleanliness (called "fitrah"). But I also note that neither of P's older brothers (Q and T), with whom he spends

time, and who are also placed in a home within the maternal family, have been circumcised.

33. I am equally satisfied, from what I have read, that Mr and Mrs R understand the importance of P's Muslim heritage, and will honour that as far as it is possible for them to do so. P's identity will quite naturally be influenced by the family within which he lives, and those who have the key parental role in his life, as well as his birth heritage and any contact with his parents. It is a matter of significance to me in this decision that Mr and Mrs R currently feel unable to support the circumcision, and propose that a decision in relation to this should be deferred until P is older.

34. I accept that both parents, practising Muslims, earnestly wish the circumcision procedure to take place in order for P to connect with his Muslim heritage. Their views are of considerable importance, and I attach significant weight to them. That said, circumcision alone is not likely to establish or enhance P's sense of cultural or religious identity; this would be best achieved at his age by regular contact with his parents who can, in the best way they consider possible, help him to understand his identity and the faith into which he has been born. When he is older, they can be on hand to help him to reach a decision on whether to be circumcised. My decision has, to some extent, been influenced by the fact that presently neither parent chooses to see P, and neither parent has (contrary to their offer to do so) provided P with age appropriate books and/or learning materials about Islam.

35. I am satisfied that were I to order the circumcision, the procedure could be completed in the next few weeks, and if so, that the "ring" procedure could/should be adopted; this would be painful and distressing to P for a number of days or weeks, but no more. If the procedure is deferred until P is older, the procedure is more complex, would require greater cooperation from P, and the recovery period would be longer. I do not regard it as an inherently risky procedure, but I do bear in mind its irreversible nature.

36. On balance, and with specific regard to the range of matters which I have summarised above, I have concluded that the decision to circumcise P should be deferred until he is able to make his own choice, once he has the maturity and insight to appreciate the consequences and longer-term effects of the decision which he reaches. I encourage the parents to resume their contact with P, so that not just his Muslim heritage, but also his experience of his wider family and origins, can be better understood and appreciated by him.

Bibliography

Ahdar, R.J. and Aroney, N. (2010), *Shari'a in the West*. Oxford: Oxford University Press.

Ahdar, R.J. and Aroney, N. (2010), 'The topography in the Western political landscape," in Ahdar, R.J. and Aroney, N. (eds.), *Shari'a in the West*. Oxford: Oxford University Press, pp. 1–31.

Akhtar, R. (2015), "Unregistered Muslim marriages: An emerging culture of celebrating rites and conceding rights," in Miles, J., Mody, P., and Probert, R. (eds.), *Marriage rites and rights*. Oxford: Hart, pp. 167–192.

Al-Adnani, M. and Scheimberg, I. (2006), "How can we improve the rate of autopsies among Muslims?," *British Medical Journal*, 332(7536), pp. 310.

Alim, N. and Yassari, N. (2016), "Between procedure and substance: A review of law making in Egypt," in Yassari, N. (ed.), *Changing God's law: The dynamics of Middle Eastern family law*. Milton Park, Abingdon: Routledge, pp. 113–130.

Allen, G., Burton, M., and Pratt, A. (2022), *Terrorism in Great Britain: The statistics*. House of Commons Library.

Allington, D. (2023), *The national research environment for the study of extremism in the UK*. Commission for Countering Extremism.

APPG on British Muslims (2018), *Islamophobia defined*. All Party Parliamentary Group on British Muslims.

Bano, S. (2012), *Muslim women and Shari'ah Councils: Transcending the boundaries of community and law*. Basingstoke: Palgrave Macmillan.

Bhatti-Sinclair, K. and Sutcliffe, "Group localised child sexual exploitation offenders: Who and why?" Available at https://papers.ssrn.com/sol3/papers.cfm?abstract_id-3248665

Black, A. (2010), "In the shadow of our legal system: Shari'a in Australia," in Ahdar, R.J. and Aroney, N. (eds.), *Shari'a in the West*. Oxford: Oxford University Press, pp. 239–254.

Bowen, J.R. (2016), *On British Islam: Religion, law, and everyday practice in shari'a councils*. Princeton: Princeton University Press.

Bowes, A. (2019), *A practical approach to planning law*. Oxford: Oxford University Press.

Brett, M. (1988), "Legislating for inequality in Algeria: The Senatus-Consulte of 14 July 1865," *Bulletin of the School of Oriental and African Studies, University of London*, 51(3), pp. 440–461.

Broyde, M.J. (2017), *Sharia tribunals, rabbinical courts, and Christian panels: Religious arbitration in America and the West*. New York: Oxford University Press.

Büchler, A. (2016), *Islamic law in Europe?: Legal pluralism and its limits in European family laws*. Farnham: Routledge.

Cabinet Office (2018), *Race disparity audit: Summary findings from the Ethnicity Facts and Figures website*. Cabinet Office. Available at https://www.ethnicity-facts-figures.service.gov.uk/static/race-disparity-audit-summary-findings.pdf

Casey, L. (2016), *The Casey Review: A review into opportunity and integration*. London: Her Majesty's Stationery Office.

Chatterjee, N. (2020), *Negotiating Mughal law: A family of landlords across three Indian empires*. Cambridge: Cambridge University Press.

Choudhury, T. (2007), *The role of Muslim identity politics in radicalisation (a study in progress)*. Department of Communities and Local Government.

Clarke, P. (2014), *Report into allegations concerning Birmingham schools arising from the 'Trojan Horse' letter*. London: Her Majesty's Stationery Office.

Coglievina, S. (2016), *Annotated legal documents on Islam in Europe: Italy*. Leiden; Boston: Brill.

CAG Consultants et al. (2008) *Responding to the needs of faith communities: Places of worship*. London.

Cranmer, F. (2015), "Paying the piper? Public funding and supervision of religion in a secularized society (United Kingdom)," in Messner, F. (ed.), *Public funding of religions in Europe*. Farnham: Ashgate, pp. 171–198.

Doward, J. (2007), "Revealed: Preachers' messages of hate," *The Guardian*, 7 January 2007.

Dupret, B. (2021), *Positive law from the Muslim world: Jurisprudence, history, practices*. Cambridge: Cambridge University Press.

Electoral Commission (2014), *Electoral fraud in the UK: Final report and recommendations*. London: The Electoral Commission.

Equalities Review Panel (2007), *Fairness and freedom: The final report of the Equalities Review*.

Euben, R.L. and Zaman, M.Q. (2009), *Princeton readings in Islamist thought: Texts and contexts from al-Banna to Bin Laden*. Princeton: Princeton University Press.

Feldman, N. (2008), *The fall and rise of the Islamic state*. Princeton: Princeton University Press.

Ferreiro, J. and Moreras, J. (2021), *Annotated legal documents on Islam in Europe: Spain*. Leiden, Boston: Brill.

Gale, R. (2005), "Representing the city: Mosques and the planning process in Birmingham," *Journal of Ethnic and Migration Studies*, 31(6), pp. 1161–1179.

Gale, R. (2007), "Planning law and mosque development: The politics of religion and residence in Birmingham," in Shah, P. (ed.). *Law and ethnic plurality: Socio-legal perspectives*. Leiden: Brill Nijhoff, pp. 127–144.

Giunchi, E. (2014), *Muslim family law in Western courts*. Abingdon: Routledge.

Greer, S. (2023), *Falsely accused of Islamophobia: My struggle against academic cancellation*. Washington: Academica Press.

Griffith-Jones, R. (ed.) (2013), *Islam and English law: Rights, responsibilities and the place of Shari'a*. Cambridge: Cambridge University Press.

Griffith-Jones, R. (2013), "The 'unavoidable' adoption of shariʿa law—the generation of a media storm," in Griffith-Jones, R. (ed.), *Islam and English law: Rights, responsibilities and the place of Shari'a*. Cambridge: Cambridge University Press, pp. 9–19.

Grillo, R.D. (2015), *Muslim families, politics and the law: A legal industry in multicultural Britain*. Farnham: Ashgate.

Grillo, R.D. and Shah, P. (2012), *Reasons to ban? The anti-burqa movement in Western Europe*. MMG Working Paper 12-09. Göttingen: Max Planck Institute for the Study of Religious and Ethnic Diversity.

Guild, E. (2016), *BREXIT and its consequences for UK and EU citizenship or monstrous citizenship*. Leiden: Brill Nijhoff.

Hamoudi, H.A. (2009), "The death of Islamic law," *Georgia Journal of International and Comparative Law*, 38, pp. 293–337.

Heath, A.F., Fisher, S.D., Rosenblatt, G., Sanders, D., and Sobolewska, M. (2013), *The political integration of ethnic minorities in Britain*. Oxford: Oxford University Press.

Hill, E., Sobolewska, M., Wilks-Heeg, S., and Borkowska, M. (2017), "Explaining electoral fraud in an advanced democracy: Fraud vulnerabilities, opportunities and facilitating mechanisms in British elections," *The British Journal of Politics and International Relations*, 19(4), pp. 772–789.

Hlaimi, S. and Littlewood, C. (2023), "Too Muslim to be homosexual or too homosexual to be Muslim: Belonging experiences of British homosexual Muslims," *Journal of Muslims in Europe*, 13(2), pp. 162–192.

Hofri-Winogradow, A.S. (2010), "A plurality of discontent: Legal pluralism, religious adjudication and the state," *Journal of Law and Religion*, 26(1), pp. 57–89.

Jacobson, J. (1998), *Islam in transition: Religion and identity among British Pakistani youth*. London: Routledge.

Jamal, A. and Panjwani, F. (2016), "Having faith in our schools: Struggling with definitions of religion," in Hunter-Henin, M. (ed.), *Law, religious freedoms and education in Europe*. Abingdon: Routledge, pp. 69–86.

Janssens, Y. (2016), *Annotated legal documents on Islam in Europe: Belgium*. Leiden; Boston: Brill.

Johansen, B. (2011), "Islamic law," *Oxford International encyclopedia of legal history*. Oxford: Oxford University Press, vol. 3, pp. 315–318.

Jones, J. (2020), "Muslim alternative dispute resolution: Tracing the pathways of Islamic legal practice between South Asia and contemporary Britain," *Journal of Muslim Minority Affairs*, 40, pp. 48–66.

Khan, S. and McMahon, T. (2016), *The battle for British Islam: Reclaiming Muslim identity from extremism*. London: Saqi.

Knights, S. (2021), *Law, rights, and religion*. 2nd edition. Oxford: Oxford University Press.

Korteweg, A.C. and Selby, J.A. (eds.) (2012), *Debating Sharia: Islam, gender politics, and family law arbitration*. Toronto: University of Toronto Press.

Lester, A. and Lyle, T. (2009), "History and context," in Lester, A., Pannick, D., and Herberg, J. (eds.), *Human rights law and practice*. 3rd ed. London: LexisNexis, pp. 1–26.

Levey, G.B. (2019), "The Bristol school of multiculturalism," *Ethnicities*, 19(1), pp. 200–226.

Maher, S. and Frampton, M. (2009), *Choosing our friends wisely*. London: Policy Exchange.

Marotta, A. (2021), *A geo-legal approach to the English Sharia courts: Cases and conflicts*. Leiden: Brill.

McGoldrick, D. (2013), "The compatibility of an Islamic shari'a law system or shari'a rules with the European Convention on Human Rights," in Griffith-Jones, R. (ed.), *Islam and English law: Rights, responsibilities and the place of Shari'a*. Cambridge: Cambridge University Press, pp. 42–71.

Meer, N. (2010), *Citizenship, identity and the politics of multiculturalism: The rise of Muslim consciousness*. Basingstoke: Palgrave Macmillan.

Mehdi, R., Menski, W., and Nielsen, J.S. (eds.) (2012), *Interpreting divorce laws in Islam*. Copenhagen: DJØF.

Mehdi, R., and Nielsen, J.S. (eds.) (2011), *Embedding mahr (Islamic dower) in the European legal system*. Copenhagen: DJØF.

Menski, W. (2006), "Rethinking legal theory in the light of South-North migration," in Shah, P. and Menski, W. (eds.), *Migration, diasporas and legal systems in Europe*. Abingdon: Routledge-Cavendish, pp. 13–28.

Menski, W.F. (2006), *Comparative law in a global context: The legal systems of Asia and Africa*. Cambridge: Cambridge University Press.

Ministry of Justice (2020), *A guide to coroner services for bereaved people*.

Mirza, M., Senthilkumaran, A., and Ja'far, Z. (2007), *Living apart together: British Muslims and the paradox of multiculturalism*. London: Policy Exchange.

Modood, T. (2013), *Multiculturalism: a civic idea*. Cambridge: Polity.

Munby, S.J., (2013) "Law, morality and religion in the family courts," Speech at the conference on *The sacred and the secular: religion, culture and the family courts*, London, 29 October 2013.

Naqshbandi, M. (2017), *UK mosque statistics*. Available at: https://www.muslimsinbritain.org/resources/masjid_report.pdf.

Nash, P. (2022), *British Islam and English law: A classical pluralist perspective*. Cambridge: Cambridge University Press.

Nash, P.S. (2024), "The case for banning cousin marriage," *Oxford Journal of Law and Religion*, 13(1), pp. 98–118.

Nielsen, J.S. and Otterbeck, J. (2016), *Muslims in Western Europe*, 4th edition. Edinburgh: Edinburgh University Press.

O'Toole, T., DeHanas, D.N., Modood, T., Meer, N., and Jones, S.H. (2013), *Taking part: Muslim participation in contemporary governance*. University of Bristol.

Oskooii, K.A.R. and Dana, K. (2018), "Muslims in Great Britain: The impact of mosque attendance on political behaviour and civic engagement," *Journal of Ethnic and Migration Studies*, 44(9), pp. 1479–1505.

Pannick, D. and Steele, I. (2009), "Human Rights Act 1998," in Lester, A., Pannick, D., and Herberg, J. (eds.), *Human rights law and practice*. 3rd ed. London: LexisNexis, pp. 27–129.

Pearl, D. and Menski, W. (1998), *Muslim family law*. London: Sweet & Maxwell.

Perry, D.L. (2019), *Mainstream Islamism in Britain: Educating for the "Islamic revival"*. Commission for Countering Extremism.

Perry, D.L. and Stott, P. (2022), *The Trojan Horse Affair: A documentary record*. London: Policy Exchange.

Poulter, S. (1986), *English law and ethnic minority customs*. London: Butterworth.

Poulter, S. (1998), *Ethnicity, law, and human rights: The English experience*. Oxford: Clarendon.

Probert, R. and Saleem, S. (2018), "The legal treatment of Islamic marriage ceremonies," *Oxford Journal of Law and Religion*, 7(3), pp. 376–400.

Rivers, J. (2010), *The law of organized religions: Between establishment and secularism*. Oxford: Oxford University Press.

Robilliard, S.J.A. (1984), *Religion and the law: Religious liberty in modern English law*. Manchester: Manchester University Press.

Rohe, M. (2014), "Family and the Law in Europe: Bringing together secular legal orders and religious norms and needs," in Shah, P.S., Foblets, M.-C., and Rohe, M. (eds.), *Family, religion and law: Cultural encounters in Europe*, pp. 49–78.

Rohe, M. (2014), *Islamic law in past and present*. Leiden: Brill.

Saeed, A. (2010), "Reflections on the establishment of Shari'a courts in Australia," in Ahdar, R.J. and Aroney, N. (eds.), *Shari'a in the West*. Oxford: Oxford University Press, pp. 223–238.

Sandberg, R. (2011), *Law and religion*. New York: Cambridge University Press.

Sardar Ali, S. (2016), "Family law reform in postcolonial Pakistan," in Yassri, N. (ed.), *Changing God's law: the dynamics of Middle Eastern family law*. Milton Park, Abingdon: Routledge, pp. 34–67.

Shah, P. (1994), 'Legal pluralism—British law and possibilities with Muslim ethnic minorities," *Retfærd (Nordisk jurdisktidsskrift)*, 17 (66/67), pp. 18-33.

Shah, P, (2003), "Attitudes to Polygamy in English Law,", *International and Comparative Law Quarterly*, 52, pp. 369-400.

Shah, P. (2009), "Activism in the European Court of Justice and changing options for Turkish citizen migrants in the United Kingdom," in Hailbronner, K., Tiryakioğlu, B., Schneider, K., and Küçük, E. (eds.), *Vatandaşlık, göç, mülteci ve yabancılar hukukundaki güncel gelişmeler* (*Current developments in citizenship, immigration, refugee law and law of foreigners*). Ankara: Union of Turkish Bar Associations, pp. 299–326.

Shah, P. (2010), "Between God and the Sultana? Legal pluralism in the British Muslim diaspora," in Nielsen, J. and Christoffersen, L. (eds.), *Shari'a as Discourse: Legal traditions and the encounter with Europe*. Farnham: Asghate, pp. 117–139.

Shah, P. (2017), "Does Channel 4's Documentary Provide the Truth about Muslim Marriage?," *Areo Magazine*. 7 December 2017.

Shah, P. (2017), "South Asian legal systems and families in foreign courts: The British case," in Garimella, S.R. and Jolly, S. (eds.), *Private International Law: South Asian states' practice*. Singapore: Springer Singapore, pp. 3–18.

Shah, P. (2020), "Are there Asian diasporic laws in Britain? Reconsidering the presuppositions of legal pluralism," *Quaderni di diritto e politica ecclesiastica, Rivista trimestrale*, (1/2020), pp. 201–220.

Shah, P., Foblets, M.-C., and Rohe, M. (eds.) (2014), *Family, religion and law: Cultural encounters in Europe*. Farnham: Ashgate.

Shaw, A. (2014), "Drivers of cousin marriage among British Pakistanis," *Human Heredity*, 77(1–4), pp. 26–36.

Shaw, A. (2018), "Consanguineous marriage and the psychopathology of the progeny of first-cousin couples," *JAMA Psychiatry*, 75(5), pp. 426–427.

Shaw, D. (2015), "Why the surge in Muslim prisoners?," *BBC News*, 11 March 2015.

Siddiqui, M. (2018), *The independent review into the application of sharia law in England and Wales*. London: Her Majesty's Stationery Office.

Singh, H. (2023), *"Islamophobia" revisited*. London: Civitas.

Sobolewska, M., Heeg, S.W., Hill, E., and Borkowska, M. (2015), *Understanding electoral fraud vulnerability in Pakistani and Bangladeshi origin communities in England*. Electoral Commission.

Sturge, G. (2024), *UK prison population statistics*. House of Commons Library.

Syrett, K. (2015), "The United Kingdom," in Roach, K. (ed.), *Comparative counter-terrorism law*. Cambridge: Cambridge University Press, pp. 167–202.

Taher, A. (2008), "A third of Muslim students back killings," *The Sunday Times*, 27 July 2008.

Tamanaha, B.Z. (2021), *Legal pluralism explained: History, theory, consequences*. New York: Oxford University Press.

Torrance, D. (2024), *The royal prerogative and ministerial advice*. House of Commons Library.

Torremans, P., Grušić, U., Heinze, C., Merrett, L., Mills, A., García-Castrillón, C.O., Tang, Z.S., Trimmings, K., and Walker, L. (2017), *Cheshire, North & Fawcett: Private international law*. 15th edn. Oxford: Oxford University Press.

Tsitselikis, K. (2016), *Annotated legal documents on Islam in Europe: Greece*. Leiden: Brill.

Uddin, I. (2020), "Reformulation of Islamic matrimonial law: British Muslims, contemporary understandings and normative practices," *Journal of Muslim Minority Affairs*, 40(1), pp. 6–25.

Wadham, J., Mountfield, H., Prochaska, E., and Brown, C. (2011), *Blackstone's guide to the Human Rights Act 1998*. 6th edn. Oxford: Oxford University Press.

Walker, T. (2016), *Shariʿa councils and Muslim women in Britain: Rethinking the role of power and authority*. Leiden: Brill.

Williams, R. (2008), "Civil and religious law in England: A religious perspective," *Ecclesiastical Law Journal*, 10(3), pp. 262–282.

Williams, R. (2013), "Civil and religious law in England: a religious perspective," in Griffith-Jones, R. (ed.), *Islam and English law: Rights, responsibilities and the place of Shari'a*. Cambridge: Cambridge University Press, pp. 20–34.

Index

Printed in the United States
by Baker & Taylor Publisher Services